THE
FUNDAMENTALIST
PHENOMENON

THE FUNDAMENTALIST PHENOMENON

The Resurgence of Conservative Christianity

Edited by JERRY FALWELL
with Ed Dobson and Ed Hindson

A DOUBLEDAY-GALILEE ORIGINAL
DOUBLEDAY & COMPANY, INC.
GARDEN CITY, NEW YORK
1981

Library of Congress Cataloging in Publication Data

Dobson, Ed.
    The fundamentalist phenomenon.

    Bibliography: p. 254
    1. Fundamentalism. 2. Christian sects. 3. United
States—Church history. I. Falwell, Jerry. II. Hindson,
Edward E. III. Title.
BT82.2.D6   280'.4
ISBN 0-385-17383-0   AACR2
Library of Congress Catalog Card Number 80–2616

In memory of G. B. Vick (1901–1975)
and
In honor of Lee Roberson (1909–   )
Great Fundamentalists

To two Great Fundamentalist Evangelists
In memory of John R. Rice (1895–1980)
In honor of B. R. Lakin (1901–   )

FOREWORD

Fundamentalism is certainly alive and well! The conservative religious movement has resurged as a dynamic spiritual force today. Its impact has brought a renewed hope to millions of God-fearing, family-loving people of our nation. It is a hope for a better life, a better government, a better society, and a better America.

Recently I asked two of my key pastoral associates, Dr. Ed Hindson and Rev. Ed Dobson, to write a book that would trace the rise, growth, development, and contemporary impact of Fundamentalism. I believe that they have done a masterful job of weaving the historical facts with honest criticism and a readable narrative. I am excited about this book because I believe it "sets the record straight" regarding Fundamentalists and what we are doing today to make America a morally and spiritually strong leader among the nations of the world.

Fundamentalism has come of age. Born in the heat of controversy between Evangelicals and Liberals at the turn of the century, the Fundamentalist Movement has not only survived—it has now arrived with long-overdue national recognition. With a gracious and humble spirit, we must be willing to be used by God to represent the cause of biblical principles and values in American society. We must continue to preach the truth, but we must preach it with love and compassion to a lost world that desperately needs our message.

I have closed this book with "An Agenda for the Eighties." In it I have articulated the issues that we must deal with in this decade. I am optimistic as I look to the future. We have a greater opportunity than ever before to be used by God to bring about a genuine spiritual awakening in America and the world in our lifetime. Let us commit all of our energies to the task ahead.

Jerry Falwell

CONTENTS

PREFACE

This book is long overdue. As Fundamentalists, we have failed to document our progress and evaluate our direction adequately. This book is an honest attempt to do both from within the movement itself. We acknowledge our bias. We are excited about Fundamentalism and its resurgent impact upon American society. Yet we have here attempted an objective, critical self-evaluation. It is our sincere hope that this study will provide a better understanding of Fundamentalism as we face the crucial years ahead at the end of this century.

Our purpose has been threefold. First, we have presented Fundamentalism from a historical perspective, tracing its roots in religious nonconformity throughout church history. We have followed its development through nineteenth-century Evangelicalism up until the eve of the modernist controversy which erupted in the early twentieth century.

Second, we have attempted to evaluate the impact of the Fundamentalist Movement from the time of the "War with Liberalism," through the period of the "aftermath," until the present day. Self-evaluation is uncomfortable and sometimes undesirable, but it is absolutely necessary. We have mixed humor with our criticism and temperance with our analysis. It is not our intent to cause any further divisions or generate any further controversy.

Third, we have dealt with the contemporary challenges that face Fundamentalism. We have presented both the strengths and weaknesses of our own movement. In order to set Fundamentalism in its proper perspective, we have necessarily dealt with Liberalism and Evangelicalism as well.

In the final chapter, Dr. Falwell articulates the issues facing all conservatives today in his "Agenda for the Eighties." These issues cannot be ignored by genuine Christians. The Fundamentalist Movement must address these vital concerns. Dr. Falwell concludes his agenda with a revolutionary appeal to both Fundamentalists and Evangelicals that could reshape the forces of conservative Christianity in the 1980s.

We recognize that this book is not an exhaustive study of Fundamentalism. We offer it as a valid starting point. Writing an assessment of the movement has not been easy because of the very nature of independent separatism and its multiplicity of subcultures. However, we make no apology for our name or doctrinal position. We are proud of our fundamentalist heritage. It is time that we define and defend our movement, which has been the spiritual backbone of America throughout her history.

Ed Dobson and Ed Hindson
Liberty Baptist College
Lynchburg, Virginia
December 15, 1980

THE
FUNDAMENTALIST
PHENOMENON

1

****

FUNDAMENTALISM IS
ALIVE AND WELL!

Fundamentalism is the religious phenomenon of the twentieth century. The media, the political system, and the grass roots of America have recognized that it is here and it is here to stay.[1] For years it was ignored, criticized, and relegated to the backwoods of Appalachia. But like a rushing mighty wind, it has moved across the tide of secularism in America and left its sweeping imprint on virtually every level of society. The movement that was once despised and rejected has now resurged as the religious phenomenon of the 1980s. Theologian and social critic Martin E. Marty has admitted that "before 1980 ends, not a few candidates will have ducked for cover to escape the fundamentalist barrage."[2]

Marty emphasizes the breadth and strength of the fundamentalist barrage, observing that "militant fundamentalists control a large percentage of the 1,400 radio and 35 television stations that make up the Protestant media network. . . . Moreover, fundamentalist leaders like Jerry Falwell and Pat Robertson—who take in more money than the Republican and Democratic parties—are mastering the mails."[3] Resurgent Fundamentalism is being recognized by friend and foe alike. It is a movement that is gathering momentum and growing to such proportions that it cannot be denied. *Newsweek* stated: "What is clear on both the philosophical level—and in the rough-and-tumble arena of politics—is that the Falwells of the nation and their increasingly militant and devoted flock are a phenomenon that can no longer be dismissed or ignored."[4]

Fundamentalists view themselves as the legitimate heirs of historical New Testament Christianity. They see themselves as the militant and faithful defenders of biblical orthodoxy. They oppose Liberalism, communism, and left-wing Evangelicalism. True Fundamentalists hold strongly to the same basic tenets that they were debating seventy-five years ago. These defenders of the faith range from well-educated professors to backwoods preachers.

THE PROBLEM OF DEFINITIONS

Fundamentalism has often been castigated, maligned, and defined in the most hideous terminology possible. The eminent British theologian James Barr boldly states: "Now Fundamentalism is a bad word: the people to whom it is applied do not like to be so called. It is often felt to be a hostile and opprobrious term, suggesting narrowness, bigotry, obscurantism and sectarianism. The people whom others call fundamentalists would generally wish to be known by another term altogether."[5] A careful reading of Barr's work quickly reveals that he confuses British Evangelicalism with American Fundamentalism. (Admittedly, his observation that there is really little philosophical difference between the two is quite appropriate.) His statements also reveal that he knows virtually nothing about real American Fundamentalism! It hardly seems appropriate for such a supposedly careful scholar to make such sweeping statements in light of the fact that thousands of American preachers gladly and loudly claim the title "Fundamentalist."

Even on this side of the Atlantic, Fundamentalists have been described as backward, cultic, obscurantist, and even Nazis![6] Sandeen totally limits Fundamentalism to an offshoot of Millenarianism.[7] Stevick, however, more correctly observes that it was an "uneasy coalition" of divergent groups of conservative Evangelicals, reacting against the common threat of theological Liberalism.[8] No honest historian can equate real Fundamentalism with the extremist cults such as the Snake Handlers, which Fundamentalists themselves totally reject. A careful study of the origins of the fundamentalist controversy will show, as Barr has already observed, that the Fundamentalist Movement went far beyond the crisis of the 1920s. It was the existence of that movement which precipitated the crisis.

Virtually all historians recognize that the Fundamentalist Movement received its name and impetus from the publication of the volumes known as *The Fundamentals,* which were widely circulated between 1909 and 1919. The preface to the four-volume paperback edition issued by the Bible Institute of Los Angeles in 1917, written by R. A. Torrey, offers no definition or historical explanation for Fundamentalism whatever. The Preface merely states: "In 1909 God moved two Christian laymen to set aside a large sum of money for issuing twelve volumes that would set forth the fundamentals of the Christian faith, and which were to be sent free to ministers of the gospel, missionaries, Sunday School superintendents, and others engaged in aggressive Christian work throughout the English speaking world. . . . We were able to bring out these twelve volumes according to the original plan. Some of the volumes were sent to 300,000 ministers and missionaries and other workers in different parts of the world."[9] The Preface merely went on to say that the twelve volumes were now being reduced, with a slight abridgment, into four in order to make them continuously available at the cheapest possible price because of the continuing demand for them. Milton Rudnick provides a chart analyzing the contents of *The Fundamentals,* showing that twenty-seven articles dealt with the Bible, nine with apologetics, eight with the person of Christ, and only three with the Second Coming of Christ. The author concluded that "an examination of the contents of *The Fundamentals* reveals that their prime purpose was the defense and exaltation of traditional views of the Bible. Nearly a third of the articles (27 out of 90 [*sic*]) were devoted to this subject . . . in all of them the inspiration and infallibility of the Scriptures were vigorously maintained."[10]

George Marsden, professor of history at Calvin College, provides an excellent definition of Fundamentalism as referring to the "twentieth-century movement closely tied to the revivalist tradition of mainstream evangelical Protestantism that militantly opposed modernist theology and the cultural change associated with it."[11] While admitting that Fundamentalism shares certain traits common with other movements, such as Pietism, Evangelicalism, Revivalism, Millenarianism, and even Holiness and Pentecostalism, he points out that it must be clearly distinguished from these movements by its militant opposition of Liberalism. The Liberal empha-

sized the natural, whereas the Fundamentalist stressed the supernatural.

Marsden also correctly observes that during the 1920s Fundamentalists in America were engaged in a furious, and at times sen-
sationalistic, battle to control the denominations and the wider culture. Unlike most scholars who have attempted to understand
Fundamentalists from a position almost totally outside the movement, the Calvin professor (whose roots are much closer to Fundamentalism) correctly states: "When these efforts failed they became increasingly separatist, often leaving major denominations
and flourishing in independent churches and agencies." We totally
agree with his observation that "the phenomenon that I have
defined as 'fundamentalism' was overwhelmingly American in the
sense that almost nowhere else did this type of Protestant response
to modernity have such a conspicuous and pervasive role both in
the churches and in the national culture."[12]

THE REAFFIRMATION OF EVANGELICAL CHRISTIANITY

It will be demonstrated in the subsequent chapters that Fundamentalism shares a common heritage with evangelical nonconformist movements that have existed at various times and expressed
themselves in diverse ways throughout the history of Christianity.
However, it is our observation that Fundamentalism, as it came to
be known in the early twentieth century, was in fact reactionary
Evangelicalism. The theological concepts that brought the Evangelical Movement to where it was at the end of the nineteenth century were carried over into the next century by its leading spokes-
men as an attempt to keep the Church standing true to the older
line of evangelical tradition. They opposed the Modernists' accommodation to cultural change. In that sense, Fundamentalism was
truly a nonconformist movement. The explosive impact of Dar-
winism, higher criticism, and liberal theology together did not
shake the Fundamentalists' strong commitment to Christ and the
Scriptures. They viewed themselves as affirming genuine historical
and biblical Christianity. They saw Modernism as a compromise
with the new forms of rationalism and secularism that were threatening the historical message of the Church at that time. It was the

threat of a common enemy that caused Bible-believing Christians from every conceivable kind of denominational background to form a mutual alliance of self-defense. What else could bring together Episcopal bishops, Methodist evangelists, Baptist pastors, Presbyterian theologians, rectors, curates, Egyptologists, authors, editors, vicars, chancellors, moderators, and attorneys? It was certainly not a common commitment to cultic-millenarianistic-obscurantist-Nazi tendencies!

The contributors to the original *Fundamentals* included such outstanding evangelical scholars as James M. Gray, Benjamin B. Warfield, James Orr, W. J. Erdman, W. H. Griffith Thomas, Melvin Grove Kyle, H. C. G. Moule, and G. Campbell Morgan. These men can hardly be looked upon as a group of wild-eyed fanatics who were against scholarship and learning. The point is that they were against the conclusions that were being drawn by the critical scholarship of that day.[13] The Modernists' exaltation of what they called "scholarship" naturally caused the Fundamentalists to disdain "scholarship" in an equally rhetorical fashion. The confrontation was assuaged during the 1930s, owing to the extensive withdrawals of Fundamentalists from the Baptists and Presbyterians in particular. The Fundamentalists then set about building their own structures, which included churches and schools. These schools were not really against scholarship. They were against the kind of scholarship that had led to the conclusions of the Modernists which had taken Christianity far from its biblical foundations.

It was during this time that the outstanding contribution of the Princeton scholar J. Gresham Machen was made in his now classic work *Christianity and Liberalism,* first published in 1923.[14] In this epic work Machen argued that the conclusions of liberal scholarship actually denied the basic message of the Christian faith. To him their denial of the supernatural inspiration of the Bible and the deity, atonement, and resurrection of Jesus Christ was tantamount to a denial of everything that the Church (Catholic or Protestant) had always held to be Christian throughout the centuries. Machen argued that what the Liberals were proposing was, not a modernization of Christianity, but the elimination of it in favor of a brand-new religion. Liberals were now waving a Bible that they did not believe had its origin from God, proclaiming a Christ who they were not sure ever lived, or died for the sins of humanity, or rose again! To Machen and the other Fundamentalists this was not a question of "backwoods mentality" but an open denial of biblical Christianity. He wrote:

> But at this point a fatal error lies in wait. It is one of the root errors of modern liberalism. Christian experience, we have just said, is useful as confirming the gospel message. But because it is necessary, many men have jumped to the conclusion that it is all that is necessary. . . . No matter what sort of man history may tell us Jesus of Nazareth actually was, no matter what history may say about the real meaning of His death or about the story of His alleged resurrection, may we not continue to experience the presence of Christ in our souls? The trouble is that the experience thus maintained is not Christian experience. Religious experience it may be, but Christian experience it certainly is not.[15]

DOCTRINE: THE REAL ISSUE!

Fundamentalism was born out of a doctrinal controversy with Liberalism. The ultimate issue is whether Christians who have a supernatural religion are going to be overpowered by Christians who have only a humanistic philosophy of life. Fundamentalism is the affirmation of Christian belief and a distinctively Christian lifestyle as opposed to the general secular society. It is the opposite of radical liberal Protestantism, which has attempted both to secularize Christianity and to Christianize secularism at the same time.[16] Viewed from the standpoint of supernaturalism vs. secularism, Barr is right when he observes that there is ultimately very little difference between the theological framework of Fundamentalists and that of Evangelicals. While acknowledging that a difference of attitude does exist between the two, he nevertheless exposes the Evangelical Movement for attempting to hide its Fundamentalism behind the "conservative Evangelical" label. He asks the rather searching question: "Has Evangelicalism succeeded in developing a conceptual framework recognizable, distinct from the Fundamentalist one?" Then he answers his own question: "It is not clear that modernized and updated Evangelicalism has yet attained to any conceptual framework that is intrinsically different from the

Fundamentalist one, or that it has even tried."[17] This point is exactly what contemporary Evangelicalism needs to face—the fact that it is not intrinsically different from the mainstream of Fundamentalism!

To an outsider such as Barr, Evangelicalism and Fundamentalism seem to be in fact one and the same. While we Americans recognize strong differences between the extremities within the two movements, we too must face the fact that we share a common heritage which goes back to the fundamentalist controversy of the 1920s. The time has come for the Evangelicals to quit pretending that they do not know who we Fundamentalists are and to stop denying their relationship to us. We need to present a unified effort to stand for the basic truths of Scripture that we both hold dear.

Most people trace the basics of Fundamentalism back to the five fundamentals that became crucial in the fundamentalist-modernist controversy. These are usually expressed as:

1. The inspiration and infallibility of Scripture.
2. The deity of Christ (including His virgin birth).
3. The substitutionary atonement of Christ's death.
4. The literal resurrection of Christ from the dead.
5. The literal return of Christ in the Second Advent.

This list of Christian essentials has been expanded and amplified many times, including such issues as the doctrine of the Holy Spirit, the depravity of humankind, belief in a literal heaven and hell, the importance of soul-winning and evangelism, the existence of the person of Satan, and the importance of the local church.[18] Nevertheless, it is more correct to limit the definition of doctrinal Fundamentalism to the essential fundamentals that have been the heart of the movement for nearly a century now.

Inspiration and Infallibility of Scripture

The fundamentalist position on the inspiration of Scripture is essentially that of the main-line Evangelical Movement.[19] Both groups ultimately go back to the plenary-verbal inspiration concept of Warfield and the Princeton theologians of the nineteenth century. Believing this to be the historical Christian understanding of Scripture, Fundamentalists and Evangelicals alike hold to a basic belief in the inerrancy of the Scriptures in their original autographs. To Fundamentalists, the inerrancy of Scripture is ultimately linked to the legitimacy and authority of the Bible.[20] They view the Bible as being God-breathed and thus possessing the quality of being free from error in all of its statements and affirmations. Robert Lightner asks: "How can an errant Bible be God's revelation? How can it be God-breathed? How can it possibly be authoritative and therefore trustworthy? How can Scripture possibly be inerrant in some parts and errant in others at the same time? In a book which claims God as its author, inspiration must extend to all its parts. If it does not, how does one go about determining what is and what is not God-breathed and therefore free from error?"[21] He rightly observes that the trend among radical Evangelicals away from the total inerrancy of the Scriptures is really nothing more than an intellectual accommodation to contemporary society.

Deity of Christ

The deity of Christ is really the most essential fundamental of all.[22] Attention has shifted in the past decade to the issue of the inspiration of Scripture, since it is from Scripture that Evangelicals derive their basic doctrinal beliefs. Nevertheless, the basic issue that was strongly defended by the early Fundamentalists was the person of Christ. This is evidenced in the article by William G. Moorehead, then president of Xenia Theological Seminary, entitled "The Moral Glory of Jesus Christ, a Proof of Inspiration."[23] Fundamentalists have always felt that belief in the deity of Christ was impugned by a denial of the inspiration of Scripture, since Christ Himself quoted Old Testament Scripture as being inspired of God and even referred to "questionable" individuals as having actually existed (Adam, Jonah, and others). The article on the deity of Christ in *The Fundamentals* was written by Warfield himself. In this article he argued that the proof of the deity of Christ was more than evident in Scripture. Christ Himself claimed to be God, accepted worship from others, and was looked upon as divine by the apostles and the early Church. To this Warfield added the argument of the personal experience of the believer. Though admittedly subjective, Warfield, like all true Christians, announced: "The supreme proof to every Christian of the deity of his Lord is in his own inner experience of the transforming power of his Lord upon the heart and life. Not more surely does he who feels the present warmth of the sun know that the sun exists, than he who has experienced the recreative power of the Lord know Him to be his Lord and his God."[24]

The strength of this argument cannot be underestimated when evaluating the commitment of Bible-believing Christians to the Christ of Scripture. For it goes far beyond their intellectual adherence to the inspiration, infallibility, and inerrancy of Scripture. It is their deep and personal devotion to the person of Jesus Christ Himself that will not enable them ever to let go of the Bible. It is this love for Jesus that drives Fundamentalist-Evangelicals to cling to the truth of Scripture beyond all the rational arguments of all the critics of all of time. This truth has been virtually unobserved because it is not understood by those who do not share it. Evangelical-Fundamentalists will not let go of the Scripture because it is the Scripture that has led them to their personal experiential relationship with the living Christ. For them to deny the Scripture, which brought them to Christ, would be like the scientist denying the formula that proved the results of an experiment.

A related issue is that of the virgin birth of Christ, which Fundamentalists view as having definite implications regarding the doctrine of the deity of Christ. This article in *The Fundamentals* was written by the Scottish theologian Dr. James Orr. To him, and the other Fundamentalists, this was no optional doctrine which had no real significance in relation to the doctrine of the person of Christ. Orr emphatically states: "Doctrinally, it must be repeated that the belief in the Virgin birth of Christ is of the highest value in the right apprehension of Christ's unique and sinless personality."[25]

Substitutionary Atonement

The doctrine of the substitutionary atonement of Christ's death is also intertwined with that of His deity. At the time of the fundamentalist controversy several new theories regarding the atonement of Christ were being propagated relative to the idea of His death being little more than a moral influence on society. To Fundamentalists, this struck at the very heart and core of Christianity. The entire message of the Gospel centers around the death, burial, and resurrection of Christ. If He did not die for sin as God's substitute for man and if He were not literally raised from the dead, then there would be no Good News to proclaim to the world. The entire evangelistic imperative of the Evangelical-Fundamentalist Movement must be seen in light of the belief in the death and resurrection of Christ.[26]

Resurrection of Christ

Closely interrelated to the other fundamentals is the doctrine of the literal resurrection of Christ. To Fundamentalists, the so-called spiritual resurrection of Christ was a totally inadequate concept. Biblically, the Scriptures clearly indicate that Christ rose bodily from the dead and appeared in a literal body form to His disciples.[27] If the justification of Christians was sealed by the death of Christ, then their ultimate regeneration was confirmed by His resurrection. Apart from the resurrection of Christ from the dead there is no Good News to tell to the world. Where Modernism was content to proclaim the moral message of Christ as summarized in the Sermon on the Mount, Fundamentalists were committed to the Gospel (the Evangel) itself. They had a message to tell to the nations because they shared with the early Church its overwhelming conviction that Jesus Christ was alive. Through their evangelistic and missionary endeavors, Fundamentalists offer to the world no mere dead moralistic teacher of the past but a living Savior who could transform a person's life today. Thus Fundamentalist-Evangelicals view themselves as relevant to humanity's needs while superseding the philosophical trends of the contemporary world.

Second Coming of Christ

Belief in the literal, bodily return of Christ is also essential to the belief of Fundamentalism. Since Jesus promised to return, and the Scriptures indicated that He would return "in like manner as ye have seen him go," the literal return of Christ is interrelated theologically to the literal resurrection of Christ. Denying modern theology's questioning whether the historical Jesus ever lived or rose again, the Fundamentalist believes that He will definitely and literally return to bring all of history to its ultimate culmination. While this doctrine is the most debated and divergent of all the fundamentals (one may choose among premillennial, postmillennial, amillennial, pretribulational, midtribulational, posttribulational, partial rapture, and other views), nevertheless all conservatives agree that Christ is coming again to judge the world and vindicate the righteous.[28] There can be no doubt that this belief has left its marked impression on American culture in general with our national insistence that a superhero will one day intervene in human history and save the world. That person will in fact be Jesus Christ Himself!

THE FUNDAMENTALIST IMPULSE

Doctrinally, Fundamentalism is really traditional and conservative Christian orthodoxy. It arose as a defense of minimal doctrinal essentials, apart from which Christianity ceases to be Christian. The basic beliefs of the majority of fundamentalist and evangelical Christians are essentially the same as those of the majority of religious Americans. Christianity today is virtually holding to the same beliefs that were expressed by the Fundamentalists at the time of the modernist controversy earlier in this century.

Young People

Since the future of Fundamentalism rests with young people, it is interesting to note the latest statistics regarding their religious beliefs. A recent survey by George Gallup indicated that almost nine out of ten teenagers pray and only one out of a hundred has no religious preference. Four out of ten admit that religion occupies an important role in their life. In a 1976 study of young adults in Dayton, Ohio, several interesting facts were discovered: "26 percent said their religious beliefs affected their daily thinking and ethics, and another 39 percent suggested that they had some effect on their daily behavior . . . 62 percent said that during a twenty-four hour period God and religion had been on their mind; 20 percent saying it was through prayer, 19 percent through church or family devotions . . . 75 percent of those who responded noted that religious beliefs would be fairly or very important in their lives. . . . Since 1976, when this poll was taken, church attendance among the young adult group has significantly increased nationally by more than 10 percent."[29] While religious trends in general do not totally prove the impact of Fundamentalism in America, they certainly do show the resurgence of conservative Christianity in our nation.

Family Living

This strong commitment to religion can also be observed in the family. Although the family has been under great stress, it appears that the current mood among American people is a trend back to the traditional family. Concurrent with that trend is an increased interest in religion. Surveys show that:

- 42 percent of parents said grace before meals with their children
- 38 percent attended church services with their children
- 28 percent attended church-related activities with their children

- 17 percent of parents read the Bible together with their children

- 44 percent of parents talked about God and religion with their children

- 31 percent of parents prayed or meditated with their offspring

- 23 percent watched or listened to religious programs on TV or radio[30]

The flood of conservative books, manuals, and study guides on the family is beginning to make an impact. Since the early sixties the influence of Bill Gothard's "Institutes" has spawned over three hundred titles on the family by Christian writers.[31] Gothard has taught his basic and advanced family principles to well over 1 million people. More materials on the family have been produced in the last ten years than in the entire history of Christianity. In addition to books, tapes, and records, there are now several film series on family living, with James Dobson's *Focus on the Family* being the most popular. It was shown in over ten thousand churches to nearly 5 million people in its first year (1980) on the market.

Professional Clergy

There is also a conservative trend among the young clergy (ages eighteen to twenty-nine). Seventy percent believe in the Genesis account of the creation of Adam and Eve, compared to only 57 percent of the older clergy. They believe (87 percent) that Christ is the only hope for heaven, and 91 percent attest to a personal religious experience involving Jesus Christ. The trend in the eighties appears to be moving strongly in the conservative direction. While the liberal seminaries are suffering from diminishing enrollments, the conservative schools are bursting at the seams. Record enrollments have been reported in 1980 at Dallas Theological Seminary (1,500), Grace Theological Seminary (500), Southwestern Baptist Theological Seminary (3,700), Trinity Evangelical Divinity School (900), and at the college level at Baptist Bible College (2,500), Bob Jones University (6,000), Calvin College (4,100),

Cedarville College (1,500), Hyles-Anderson College (1,700), Liberty Baptist College (4,400), and Tennessee Temple University (5,000). In addition, the Liberty Home Bible Institute (a home correspondence program) now has 10,000 students currently enrolled in a two-year study program, while the Moody Bible Institute in Chicago annually enrolls over 100,000 people taking at least one course by correspondence.

It is now estimated that there are over 200,000 young people preparing for full-time Christian work in the conservative schools at the college and graduate level. While these schools vary greatly in their stance toward Fundamentalism, they are an indication of the growing conservative movement. Their ultimate impact on the future will enhance the influence of conservatism among the nation's clergy.

General Public

The strength of this new trend can also be observed in the surveys related to orthodox beliefs: the inerrancy of the Bible, the deity of Christ, and the necessity of faith in Jesus Christ. Eighty percent of the population believe that Jesus Christ is God or the Son of God. The response was strong to the statement "The Bible is the Word of God and is *not* mistaken in its statements or teachings." This was endorsed by 42 percent of the general public, while 34 percent of the general public also believed in a personal devil and 40 percent believed in the Genesis account of the creation of Adam and Eve.[32]

In reviewing the seventies, Gallup and Poling state: "It would be difficult to identify a decade that incorporated more crises and change for the churches than the 1970's. Yet the 1980's may far surpass the tumultuous furor we have just completed. Staggering membership losses suffered by the mainline denominations have not yet turned around in a positive growth direction. The Presbyterian, Episcopalian, and United Church of Christ communions cannot long exist as viable church organizations nationally if the declines of the 70's persist in the 1980's. On the other hand, the conservative churches appear to be in an up period, with the Southern Baptists and a variety of fundamentalist groups setting attendance and membership records almost hourly."[33] It is clear that the fundamentalist impulse is here to stay!

The rejuvenation of fundamentalist-evangelical Christianity is further substantiated by the findings of the *Christianity Today–* Gallup Poll. These statistics indicate that the roots of orthodox Christianity go deep into the fabric of American society. Although the poll centers around the term "evangelical," it is clear that many of the people represented in this group are actually Fundamentalists in their doctrinal position. The poll identified two kinds of Evangelicals. The first, the "Orthodox Evangelical Group," were those who held that (1) Jesus Christ is the divine Son of God, or is both fully God and fully man; (2) the only hope for heaven is through personal faith in Jesus Christ; and (3) the Bible is the Word of God and is not mistaken in its statements and teachings; and who (4) read the Bible at least once a month; and (5) attend religious services at least once a month. The second group identified were the "Conversionalist Evangelicals," who "read the Bible, attend religious services at least once a month, and who have had a particularly powerful religious experience that is still important to them, which they understand as a conversion experience that included an identifiable point at which they asked Jesus Christ to become their personal Saviour."

In summarizing the statistics, *Christianity Today* identified some interesting and surprising facts:

- One of every five adults 18 years old and over—31 million persons—is an Evangelical.
- Almost one in five adults (19%) considers himself or herself Pentecostal or charismatic, but of those 29.4 million persons, 23.5 million have *not* spoken in tongues.
- Better than one third of the adult population have had a life-changing religious experience. For 50 million people, this experience involved Jesus Christ, and for 39.5 million people this was a conversion that included asking Christ to be personal Saviour.
- Almost 69 million people 18 and over—are hoping to go to heaven only because of their personal faith in Jesus Christ.
- More than eight of every ten persons believe Jesus Christ is divine.

- Sixty-five million adults believe the Bible is inerrant.
- Fifty million go to the Bible first to test their own religious beliefs.
- Seven out of ten adults believe the devil is either a personal being (74%), or an impersonal force that influences people to do wrong (36%).
- Half of the adults in the U.S. believe God created Adam and Eve to start the human race.
- A whopping 84 percent—more than eight of every ten people—believe the Ten Commandments are valid today.[34]

There are several facts that are clearly evident from this poll: First, 69 million people are hoping to go to heaven because of their personal faith in Christ. Second, the vast majority of Americans believe the Bible is the Word of God and that it is a valid guide in moral and ethical issues. When one examines the religious beliefs of young people, families, young clergy, and the population in general, it is obvious that the American population has a strong personal commitment to orthodox, fundamental, evangelical Christianity. Skepticism, agnosticism, and atheism have little influence on this society. Fundamental Christianity is resurging as America begins the decade of the 1980s.

Church Growth Movement

This resurgence is most evident in the growth of fundamentalist churches. During the decade of the seventies, the major denominations experienced significant loss in their membership. Church growth strategist Peter Wagner states: "In a seven-year period (1970–1977) the United Methodists, for example, lost 886,000 members, the United Presbyterians lost 526,000, and the Episcopal Church lost 467,000. Even the Southern Baptist Convention experienced some difficulty. During the first seven years of the 1970's, they increased 17 percent, while the general population in America increased 7 percent. However, in 1976, 1977, and 1978, their baptisms decreased for the first time in the history of the convention. In 1978 Southern Baptist netted only 121 new churches—a meager

0.4 percent increase—and over 6,000 churches did not report baptisms."[35] Although the charismatic movement in general grew 48 percent, the main-line Pentecostal denominations such as the Church of God and the Assemblies of God had a two-year decline in their Sunday school attendance.

During this time of denominational decline, the Fundamentalist Movement has been experiencing unusual and staggering growth. In the last several decades Fundamentalists have placed an important emphasis on church planting. Most denominational seminaries are training ministers to assume pulpits in already established churches. Since Fundamentalism was born out of a confrontation with and withdrawal from the main-line denominations, Fundamentalists have always placed an emphasis on starting new churches. For example, the Baptist Bible Fellowship, which began in 1950 with 200 preachers, has now grown to over 3,500 churches.[36] Most of these churches have been started by graduates of the fellowship colleges. Dr. Jerry Falwell has on numerous occasions projected a plan for the planting of 5,000 new churches by the end of the century. One conservative nondenominational group in California has a goal of 10,000 new churches by the end of the decade. They plan to minister aggressively to the eighteen-to-twenty-nine-year-old population of America in the process.[37] Although these are projected, visionary goals, many of the groups are well on their way to accomplishing their objectives in new church planting. The combined impact of these church planting projections will be a phenomenon in itself as the American Church marches into the twenty-first century.

The Fundamentalist Movement has been closely identified with the Super Church. While denominational churches were declining, the Fundamentalist Movement was involved in building large churches with multifaceted ministries and extensive outreach programs. The commitment to aggressive evangelism is at the heart of all conservative church growth. Liberalism is literally dying from lack of recruitment.

In 1969 Dr. Elmer Towns listed the ten largest Sunday schools in America as follows:[38]

Church	City, State	S.S. Attendance
1. Akron Baptist Temple	Akron, Ohio	5,762
2. Highland Park Baptist Church	Chattanooga, Tennessee	4,821
3. First Baptist Church	Dallas, Texas	4,731
4. First Baptist Church	Hammond, Indiana	3,978
5. Canton Baptist Temple	Canton, Ohio	3,581
6. Landmark Baptist Temple	Cincinnati, Ohio	3,540
7. Temple Baptist Church	Detroit, Michigan	2,847
8. First Baptist Church	Van Nuys, California	2,847
9. Thomas Road Baptist Church	Lynchburg, Virginia	2,640
10. Calvary Baptist Temple	Denver, Colorado	2,453

Ten years later (1979), the top twenty Sunday schools were as follows:[39]

Church	City, State	S.S. Attendance
1. First Baptist Church	Hammond, Indiana	15,101
2. Highland Park Baptist Church	Chattanooga, Tennessee	11,000
3. Thomas Road Baptist Church	Lynchburg, Virginia	10,000
4. First Baptist Church	Dallas, Texas	6,703
5. Akron Baptist Temple	Akron, Ohio	6,700
6. Canton Baptist Temple	Canton, Ohio	4,574
7. Calvary Temple Church	Springfield, Illinois	4,379
8. Landmark Baptist Temple	Cincinnati, Ohio	4,315
9. Calvary Assembly	Winter Park, Florida	4,234
10. First Baptist Church	Jacksonville, Florida	3,828
11. Westside Assembly of God	Davenport, Iowa	3,400
12. Madison Church of Christ	Madison, Tennessee	3,357
13. Los Gatos Christian Church	Los Gatos, California	3,352
14. The Chapel in University Park	Akron, Ohio	3,200
15. Indianapolis Baptist Temple	Indianapolis, Indiana	3,100
16. Temple Baptist Church	Detroit, Michigan	3,100
17. Bellevue Baptist Church	Memphis, Tennessee	3,000
18. First Baptist Church of Van Nuys	Van Nuys, California	2,850
19. North Phoenix Baptist Church	Phoenix, Arizona	2,776
20. North Cleveland Church of God	Cleveland, Tennessee	2,739

In comparing the 1969 listing and the 1979 listing, several observations are apparent. First, many of the churches experienced extraordinary growth during this decade. Highland Park Baptist Church increased from 4,821 to 11,000. Thomas Road Baptist Church increased from 2,640 to 10,000. First Baptist Church of Dallas increased from 4,731 to 6,703. Canton Baptist Temple increased from 3,581 to 4,574. First Baptist Church of Hammond increased from 3,978 to 15,101! The second characteristic of the large church growth movement is that the number of large churches is growing. In 1969 the tenth largest averaged 2,453. In 1979 the thirtieth largest averaged that same attendance. This indicates that a number of churches around 2,400 in size tripled in the decade of the 1970s. Most of the large, aggressive churches would easily be categorized within the Fundamentalist Movement. Towns estimated that in 1973 there were about 10,000 aggressive and growing fundamental churches in America.[40]

The Electric Church

Fundamentalist, evangelical, and charismatic organizations have enjoyed almost complete domination of the media—particularly radio and television. This domination has provided crucial impetus to the resurgence of fundamental Christianity. Every Sunday morning, millions of people tune into a religious radio or television program. In the United States, religious broadcasters reach more people through their programs than all of the churches combined! At least 47 percent of all Americans tune to at least one religious program each week. The Gospel has been made available to 97 percent of the world's population through Christian broadcasting.[41]

The "Day of Discovery" attracts a weekly TV audience of 7 million. Its counterpart, the "Radio Bible Class," is distributed to over one thousand independent stations around the world. Billy Graham's "Hour of Decision," which started in 1950, is now heard on over nine hundred stations worldwide. Rex Humbard has been broadcasting on television since 1952, and Oral Roberts since 1954. Oral Roberts' prime-time television specials attract an audience of several million each.

Charismatic broadcasters have made an unbelievable impact on the media. The "700 Club" is one Christian organization that even owns and operates a satellite earth station. In 1980 it had a

budget of $50 million and utilized seven thousand prayer coun-
selors around the clock nationwide. The "PTL Club" started in
1974 and by 1978 had accumulated an outreach that included
broadcasts on over two hundred stations and also brings in an
annual income of $50 million.[42]

While many of these broadcasts are not within the fundamentalist church camp, they do reflect fundamentalistic theology in
relation to Christ, the Bible, and conversion. Fundamentalists
themselves are well represented by Jerry Falwell's "Old-Time Gospel Hour," a one-hour program seen on nearly four hundred television stations weekly; the daily thirty-minute radio version is heard
on over five hundred stations throughout the United States. The
estimated total audience (radio and TV) is the largest religious
audience in history.

Religious broadcasting is capturing the minds, hearts, and
pockets of America. Jim Montgomery invented the term "Electric
Church" in a *Wall Street Journal* article, saying: "The Electric
Church is a booming industry generating thousands of jobs and an
annual cash flow of hundreds of millions of dollars."[43] According to
Armstrong, as of 1978 one new religious radio station was being established every week and one new religious television station every
month.[44] The National Religious Broadcasters organization has
grown from 49 members in 1944 to over 800 members by 1980.

Christian School Movement

The impact of Fundamentalism can be seen in the growth of Christian education. This is demonstrated both in Christian day schools
and in higher education. One of the most important requirements
for the perpetuation of any movement is that the movement provides an opportunity for the training of new leaders. Any organization that fails to prepare and train new leadership will ultimately
deteriorate and die. The extent of the higher education movement
can be seen by analyzing the Christian Association for Student
Affairs, which was organized in 1957. This organization has approximately two hundred member schools, representing Christian liberal
arts colleges, Bible colleges, and Bible institutes in the United States
and Canada. It has a strongly fundamentalist doctrinal statement
to which all members of the association must adhere:

1. We believe that there is one God, eternally existing in three persons: Father, Son, and Holy Spirit.
2. We believe the Bible to be the inspired, the only infallible, authoritative Word of God.
3. We believe in the deity of our Lord Jesus Christ, in His miracles, in His vicarious death and atonement through His shed blood, in His bodily resurrection and ascension to the right hand of the Father, and in His personal, visible return to power and glory.
4. We believe that man was created in the image of God, that he was tempted by Satan and fell, and that, because of the exceeding sinfulness of human nature, regeneration by the Holy Spirit is absolutely necessary for salvation.
5. We believe in the present ministry of the Holy Spirit by Whose indwelling the Christian is enabled to live a Godly life, and by Whom the church is empowered to carry out Christ's great commission.
6. We believe in the bodily resurrection of both the saved and the lost; those who are saved unto the resurrection of life, and those who are lost unto the resurrection of damnation.[45]

The study of the modern Christian day school movement finds that its growth is equally as explosive as that of the churches. In 1954–55 there were 123 Christian schools in the United States, representing a combined enrollment of 12,187 students. Since then the growth of Christian schools has been mounting toward a shattering crescendo. There are now some 18,000 Christian day schools in America, and several new ones coming into existence every day! California and Florida were early pioneers among the states that have generated large populations of Christian schools. For example, over 20 Christian schools are located within fifty miles of Miami, Florida, alone. The largest schools in the state, however, are located in Jacksonville and Pensacola. California has more Christian schools than any other state and is the home of the fastest-growing Christian school association in the world: the Association of Christian Schools International.[46]

Christian school people have been more preoccupied with the problems of dramatic growth than with documenting the educational movement of which they are a part. Conservative estimates conclude that there are presently 18,000 Christian schools, 125,000 teachers, and over 2 million students. All of this indicates the strength of this burgeoning movement, which promises to provide conservative Christianity with ample leadership for the future.

Christian school associations such as Christian Educators Association of the Southeast, Accelerated Christian Education, American Association of Christian Schools, and Association of Christian Schools International enjoy the support of many schools which also actively serve in state organizations. These state organizations often employ lobbyists to represent their interests in their state capitals. They also handle their own accrediting procedures and standards.

The modern Christian school movement is distinctively religious in orientation, is definitely not racially motivated, and is dedicated to quality education. The movement is marked by parent participation, zealous teachers and administrators, and lots of grass-roots enthusiasm and community support.

Christian school textbook and curriculum publication is experiencing a corollary growth to the movement. Christian school textbooks are usually academically sound while also being biblically oriented. While some might call these texts authoritarian and narrow, Christian school parents and students are delighted that they reinforce parental values rather than undermining them.

Nonpublic, Protestant, Christian-oriented educational schools are on the rise. Those already in existence are growing even larger. Nationally known Christian educator Dr. Ronald Godwin says: "Their safe, academically sound, spiritually oriented atmospheres are much appreciated as a responsible alternative to deteriorating public school education."[47] Their combined impact has generated momentum for the emerging force of Fundamentalism in the future.

SUMMARY

Liberalism in Reverse

The facts cannot be ignored. When added together, they total a conclusion that is evident: Fundamentalism is *the* Force of the 1980s. The Gallup Poll findings, the church growth statistics, the massive influence of the Electric Church, and the extensive impact of Christian education are the ingredients of a rejuvenated, dynamic, and resurgent movement. Its size and strength alone demand public attention. Its vision and fervor may change the course of American history in the next two decades.

The resurgence of Fundamentalism into the mainstream of American religious life must ultimately be viewed in relation to the declining influence of Liberalism. The roots of religious Liberalism go back to the influence of the German theologian Friedrich Schleiermacher (1768–1834), who considered the ultimate authority in religion to be founded in the experience of the soul rather than in the content of Scripture. Eventually liberal theologians transferred religious authority from the Bible to the psycho-spiritual experience of the individual. Coupled with the emerging influence of Higher Criticism, this movement ultimately led to a wholesale rejection of absolute biblical authority.[48]

In America, Liberalism began to take a turn toward what became known as the "social gospel" under the influence of Walter Rauschenbusch (1861–1918) and Horace Bushnell (1802–76). Following Schleiermacher's lead, they placed Christian "nurture" above confrontational evangelism and promoted an experience of Christianity that was not dependent upon any biblical verification. In his evaluation of Liberalism and its stepchild neo-orthodoxy, Charles Ryrie observed: "Insofar as the Bible was true it was inspired, but it was the task of the liberal critic to determine at what points the Bible was true."[49] This attitude eventually led to a disdain for biblical truth and undermined the Christian foundation of Liberalism. The result left the movement with no real authoritative message for the American public, and after one hundred years of vague theologizing, Liberalism is now losing its grasp on the people of America.

J. I. Packer has identified the basic characteristics of American liberalism at the turn of the century:

1. God's character is one of pure benevolence—benevolence that is without standards. . . .
2. There is a divine spark in every man. . . .
3. Jesus Christ is man's Saviour only in the sense that He is man's perfect Teacher and Example. . . .

4. Just as Christ differs from other men only comparatively, not absolutely, so Christianity differs from other religions not generically, but merely as the best and highest type of religion that has yet appeared. . . .

5. The Bible is not a divine record of revelation, but a human testament of religion; and Christian doctrine is not the God-given word which must create and control Christian experience.[50]

The later synthesis of neo-orthodoxy did not help the situation much. Ryrie observes that "neo-orthodoxy is a theological hoax. It attempts to preserve the message of the Bible while denying the facts of the Bible."[51] Neo-orthodox Liberals, like their modernist counterparts, see no real basis in fact in much of the Bible. Van Til identifies the movement as nothing more than Modernism with a new twist. He writes: "The new Modernism and the old are alike destructive of historic Christian theism and with it the significant meaning of human experience."[52]

The inherent lack of absolute truth is the leading cause for the demise of Liberalism and the dissolution of its impact on American society. When the extreme left wing of Liberalism tended toward the God Is Dead movement in the 1960s, even many Liberals became concerned about the drift of their own movement.[53] Since then, neo-Liberalism seems to be swinging back to the right and making strong appeals to left-wing Evangelicalism.[54] However, lack of authoritative direction has left the Evangelical Movement drifting.

Evangelicalism in Neutral

After main-line Evangelicalism reacted to Liberalism and produced Fundamentalism, it reacted to Fundamentalism and produced New Evangelicalism. In its original form, this sought to develop a new attitude and outlook that were missing in many Fundamentalists. Attempting to avoid the extremely negative separatism of the Fundamentalists, the New Evangelicals emphasized theological tolerance, infiltration of the denominations, and a commitment to social problems.[55]

However, overtolerance has left the Evangelical Movement in neutral. Webber evaluates its status as: "This branch of Christianity is waiting for direction, longing for a leadership that will help it become a potent world influence for the historic faith."[56] Unfortunately, that leadership has been missing. Evangelicals have been drifting for so long, they now lack a cohesive unity. The entire movement is in danger of drifting into moderate Liberalism. It has drifted from Evangelicalism to *New* Evangelicalism to *Young* Evangelicalism to *Worldly* Evangelicalism, continuing on toward the theological left. It is now beginning to warm its hands by the fires of Liberalism and neo-orthodoxy.[57]

Carl F. H. Henry, one of the founders and leading proponents of Evangelicalism, states: "Evangelicals seem to be in a holding pattern, sometimes approaching a long-awaited landing, then circling 'round and 'round a cooperative objective, even at times moving exasperatingly away from it. We perform a series of maneuvers whose outcome is complicated by gathering storms that may divert us to an unforeseen and unintended destination."[58] Unless the Evangelical Movement requests an instrument-flight-rules (I.F.R.) flight plan that commits it to the doctrinal absolutes of Scripture, its "unforseen and unintended destination" may include polarization from true Evangelicalism, disintegration of its biblical distinctives, and eventual integration with Liberalism. It may well land at the wrong airport. In light of this current dilemma, while the evangelical jumbo jet has been lumbering down the runway for years trying to maneuver a takeoff, it has been suddenly hijacked by fundamentalist pilots![59]

Fundamentalism in Overdrive

While dissolute Liberalism has been dissolving, and drifting Evangelicalism has been trying to decide where to drift next, Fundamentalists have continued to preach the same basic message they have always been preaching. Webber correctly observes that "between 1930 and 1960, Fundamentalism spread, almost unnoticed, throughout the United States and the World. Fundamentalists founded numerous Bible schools, colleges, and seminaries, a number of new denominations, mission boards, publishing houses, evangelistic associations, and other Christian enterprises."[60]

While, according to Quebedeaux, Evangelicals have been trying to become "respectable by the world's standards," Fundamentalists, who couldn't care less about respectability, have suddenly recaptured the heart and spirit of the American religious community.[61] In spite of Quebedeaux's prediction that the world can "no longer take the message and lifestyle of fundamentalism seriously," conservative middle-American Christians are once again leading the moral and social impact of Christianity on society.

The ethereal theorizing of the Evangelicals has left them reluctant (perhaps even unable) practically to produce the organizational structure necessary to change the American life-style. By contrast, Fundamentalism has learned how to put its dynamic force into the political arena and does not intend to withdraw. Committed to absolute truth of Scripture, and undaunted by criticism and public opinion, it has resurged into the mainstream of American life. It may be said that the Fundamentalists, although often falsely ridiculed as "backwoods hillbillies," have their eighteen-wheeler rolling and with their electronic C.B. in hand are broadcasting their message to the world. They've got the "hammer down," the "pedal to the metal," and they intend to "keep on truckin'." Ten-four, good buddy!

2

ROOTS OF RELIGIOUS NONCONFORMITY

Religious nonconformity goes back to the very birth of the Church itself. The New Testament Christian Church was given birth at Pentecost by the coming of the Holy Spirit in baptism upon the early disciples (Acts 2). It represented a break with first-century Judaism, and ultimately with the Jewish religion under the Old Covenant. Christian believers view themselves as possessing a New Covenant sealed in the blood of Jesus Christ and enacted by His resurrection. They see themselves as recipients of His "Great Commission" to go into all the world and preach the Gospel (Acts 1:8). Certainly this evangelistic imperative characterized the essential nature of the early Church. Its methods included personal testimony, synagogue preaching and open-air preaching, house evangelism and literary evangelism (apologetic and polemic).[1]

Most Fundamentalists, especially within the Baptist and Free Church traditions, view the early New Testament Church as an independent, autonomous fellowship of local believers banded together for the purpose of carrying out the Great Commission. In this context, the "Church" has reference to a distinct group within history who through the medium of preaching has accepted the Gospel of Jesus Christ by faith and has separated itself unto righteousness. The Free Church Swedish scholar Gunnar Westin states: "The 'accepted word' was the foundation of the church, and without this acceptance there would have been no local assemblies." He goes on to remark: "These congregations may be defined, therefore, as free churches because they won adherance and members who, when they freely accepted the word, turned away from the life of sin and voluntarily were baptized."[2]

The Church itself is called in the Greek language of the New Testament God's *ekklesia* ("called-out assembly"). This early Church knew no constituted hierarchy, but rather was an autonomous assembly that had no relationship, subordinate or coordinate, with any ecclesiastical or civil authority. It was a local fellowship of believers scattered throughout the Roman Empire, at various points making known the good news of Jesus Christ and the salvation that He offered. For the most part, the early Christians considered themselves as strangers and pilgrims on the earth. Their citizenship (*politeuma*) was in heaven. Thus they held a kind of dual citizenship as citizens of earth and heaven at the same time.

It is clear that, until the latter part of the second century, the various apostolic and postapostolic churches were still autonomous and that no centralized church authority existed. In the writings of the Apostle Paul, his letters were directed to local congregations and/or their pastors, not to any hierarchy of authority. This same policy is also seen in the *First Epistle* of Clement of Rome, in Polycarp's *Letter to the Philippians,* and the Ignatian *Epistles* to the churches in Asia Minor, written during the latter part of the first and early part of the second centuries.[3] During this same time itinerant prophets, evangelists, and teachers exerted considerable influence on the various local churches and their missionary expansion throughout the Roman Empire.

NONCONFORMITY IN THE EARLY CHURCH

The process of centralization of church authority did not begin until the local leaders (bishops) came together for synod meetings in the second and third centuries. It was during this time that the bishop at Rome began to assert authority over the other bishops. In time he would issue statements implying that he was the head of the churches, though this doctrine was not formally adopted until the sixth century A.D. Before this, Christian gatherings were comparatively simple and free of ritualistic accompaniments. This can be seen in the letter from the governor of Bithynia to Emperor Trajan referring to early Christian gatherings: "They were in the habit of meeting on a certain day before sunrise and reciting an antiphonal hymn to Christ as God." In his famous *Apology* (c. A.D. 150) Justin Martyr of Rome gave the following account of the early Christian services: "On the day called Sunday, all who live in the cities or in the country gather together in one place, and the memoirs of the apostles or the writings of the prophets are read for so long as time permits. Then, when the reader has ceased, the overseer instructs us by word of mouth, exhorting us to put these good things into practice, then we all rise together and pray."[4] Justin's comments go on to explain that this was followed by communion, which was always held on Sunday because that was the day that Jesus Christ rose from the dead. Other meetings were conducted to help deal with the needs of various members, as well as to proclaim the Gospel. He also describes a process of careful recording of membership "name for name" in order to maintain proper church discipline.

Marcionism

It was during this time that the Church, though often under persecution, made tremendous gains within the Roman Empire. Early Christianity, with its emphasis that all people were equal in Christ, stood in direct contrast to the strong social structure of the Roman Empire. In less than three centuries, without ever mustering an army, Christianity conquered the fading empire through its strong emphasis upon Gospel proclamation and personal godly living. Simple Christianity had made a permanent impact upon the Roman world.

Long before the Catholic Church was formed as a legal institution within the Roman Empire, there were divergent groups that were separating from the structured Church. As early as A.D. 140, Marcion opposed the trend that the Church was taking in accommodating to what he saw as a return to Judaism. He attempted to purify the Church along the lines of Pauline Christianity. Some have suggested that the Marcionites may have called themselves Paulicians, since the Paulicians who appear in the Middle Ages were "easily transformed Marcionites."[5] However, Marcion's total opposition to the Old Testament and Judaism misled him into taking a dualistic approach to his understanding of the Person of God. The strict discipline of the Marcionite movement caused it to grow to widespread popularity by A.D. 200. Though originating in Rome, the Marcionite movement was a major competitor to the primitive Catholic Church in the East. In time it fell under the ban of severe imperial edicts against heretics.

Montanism

Another separatist church movement that arose during the same period was known as Montanism. Westin notes: "It also became a well-defined opposition movement against ecclesiasticism in the official and institutionalized church, which developed during the latter portion of the second century."[6] The movement began in the city of Pepuza, in Phrygia, in central Asia Minor. It had an exciting and dynamic beginning but was marked with several excesses, including speaking in tongues and the claim of direct revelation in establishing a "new order of prophets." The movement spread as far as North Africa and ancient Gaul. It also fell under the ban of the Roman emperors, and in A.D. 407 Honorius decreed the death penalty for all Montanists.

Novatianism

During the third and fourth centuries there continued to be nonconformist groups within the imperial Roman Church. This controversy centered on two separatist groups known as Novatians and Donatists. The issue of this controversy, which erupted during the Decian persecution in the middle of the third century, had to do with the disposition of those who capitulated to the government during times of persecution. These backsliders were known as *lapsi*. The question was whether or not they should be received back into the congregation upon their professed repentance.

In about A.D. 250, Novatian, a presbyter, was elected the bishop of Rome. He stood for strict enforcement of discipline upon deserters of the faith. Calling the Church back to the strict discipline of its earlier days, he demanded a more severe approach than was then popular with the majority of believers. His strict position caused him to be dismissed by an orthodox bishops' synod, which excommunicated him as well.[7] However, many still agreed with the position of Novatian, and he became the leader of a group in opposition to the accepted Church. His followers came to call themselves *Katharoi* ("pure ones"). Their movement spread widely throughout North Africa and Asia Minor. In many places the Montanists forsook their own cause and joined forces with the new opposition movement in great numbers. Even in Carthage the Montanists supported Novatian's claim to the episcopate of Rome. Novatian churches developed into a well-knit unit that spread throughout the empire and rivaled the Catholic Church even in the days of Emperor Constantine and his successors.

Donatism

Following another persecution under Emperor Diocletian, a controversy similar to Novatianism arose; it became known as Donatism. The issue began when a new bishop, Caecilian, was elected in Carthage who had been consecrated by one who had denied his faith during the Diocletian persecution. Several people refused to recognize the legitimacy of the new bishop, and a group of dissenters eventually elected Donatus to take his place. This caused a split in the North African churches that resulted in Donatus' controlling the schismatic group. Future attempts to win over the Donatists to the Catholic Church proved to be fruitless. Constantine himself dispatched an edict in A.D. 321 granting them toleration within the empire. He even granted money to Roman congregations to build new church buildings in instances where the Donatists had maintained possession of the older churches.

In A.D. 330 some 270 Donatist bishops gathered for a synod in Carthage. It is clear that there were now two divergent influences in the Church, one committed to the nonconformist tradition and the other emphasizing the solidarity of the Church. Later some of the Donatists went so far as to rebaptize individuals who had come from the Roman, or orthodox, Church, which had now become the state-supported Church.[8] Their influence was eventually greatly reduced by the outstanding Catholic theologian Augustine, who con-

fronted the Donatists in a church council held in Carthage in A.D.
411. This confrontation between 286 Catholic bishops and 279
Donatist bishops was followed by severe persecution. As a result,
the Donatists' meetings were forbidden at the threat of the death
penalty, their churches closed, and their property confiscated.
Though greatly weakened, the Donatists continued to exist in
North Africa alongside the Catholic Church until the time of the
Moslem invasion.

NONCONFORMITY IN THE MEDIEVAL CHURCH

Paulicians

The Paulicians appeared in Syria and Armenia as early as the seventh and eighth centuries. In time they became numerous even in
the city of Constantinople and became the object of persecution by
the Byzantine emperors. The Paulicians emphasized personal holy
living and separation from the nominal Christian population. They
had their own pastors and opposed the system of church hierarchy.
Preferring to call themselves "simply Christians," they opposed the
use of the symbol of the cross, clerical vestments, and the celebra-
tion of the Mass.[9]

During the tenth century a branch of the Paulicians, which became known as the Bogomils, appeared in Bulgaria. By the eleventh century another movement, known as the Cathari ("pure
ones"), also appeared in Eastern Europe, with viewpoints similar to
those of the Paulicians and the Bogomils. Baptist and Free Church
historians are quick to point out that the Cathari were called Bul-
gari in France and show the common ancestral relationship of all
of these movements, which probably in one form or another goes
back to the Novatians.

Albigenses

In France the Cathari were called Albigenses, because they centered around the city of Albi. They emphasized the New Testa-

ment as their only basis for faith and worship, but they also incorporated many dualistic concepts similar to those of Gnosticism. So extreme were they in their rejection of the physical and the material that they were even opposed to the reproduction of the race. They also rejected the concept of the physical presence of Christ in the Eucharist, as well as the doctrine of a literal hell and a physical resurrection. By making the New Testament their authoritative expression of faith, the Albigenses offered a challenge to the Roman Church, which claimed authority through the line of popes, going back to Christ Himself.[10] They were virtually exterminated in a crusade, sponsored by Pope Innocent III in 1208, which was led by Simon IV de Montfort.

Waldensians

At about the same time, a stronger and more influential nonconformist group called the Waldensians (or Waldenses) attracted a large following in northern Italy.[11] Known also as "the poor men from Lyons," they were followers of Peter Waldo, a prosperous merchant who turned his back on his business and the things of the world to devote himself to a life of itinerant preaching. While the Waldensians had similarities to the Cathari, there is no historically verified lineal relation between the two groups. The followers of Waldo did not hold to the dualistic approach of the Albigenses, but as early as 1184 they were excommunicated for their refusal to stop preaching as a band of laymen, popularly called the "Poor in Spirit."

Waldo formed his movement into a band of wandering preachers, ranging from Italy to France, who operated as missionaries to the people within the Church, in spite of the ban of the Pope. Their viewpoints certainly marked the Waldensians as prereformers: they opposed the Mass, the concept of purgatory, the hierarchy, the priesthood, the worship of the saints, and pilgrimages. Following the example of Christ, they went out by twos, dressed in simple clothing, and preached the Gospel to the poor in the vernacular. The Waldensians strongly believed that every man should have the Scripture in his own tongue and that it should be the final authority for one's faith and life. In various places they organized societies and called their churches "congregations." Many Free Church groups, including the Baptists, trace their origins to this movement.[12] Technically the Waldensian church still exists today in northern Italy. However, at the time of the Reformation, most of the Waldensians, as well as the Bohemian Brethren (Hussites), were influenced by the Calvinistic Reformation and merged into the Reformed Church.

Wycliffe and the Lollards

In the fourteenth century, owing to the preaching and writing ministry of John Wycliffe in England, another lay-reforming movement arose known as the Lollards. During his studies at Oxford, Wycliffe came under the influence of the Augustinian theologian Thomas Bradwardine, who taught justification by faith as opposed to salvation by works. Later, as a professor at Oxford, Wycliffe used his influential position to criticize the Pope's levying taxes in England while actually residing in Avignon, France. A strong nationalistic feeling had spread through the royal house and the middle classes of England because the Pope was now dispossessed from Rome and living in Avignon under the protection of the French king, who was England's mortal enemy. Wycliffe wrote *Of Civil Dominion* in 1376, in an attempt to reform the Church from within by the removal of immoral clergy and the removal of all property from church ownership. By these means he hoped to refocus the Church's emphasis on people's spiritual needs. He later wrote an apology for the Bible, *The Truth of the Scripture*, in which he emphasized that the Bible alone was valid in matters of faith and practice. This was followed by his treatise *On The Church*, which would later have tremendous influence on the Bohemian (Hussite) reform movement as well.

By 1382 Wycliffe was openly attacking the authority of the Pope, by insisting that Christ alone was the true Head of the Church. He also asserted that the Bible, and not the Church, was the sole authority for the believer. The Oxford professor went even further, openly opposing the doctrine of transubstantiation. He was condemned in London in 1382 by the Catholic Church and forced to retire to his rectory at Lutterworth. However, the group of lay preachers that he had founded, the Lollards, proclaimed his ideas all over England until they were condemned by Parliament in 1401 as heretics and placed under the death penalty. Wycliffe's greatest contribution was the translation of the Bible into the English language, which provided the basis for the proclamation of evangelical ideas throughout the British Isles in years to come. His views also laid the foundation for the teachings of John Huss and the Bohemian reformers.[13]

Huss and the Unity Brethren

When Richard II of England married Anne of Bohemia, students from the Continent came to England to study. Upon their return to Bohemia, they carried Wycliffe's ideas back to their homeland. John Huss studied at the University of Prague (in what is now Czechoslovakia) and eventually became its rector in 1402. His preaching paralleled the rise of Bohemian nationalism against the control of the Holy Roman Empire. Huss proposed to reform the Roman Church in Bohemia on the lines of the similar concepts proposed earlier by Wycliffe in England. Tensions between Czechs and the Germans became so severe that the Germans withdrew from the university in 1409 to establish their own institution at Leipzig. In 1414 Huss was ordered by civil authorities to go to the Council of Constance under a safe-conduct promise from the emperor, which was, however, not honored: he was condemned as a heretic. When he refused to recant, he was burned at the stake by order of the council in July of the same year.[14]

The followers of Huss eventually divided into several groups. The more radical wing were known as Taborites. They rejected all the practices of the Roman Church that could not be found in Scripture. Another branch, the Utraquists, held the position that only that which the Bible actually forbade should be eliminated. By the middle of the fifteenth century the Bohemian Brethren, or *Unitas Fratrum,* was formed under the leadership of Peter Chelčický. Emphasizing the separation of Church and State, he took a definite stand against both the ultraconservative and the ultraradical parties within the movement because of their use of the sword. Thus the "United Brethren" began as a pacifist movement within the troublesome atmosphere of medieval Europe.

The Hussite historian Peter Brock links Chelčický's views to

Waldensian influences, which had reached Bohemia at least a century before this time.[15] In defending his position of nonresistant pacifism, Chelčický wrote in his most important work, *The Net of Faith*, "Whosoever is not sincerely brought to the Christian faith through preaching of the Gospel will never be brought by force." He viewed governmental authority as necessary to control people in their wicked condition, but held that Christians should not involve themselves directly in the state, nor should the state attempt to rule the Church. His ideas laid the groundwork for what would later become the Brethren and Moravian Church movement in central Europe. Although the Brethren practiced baptism of both adults and infants in their earlier days, they later gave up the practice of baptizing adults at the time of the Roman Church's persecution of the Anabaptists.

Savonarola of Florence

Toward the end of the fifteenth century a Dominican monk named Savonarola attempted to reform the Church in Florence, Italy. While he did not advance the strong reformed positions of Wycliffe and Huss, he nevertheless brought the wrath of the Church down upon him by his preaching against the evil life of the Pope. This resulted in his death by hanging. Though Savonarola did not organize a group of followers to encourage reform within the Church, it must be observed that his attempted correction of the Church's failures coincided with a series of reforming councils that were held at Pisa (1409), Constance (1414–18), Basel (1431–49), and Ferrara and Florence (1437). These attempted reforms were put to an end by the papal bull entitled *Execrabilis*, issued by Pope Pius II in 1460, which condemned any further appeals to future general councils.[16]

NONCONFORMITY AND THE RENAISSANCE

Most studies of Free Church dissent and nonconformity at this point skip ahead to the Reformation. It should, however, be observed in the study of history that the Renaissance developed in

Europe between 1350 and 1650 and marked the transition from the medieval to the modern world. During the fourteenth century in Italy this "rebirth" of culture began with the rediscovery of the old classical works of the Greeks and Romans. In Italy this resulted in the development of classical humanism, which was matched by the development of religious humanism in Germany and Holland. In its fullest sense, the Renaissance involved an era of cultural reorientation in which people substituted an anthropocentric view of life for the medieval theocentric view. Thus man, and not God, became the measure of all things in the center of the rising urban middle-class society.[17]

The Italian Renaissance was humanistic, optimistic, and experimental in its approach to discovering the meaning of life. Spurred on by writers such as Petrarch, Cellini, and Machiavelli, and artists such as Michelangelo and Leonardo da Vinci, the new wave of secularism took its toll upon the medieval Church. The Renaissance Popes became predominantly interested in literature and the arts to the point that they made a cult of beauty. Toward the end of this period, Pope Julius II (Pope 1503–13) commissioned Michelangelo to paint the ceiling of the Sistine Chapel, and Pope Leo X (Pope 1513–21) sanctioned the sale of indulgences to raise money for the building of St. Peter's Basilica in Rome.

In the North the religious humanists, led by Colet, Reuchlin, and Erasmus emphasized the importance of the original languages of the Bible, Hebrew and Greek. Erasmus produced the first printed Greek New Testament in 1516, as well as a theological treatise, entitled *Free Will*, in 1524. Their studies eventually opened new vistas of interpretation for informed scholars who could once again read the Bible in its original languages and find therein the true Church of the New Testament era.

The Reformation and the Radical Reformation

The ultimate nonconformity came with the Protestant Reformation, whose beginnings are generally dated to between 1517 (when Luther nailed his Ninety-five Theses to the church door at Wittenberg) and 1520 (when he was excommunicated by the Catholic Church).[18] The Lutheran break was precipitated by the Indulgence

Controversy. Luther, as a professor of theology at the University of Wittenberg, openly opposed the sale of indulgences to sin. Intending his original criticism merely for the indulgence system itself, Luther soon found himself embroiled in a great conflict with the Catholic authorities. He attacked the sacramental system of the Roman Church, emphasizing that only the Lord's Supper and Baptism were valid sacraments of the Church. He emphasized that the New Testament was the basis of one's faith, and not the church fathers, councils, or papal decrees. He was excommunicated in June 1520, by Leo X. In the spring of 1521 he was summoned to the imperial council at Worms by Charles V of the Holy Roman Empire. He later escaped to Wartburg Castle, where he translated the New Testament into German in less than one year, making use of Erasmus' edition of the Greek New Testament.

Almost immediately, however, Luther came into conflict with a radical group of Anabaptists. They were so called because they were known as "rebaptizers." They insisted that only a believer's baptism by immersion was legitimate New Testament baptism. This view posed a threat to both Catholic and Protestant national churches. Luther's conflict involved a group of radicals led by Thomas Müntzer (1489?-1525), who were centered in the mining town of Zwickau in central Germany. These early Zwickau "prophets" visited Wittenberg during Luther's stay at Wartburg and caused a great deal of confusion, which ultimately led to Luther's open opposition of their preaching.

This excessive group has often been connected to the Swiss Anabaptists, but this view has now been proved false by the Radical Reformation scholar Donald Durnbaugh, who observed that the Zwickau radicals were a separate phenomenon unto themselves and that no personal contact existed between Müntzer and the Swiss Brethren. He remarks that a series of documents recently discovered clearly indicates that "the two movements can only be placed in the same camp by ignorance or prejudice."[19]

Anabaptists

The real story of the Swiss Anabaptists (or Brethren) begins with the Reformation movement of Ulrich Zwingli (1484-1531). An eloquent preacher and humanist, in 1519 he was called to become the pastor of the great cathedral church in Zurich, whereupon he began to preach straight through the New Testament. During that year he later confessed a conversion experience. In 1522 he began an active reform effort, married a widow, Anna Reinhard, and prepared *Sixty-Seven Articles* to emphasize salvation by faith and the authority of Scripture. By 1525 the Mass was abolished in Zurich, and eventually in Bern and Basel as well.

As time passed, his followers became greatly disappointed that he did not carry through even more severely on some of his beliefs. He became a sort of "halfway" man afraid to face the consequences of his own teaching. Virtually all church historians ascribe the concepts of a Free Church, baptism of believers by immersion, and the viewing of the communion service as a "memorial feast" to the influence of Zwingli.[20] It should be noted, however, that Zwingli himself opposed the Anabaptists after 1525, and the Zurich city council forbade their views and banished them from the city on threat of execution by drowning (an obvious parody on their practice of baptism by immersion). In 1531 Zwingli was killed while trying to conquer the city of Geneva by force in an attempt to win it over to the Protestant cause. He was succeeded by Heinrich Bullinger (1504–75), and eventually his followers merged with the Calvinistic movement into the Reformed Churches of Switzerland.[21] In spite of his personal limitations and excesses, Zwingli is looked upon by many Baptist historians as the "father" of the Baptist movement because of his views on believers' baptism and the commemoration concept of the Lord's Supper.

In the meantime, Zwingli's students Conrad Grebel and Felix Manz picked up where he left off and became the prophets of the more radical Anabaptist movement. One of the German Anabaptists, Balthasar Hubmaier (1481–1528), became the leader of the Free Church movement in Moravia and won thousands of Moravian converts to his Anabaptist views. Tragically, he was burned at the stake by order of the emperor and his wife was drowned in the Danube River by church authorities. Some of the Anabaptists unfortunately went even further in their radical views; they included Melchior Hoffman, who arrived in Strasbourg, France, to await the coming of the millennium in 1533.

Mennonites

In Holland, the Anabaptist movement was directed under the capable and mature leadership of Menno Simons (1496–1561). He had given up his priesthood in the Roman Church in 1536 and embraced Anabaptist views. Thereupon he assumed leadership of the "Brethren," the name taken by Anabaptists in the Netherlands. After his death, his followers were known as Mennonites. They insisted upon the authority of the Bible, literally interpreted, and believed that a pure church of regenerated members was the only true Church. They practiced baptism by pouring at first, and later by immersion. Their opposition to infant baptism and their insistence on rebaptism gave them the Anabaptist label, anyway. In time the Mennonites divided into several different groups (there are at least nineteen branches in North America alone) and numbered over half a million, spreading as far as Russia by 1788.[22] Whatever their variations, they have remained true to their basic contention favoring an autonomous, believers' church of redeemed and baptized adults. Their history became one of the most tragic chapters in all the pages of church history. Martyrs by the thousands gave their blood for their Baptistic beliefs.

Baptists

Many trace the origins of the Baptist Church movement to that of the Anabaptists.[23] Certainly it can be demonstrated that they did have a significant influence upon the Baptists in England. The first Baptist church in England was organized in 1612 by Thomas Helwys and John Murton, following the earlier influence of John Smyth, an Independent-Separatist Puritan.[24] Their roots go back to the same group that became the Pilgrims who sailed to America on the *Mayflower*.[25] The later group came from Scrooby and fled to Holland in 1609 under the leadership of Smyth. There they came under the influence of the Mennonites.

Thomas Helwys and several others, however, eventually returned to England in 1612 and organized a Baptist church that

practiced baptism by affusion (pouring) and held to Arminian doctrines with which they had become familiar during the Calvinist-
Arminian dispute in Holland. Because of their theological view of a
general atonement, they were later known as General Baptists. In
the same year, Helwys issued the first appeal for freedom of worship ever to be published in the English language.[26] The treatise
was entitled *A Short Declaration of the Mystery of Iniquity*. In it
the Baptist pastor penned a special inscription for a presentation to
King James I, a notorious supporter of the divine right of kings and
the necessity for a state church. It read: "The king is a mortall man
and not God, therefore hath not power over the immortall soules of
his subjects to make lawes and ordinances for them and to set spiritual lords over them." This bold declaration led to the author's
being thrown into Newgate Prison, and he was never heard from
again.[27]

The leadership of the General Baptists was taken up by John
Murton and Leonard Busher. In the early years of the movement
they remained in constant communication with the Dutch Mennonites. At times the English Baptists even proposed organic union
with the Dutch, but differences regarding allegiance to civil magis-
trates and support of national governments separated them. The
Baptists were in favor of allowing such practices, while the Mennonites were strickly opposed to them. By 1644 the General
Baptists numbered forty-seven congregations and formally united
as a denomination in England.

The Calvinistic, or Particular, Baptists arose in 1638 from
within an Independent Puritan congregation begun in Southwark,
London, by Henry Jacob. Some members of the Southwark congregation, led by John Spilsbury, became convinced that baptism of
believers by immersion was the only valid form of baptism. They
withdrew from the Independent congregation and formed what
would eventually become the First Particular Baptist Church in
England. Hearing of a group of Christian believers in the Netherlands who practiced baptism by immersion, they sent over one of
their members, the Dutch-speaking Richard Blunt. He arrived at
Rhynsburg near Leiden, Holland, in 1642. There he was influenced
by a Pietist group with close Mennonite affiliations, known as the
Collegiants. He was immersed himself, and upon his return to England fifty-one members of the church were also baptized by immer-

sion. By 1644 there were already seven congregations of Particular Baptists in England.[28]

Nowhere in church history will one find a group more bent toward nonconformity than Baptists. By 1689 there were already eight major Baptist confessions of faith in existence. With the restoration of Charles II to the English throne after the Commonwealth period under Oliver Cromwell, Baptists came under severe persecution. The most famous victim was John Bunyan (1628–88), who had become a Baptist in 1653 and served as an eloquent preacher despite his lack of formal education. Bunyan spent twelve years in jail for his religious convictions, during which time he wrote the famous allegory *Pilgrim's Progress.*

During the eighteenth century many of the General Baptists drifted into Arian and Socinian (Unitarian) ideas, while the Particular Baptists argued over election to the extent that they became Hyper-Calvinistic. Durnbaugh is convinced that it was not until the Wesleyan revival swept England in the late eighteenth century that new life came to the Baptist movement. After this the Baptists produced some of their greatest preachers ever, such as Andrew Fuller, John Ryland, John Gill, and the missionary statesman William Carey (1761–1834).

Carey himself is an interesting study in that he was raised an Anglican, was influenced by Methodist prayer meetings, but was baptized in 1783 by Ryland. He earned his living as a shoemaker and schoolteacher but eventually became an active pastor. Resisting the Hyper-Calvinistic strain among the Particular Baptists, in 1791 he published *The Inquiry into the Obligations of Christians to Use Means for the Conversion of the Heathen.* A year later he preached at Nottingham on his now famous theme "Expect great things from God; attempt great things for God," using Isaiah 54 as his text. He then helped form the Baptist Missionary Society with the help of Fuller and Ryland and, according to the church historian Latourette, he was the first Anglo-Saxon Protestant to propose a missionary endeavour to reach the heathen.[29] Carey himself became one of the first missionaries and spent a long and distinguished career in India. In time these Baptist nonconformists and separatists not only brought the Gospel to thousands of converts around the world, but also became leaders in the opposition to slavery within the British Empire.

Today Baptists number nearly 25 million church members in one hundred countries and over one hundred different denominations and associations. While the Baptist World Alliance, begun in 1905, links the major Baptist denominations, it by no means represents the totality of the Baptist movement. It should be observed at this point that the designation "Baptist" is not synonymous with "Fundamentalist." As we shall see, the bulk of today's Fundamentalists are certainly Baptists, but the majority of Baptists are not necessarily Fundamentalists. The major contribution of the Baptists to the history of religious nonconformity is the fact that they took a strong stand in favor of a believers' church, believers' baptism, separation of Church and State, and the individual priesthood of the believer. They represent a divergent strain from the Protestant state churches that came out of the Reformation period.

Pietists

The nonconformist emphasis in the Protestant movement at times followed parallels within the Catholic Church. Such was the case of the Pietist movement in Germany, which arose as an evangelical corrective to the cold orthodoxy of the Lutheran Church.[30] At the same time Quietism, a mystical movement within the Roman Catholic Church, was making inroads in Europe. It emphasized an intuitive approach to God by the passive soul, which opened itself to the "inner light" of God. Deriving their impetus from St. Ignatius of Loyola and St. Teresa of Ávila, the Quietists represented the mystic phase of the Counter Reformation. Francis de Sales wrote an *Introduction to the Devout Life* (1609), and Miguel de Molinos wrote his *Spiritual Guide* (1675), emphasizing the passivity of the soul in the reception of divine light from God. In time the emphasis shifted to meditative contemplation of the Divine as a means of absorption into God as the goal of the mystical experience. Following this same trend, François de la Mothe-Fénelon, tutor to the grandson of King Louis XIV of France, wrote *Christian Perfection*.

In Germany the Pietists emphasized a subjective and personal return to Bible study and prayer. The movement grew out of the ministry of Philipp Spener (1635–1705), a Lutheran pastor in Frankfurt, who organized "cottage prayer meetings" for home Bible study and prayer. Eventually August Francke (1663–1727) and some friends at Leipzig University founded a similar group, Collegia Pietatis, for Bible study. He and Spener became close friends and worked together at the University of Halle after 1691, making it the intellectual center of Pietism. They organized a *Paedagogium* in Halle and one at the University of Wittenberg. Francke eventually became the leader of the Moravian Church and took in Bohemian refugees at his Berthelsdorf estate in 1722. The missionary vision of the Moravians was unparalleled in the Western church at that time. It was their brief missionary excursion to the American colony of Georgia that left such a marked impression on the life of John Wesley. Eventually the Moravian effort in America shifted to Pennsylvania. From a spiritual and intellectual standpoint, Pietism stood as a corrective to the influence of deism and rationalism. The Pietist influence can also be traced to the revival period in American church history, especially in the ministry of Theodore Frelinghuysen, the Dutch Reformed pastor in New Jersey who in turn had such an influence upon the Presbyterian Gilbert Tennent and ultimately on Jonathan Edwards and the Great Awakening.[31]

Methodists

The Methodist movement was begun by the revival preaching of John (1703–91) and Charles Wesley (1707–88) in England during the time of the Industrial Revolution.[32] As the eighteenth century dawned in England it was a time of religious decline in every aspect of public life and morals. Drunkenness was of epidemic proportions and the conditions of the jails and factories were corrupt. The general public did not regularly attend services of the established church, and the pulpits echoed with essays on moral duties proclaimed by passionless preachers. John Wesley had been reared in an Anglican rectory, studied at Oxford, and helped organize the Holy Club there in the fall of 1729. The members of this group tried to conduct their lives in a strict, orderly fashion and soon gained the nickname of "Methodists."

In 1735 the Wesley brothers sailed to America to serve as missionaries in the colony of Georgia. However, their two years of missionary service were basically fruitless, except for the meeting with

Spangenberg and his Moravian brethren who proclaimed a personal relationship with Jesus Christ. Upon his return to London, John Wesley was greatly influenced by the Moravian leader Peter Boehler. He was converted in 1738 while attending one of the Moravian meetings at Aldersgate. Of that night Wesley records: "I felt my heart strangely warmed. I felt I did trust in Christ, Christ alone for salvation; and an assurance was given me that He had taken away my sins, even mine." Later that year he followed his friend George Whitefield into the fields and prisons, preaching the gospel and calling for an immediate and definite conversion response from his hearers. The results of Wesley's labors were unbelievable. In half a century he rode no less than 250,000 miles on horseback, preached an average of 500 times yearly, organized Methodist societies, trained lay preachers, and began to develop Sunday schools, prison reform, and organized opposition to slavery.

Wesley also preached 42,000 sermons and wrote over 50 books during his lifetime. His brother Charles wrote over 6,000 hymns. In spite of his Puritan heritage, Wesley separated from traditional Reformed doctrine in his view of prevenient grace which enables any person potentially to come to Christ.[33] Wesley held that Christ's death atoned for the sins of all and that each person was capable of resisting God's grace and could even consciously and deliberately lose salvation. He also placed great emphasis upon the experience of the believer's daily life, thus transmitting the influences of the pietistic movement on the Continent. Wesley gave the same attention and enthusiasm to the doctrine of sanctification that the older Calvinistic revivalists had given to that of justification. For Wesley, the goal of every believer was Christian perfection, which came to be known as "entire sanctification." In his early days, John Wesley worked closely with the Calvinist George Whitefield. Eventually the two parted ways over their theological differences but continued their fervent preaching ministries.

It was only after Wesley's death that the Methodists of England organized into an official Methodist Church separate from the Anglican Church. Retaining a basic episcopal polity, the Methodists included the "altar call" as a significant part of their services. Like other evangelicals, Wesley emphasized justification by faith through an instantaneous experience of conversion. He also encouraged his followers to exert a spiritual influence upon society, which was accomplished through the impact on labor and on the gin traffic, the abolition of slavery, the Sunday school movement, and prison reform in England.[34] The Methodist revival and the subsequent evangelical revival within the Anglican Church transformed the upper and lower classes of England in such a way that they caused England to become the great leader of nations and keeper of world peace during the nineteenth century. Many believe that Wesley's preaching saved England from a revolution similar to that of France. Certainly the Methodist revival ranks as the outstanding social and religious movement of the eighteenth century.

The Brethren

Also growing out of the influence of Pietism was the ministry of Alexander Mack (1679–1735), the founder of the Church of the Brethren in Germany. In summarizing the beginnings of the movement, Mack himself stated: "In the year 1708 eight persons agreed to establish a covenant of good conscience with God, to accept all the ordinances of Jesus Christ as an easy yoke, and thus follow after their Lord Jesus . . . these eight persons united together as brethren and sisters in the covenant of the cross of Jesus Christ as a church of Christian believers."[35] They were made up of people from the Palatine section of Germany, which had seen the official state religion alternate eight times in 150 years among three recognized faiths: Catholic, Lutheran, and Reformed. They were basically a simple people with an emphasis on personal and practical Bible study. They called themselves the "Brethren" and were sometimes referred to as the New Baptists.

The Brethren were strongly influenced by the writings of Gottfried Arnold (1666–1714), who urged Christians to return to the beliefs of the early Church as normative for all later Christian practice. It was from Arnold's writings that they accepted the concept of triune immersion (baptism performed three times face forward in the name of the Father, the Son, and the Holy Spirit). Though influenced somewhat by the Mennonites, the Brethren tended to look upon their pietist cousins as the "quiet ones who were too tolerant toward unbelievers." Like many of the Baptists and other nonconformist groups, the Brethren traced their origins back through various nonconformist sects to the time of Christ and the apostles.

The Brethren were severely persecuted in their own land and were forced to flee Schwarzenau, Marienborn, and Krefeld. Many of them eventually migrated to Germantown, near Philadelphia, Pennsylvania, in 1719. Mack himself led another group to America in 1729. Here they would practice their long heritage of triune immersion and the threefold communion service, which included the love feast, washing of feet, and partaking of the communion elements.[36]

Plymouth Brethren

Another Brethren group with a different origin was the Plymouth Brethren, who arose in Britain in the early nineteenth century as an attempt to restore the true New Testament Church. During this period the Oxford Movement brought about a return-to-Rome emphasis within the Anglican Church, which led to the development of the Anglo-Catholic wing and ultimately resulted in the defection of John Henry Newman to Catholicism. While some trace the evangelical reaction to the Oxford Movement back to the Primitive Methodists and the Catholic Apostolic Church (Irvingites), the Brethren themselves trace their origin to the believers' Bible study meetings held by Anthony Groves (1795–1853) in Dublin, Ireland. A similar group was begun in the same city by Edward Cronin, a medical student. In 1829 the two groups came together for the purpose of holding common services. The only requirements laid down for fellowship were a simple statement of belief in Christ and an exemplary Christian life. Any member was allowed to speak at the meetings, which followed a pattern similar to those of the Quakers.

The theologian of the movement was John Nelson Darby (1800–82), who came from a notable family, his grandfather being Lord Nelson of Trafalgar fame.[37] An excellent student, Darby entered the university at the age of fifteen and graduated with honors in law in the summer of 1819. He gave up his law practice, however, and after his conversion was ordained a deacon in the Church of England in 1825. A tireless worker who often stayed on visitation until midnight, Darby reported over six hundred Catholic defections weekly to the Anglican Church. An injury forced him to spend some time in Dublin, where he came into contact with the Brethren teachings. By 1829 he had decidedly changed his views and published a pamphlet entitled *Considerations of the Nature and Unity of the Church of Christ.* Though he did not totally break with the Church of England until seven years later, Darby resigned as curate and began an itinerant ministry of writing and speaking. He never married and used his personal estate to support himself and his newfound cause. He was extremely intelligent, dedicated, and overpoweringly influential upon most of those with whom he came into contact.

From Dublin, Darby eventually went to Plymouth, England, where he established the largest of the Brethren meetings, with over twelve hundred members by 1845. During his lifetime Darby compiled and published thirty-four large volumes. Following his example, the Brethren pastors refused the title "Reverend" and rejected all stipends and salaries. Some of the better-known men who became a part of this movement included George Müller (1805–98), who opened a large congregation and orphanage in Bristol and was known as the greatest prayer warrior of the nineteenth century. Another was Sir Robert Anderson, who had been, from 1865–1901, chief of the criminal investigation department of Scotland Yard and became known for his writings on Bible prophecy. The Plymouth Brethren were opposed to the use of musical instruments (which they traced to the influence of Cain's descendants) and were strong advocates of the doctrine of eternal security to the point that they actually reworded the well-known hymn "Just As I Am Without One Plea" to read "Just As I *Was*."

Their strongest contribution to evangelical doctrine was their teaching on the dispensations. Darby divided biblical history sevenfold into "Dispensations" (or eras) in which God dwelt in a different manner with different people. Darby strongly influenced Dwight L. Moody, the famous American evangelist, even though they differed on their attitude toward separatism. Darby's writings also had a great influence on C. I. Scofield and other American pretribulationalists. In spite of their strong belief in the soon-coming rapture of the Church, the Brethren resisted setting dates, which was already becoming the bane of such groups as the Adventists and those that would become the Jehovah's Witnesses (Russellites).

Among the early Fundamentalists, the influence of Plymouth Brethren dispensationalism can best be seen in the writings of Clarence Larkin and Harry Ironside.[38]

Quakers

Similar in church worship format but different in their theological views were the Quakers (Society of Friends).[39] They arose in England during the seventeenth century and opposed the Ranters, chiliasm, antinomianism, and individualism. Emphasizing an inner-light theology that they borrowed from the pietist movement, the early Quakers were known as "Seekers" or "Children of Light." Their followers included the well-known English statesman William Penn, who himself wrote a work entitled "Quakerism a New Nickname for Old Christianity." One of the early Quakers, John Gratton, described his personal search for truth when he said: "The Episcopalian Priests came in their white surplices and read common-prayers. . . . I saw that they had the form without the power. . . . Their worship to be in ceremony and outward things without life. The Presbyterian (Puritan) Priests, whom I had so much esteemed and admired, made their farewell sermons and left us . . . So I left them. . . . I found a people called anti-Baptist. . . . I thought they came nearest the Scriptures of any I had yet tried . . . but after they came out of the water I saw no appearance of the spirit of the newness of life and power . . . after sometime I heard of a Friends' meeting at Exton . . . and when I came I was confirmed that they were in that truth whereof I had been convinced though they were so much derided by the world."[40] During the 1650s and '60s the Quaker movement experienced explosive growth as thousands were brought into the Society of Friends.

The catalyst of the Quaker movement was the powerful person and preaching of George Fox (1624–91), who claimed to have experienced inner callings and visions from God. Fox, who is often called the father of Quakerism, was in reality one of its many preachers. Having grown up in a devout Puritan home, Fox was deeply upset by the frivolity of many of the Christians of his day. He became convinced that many professing Christians did not "possess what they professed." Finally he announced that he had come to faith in Jesus Christ alone, and this he claimed to know "experimentally." Trueblood notes that this was the key to Fox's Christianity.[41] His would be, not a religion of creed, ceremony, or practice, but one of deep personal experience. Eventually Fox embarked on a personal mission to discredit organized religion in favor of the "opening" of the soul to the inner light of God. His iconoclastic approach to dealing with organized religion was ultimately dubbed the "Lamb's War." Viewing their mission as being from God, the Quakers sent itinerant missionaries all over the known world. They went so far as to confront the Sultan of Turkey and the Emperor of China. They even went to Rome to try to convert the Pope and were probably thrown in jail! They were not always appreciated by other Christian groups; one Anglican said of them, "The Quakers compass sea and land to make proselytes; they send out yearly a vagabond of Fellows that ought to be taken up and put in Bedlam . . . their preaching of cursing and lies poisoning the souls of the people with damnable errors and heresies."[42] In defense of the movement, Robert Barclay (1648–90) wrote a classic apologetic and systematic treatment of Quaker beliefs known as the *Apology,* which, although anti-Calvinistic in content, parallels the *Institutes* in form. The methods and "messianic" mission of the Quakers were not unlike those of many Fundamentalists today, though they have little lineal relation.

The Disciples

A final nonconformist group following separatist principles became known as the Disciples of Christ. While the Christian Church movement is generally looked upon as American in nature, its British roots certainly cannot be denied. Some trace the origin of New Testament restorationism, which became the fundamental principle of the Church of Christ, to John Glas (1695–1773), and the teachings of his son-in-law, Robert Sandeman (1718–71).[43] They attempted to reestablish the Church simply, along the lines of the early New Testament Christian pattern. This practice brought them into sharp contrast with the Methodists, who were willing to accept the structure of the Church of England while attempting to reform its spiritual life.

A second impulse also originated in Scotland with the Haldane brothers, Robert and James. Both were raised as members of the Church of Scotland, but repudiated it because of Hyper-Calvinism. When the Kirk formally voted to reject the resolution "that it is the duty of Christians to send the Gospel to the heathen world," the Haldanes began to preach and distribute tracts emphasizing the application of Calvinistic doctrine to legitimate evangelism and missions. They further contacted the Anglican evangelist Rowland Hill and employed him to preach in a large tabernacle that was constructed in Edinburgh. In 1799 they formally withdrew from the Church of Scotland and organized an independent, Free Church congregation. They further set up a training school for ministers in Glasgow and even ministered for a time in Geneva. Though they are well known among Presbyterians for their Calvinistic commentaries, they are also well known among the Disciples for their influence on Alexander Campbell (1788–1866). His father belonged to the clergy of the Seceder Presbyterian Church in Ireland and migrated to America with his family in 1807. In the meantime Alexander remained in Scotland to pursue his studies at the University of Glasgow, where he was strongly influenced by the Haldanes, the writings of Sandeman, and the Plymouth Brethren. Meanwhile his father, Thomas, wrote his now famous *Declaration and Address*, which became the "Constitution" of the Church of Christ movement.[44]

Alexander eventually emerged as the dynamic preacher of the new movement and the pastor of the congregation at the Brush Run, Pennsylvania, Church. Upon the birth of Alexander's infant son, he was forced to face the question of the scriptural legitimacy of infant baptism. Intensive study by the Campbells led them to conclude that it was not a biblical doctrine. Both father and son and their wives submitted to immersion by a Baptist pastor in June of 1812. The Brush Run Church then joined the Baptist Association, and for the next seventeen years Alexander Campbell became a belligerent promoter of baptism by immersion. In 1823 he actually founded a periodical called *The Christian Baptist*. By 1830, however, the Campbells broke with the Baptists over the official confessions of faith, which they strongly opposed. From that point on, Campbell's followers were known as "Campbellites" by their enemies, while they called themselves simply "Disciples."

Alexander Campbell gained a national reputation from his well-publicized debates with Baptists, Catholics, and "Free Thinkers." He organized Bethany College, West Virginia, in 1840, published his own translation of the Bible, was elected a delegate to the Virginia State Constitutional Convention, and in general was known as an active preacher, promoter, and writer.

A similar movement became known officially as the Christian Church, emphasizing primitive church government in the form of a republic, which its members viewed as having "come down from heaven." Opposing the predestination teaching of the Particular Baptists, Elias Smith and Abner Jones organized the first independent Christian Church in Vermont in 1801. Smith later founded the *Herald of Gospel Liberty* as the periodical of the movement. The new movement received further impetus from the famous camp meetings at Cane Ridge, Kentucky, during the late eighteenth century under the preaching of Barton W. Stone (1772–1844). Though originally a licensed Presbyterian minister, Stone rejected the Presbyterian view of election in favor of what he called "Free Grace." By 1803 he had withdrawn from the Presbyterian synod of Kentucky and Ohio. Unlike Campbell, who died the richest man in West Virginia, Stone died in virtual poverty for the cause he promoted.

These variant strands of Christian Churches formally merged in 1832; Durnbaugh notes: "They shared the conviction that denominationalism was wrong, that creeds were unnecessary, that predestination was an error."[45] Always emphasizing the central importance of baptism by immersion as a major evidence of conversion, the Disciples' form of evangelism began to follow the five-step approach of Walter Scott (1796–1861), which involved faith in God, repentance, baptism, remission of sins, and reception of the Holy Spirit. Their emphasis on what became known as "baptismal regeneration" brought severe reprisals from Baptists and Presbyterians alike. Though not directly related to the fundamentalist controversy, the Church of Christ, unlike the Christian Church, still holds to very conservative doctrine today.

CONCLUDING OBSERVATIONS ON
RELIGIOUS NONCONFORMITY

It is certainly obvious that the various Free Church movements down through the years have emphasized their own particular idiosyncrasies and individualistic approaches to the Bible, theology, and ecclesiastical structure. It is equally obvious, however, that they represent a very definite strain within the history of Christianity. While not providing a clear "Trail of Blood" back through the various ages of martyrs to the apostles themselves, the nonconformists nevertheless represent a definite set of basic principles held in common opposition to main-line Christianity.

The Infallibility and
Authority of Scripture

Virtually every divergent group in the history of Christianity has based its principles upon the authority of the Bible. It may definitely be said that these movements had a basic distrust of human reason and the corporate consensus of religious ecclesiasticism. They placed the Bible above creeds, councils, papal edicts, philosophical arguments, and religious tradition. The one unifying factor in all these movements, without a doubt, is their common adherence to the basic authority of Scripture as the only dependable guide for faith and practice.

Separation of Church and State

The nonconformist approach to the issue of Church-State relations has always been one of vocal denunciation of any organic tie between the two. This conviction has often been misunderstood by English and other European Christians who come from the state church traditions. Even at the time of the American Revolution, when the Baptist Isaac Backus was urging a clear separation of

Church and State, many others feared that such a final dissolution would be the ultimate destruction of the Church itself.[46] On the contrary, the separation of Church and State by the First Amendment to the Constitution forced American preachers into aggressive evangelism in order to win converts and followers to their movements. This has become one of the unique trademarks of the American church system. No longer could any particular group depend upon state support in spite of its lack of numerical success.

In contrast to the state-supported churches of Britain and continental Europe, which have been steadily in decline (virtually to the point of death) over the past two hundred years, the independent church movement in America has grown rapidly to mammoth proportions.[47] Since no one automatically belonged to a particular church, a person's allegiance and membership had to be vigorously sought by the various churches. This healthy spirit of competition (though at times degenerating into near-disastrous ecclesiastical battles) has paralleled the similar dynamic growth of the republican and capitalistic system in American society. Thus, without deliberate intention, the United States Constitution provided the nonconformist churches with the opportunity to develop in an atmosphere of unrestricted freedom. Their aggressive message was able to be as openly applied to society as was that of the more established churches.

Religious Liberty

The clarion call for separation of Church and State was by no means intended by the early American civil or religious forefathers as an attack upon religious liberty. In fact, on the contrary, it was an appeal for religious liberty. Some argue that the absence of a national religion causes people to seek a substitute by making a religion of the nation. There can be no doubt that many Americans view the Christian impact upon our nation as a providential act of God, establishing America as a modern-day "chosen people" to be used as a vehicle for His purposes. Allegiance to America has become the unifying factor among the divergent religious groups of this nation. While this has been criticized by many, it must be observed that it is no different from the common allegiance to our national unity among our varying political groups as well. Durnbaugh correctly observes: "What is now taken for granted in much of the world as an elementary right was quite literally a revolutionary doctrine when first proclaimed as a truth by the radical reformers."[48] He goes on to refer to Chelčický's words: "Whoever is not sincerely brought to the Christian faith through preaching of the Gospel shall never be brought by force" as the watchword of religious liberty for today. The love of religious liberty by American Christians certainly originates from the history of severe persecution of the nonconformist from whom we derive our spiritual heritage.

Involvement in the State

Professor Durnbaugh further emphasizes the involvement of the believers' churches (nonconformist) in the governmental affairs of state.[49] He breaks these into three basic categories: (1) *Lutheran:* the attempt of the kingdom of Christ to transform human society; (2) *Mennonite:* witness without political involvement; (3) *Baptist:* guardians of the dividing wall of Church and State, while confronting the state through the means of proclamation of the standards of Christian truth. Unfortunately, today many secularists are attempting to criticize the involvement of Christian groups in the political arena. The history of religious groups, however, shows that they have always been very actively involved in the political and social processes of the state. Separation of Church and State does not mean separation of God from society. Religious liberty does not mean bondage to secularism. Rather, the historic position of religious nonconformity is one of spiritual confrontation with society itself.

Evangelism, Discipleship, and Missions

The uniqueness of the nonconformist Free Churches is their strong commitment to aggressive evangelism. To these churches, recruitment is the "name of the game." The very nature of the ministry involves an aggressive confrontation of Christianity with non-Christian society. Following the guideline of Scripture, conservative Christians consider themselves to be "in the world, but not of the world." Thus we believe we have a mission to the world in which we live. Christians view themselves as God's agents within society. Recognizing that the kingdom of Christ is not spread by the sword, evangelical Christians view the military as the means of defending the peace so that law and order may prevail, allowing Christians the freedom to spread the message of Jesus Christ to the world. When this distinctive commitment to the mission of the Church is lost, Christianity reverts to introspective intellectualism and retrogressive demise. It is no wonder that those Christian groups most strongly committed to missions and evangelism are the groups that are growing the most rapidly and extensively today.[50]

Regenerated Church Membership

In spite of their theological differences, the various nonconformist churches in common emphasize the concept of a believers' church, that is, one in which every member professes personal faith in Jesus Christ. To the nonconformist, church membership is not looked upon as a mere question of social manners or fidelity to the family heritage. Rather, it is viewed as the most serious associational commitment that an individual can make. Fundamentalists hold strongly to this same principle, emphasizing the importance of personal salvation for each individual. Thus their commitment to evangelism relates to their commitment to a regenerated membership.

Restoration of New Testament Church Principles

Another common feature of the Free Church movement has been the desire to return to the simplicity of the early churches. Nonconformists seek to wend their way back through the Reformation, medieval society, and Imperial Roman influence to reach the original purpose and intent of the Church in order to reestablish a church consistent with the practice of the apostles of Christ Himself.

While this commitment varies in intensity from one group to another, it is nevertheless an underlying factor in the independent movement, which tends to avoid the ritual, liturgy, and structure of the established churches.

Fundamentalism is the spiritual and intellectual descendant of the nonconformist Free Church movement. There can be no doubt that fundamentalist roots go back to the evangelicals of the late nineteenth century, who were a product of the Free Church heritage. While modern-day Fundamentalists may actually oppose some of the branches of that movement (such as Quakers), they nevertheless are common recipients of a heritage that recognized the Bible above all human ecclesiastical systems.

3

***

AMERICA'S RELIGIOUS HERITAGE

The development of religious dissent and nonconformity in Europe led to the ultimate migration of thousands of Protestants to colonial America in the seventeenth century. One cannot help but observe that Columbus' discovery of America came less than twenty-five years before the beginning of the Reformation in Europe. It was as if God had preserved a great "Island in the Sea" as a place of refuge for the persecuted believers from continental Europe. While it is true that the early colonists came to North America in search of economic wealth, it must also be observed that their religious motivation was of great importance, too. As Cairns observes, "the transplanting of Europeans to North America cannot be disassociated from the transplanting of their religion to the same land."[1]

ANGLICAN BEGINNINGS

The first permanent English settlement in America was established at Jamestown in 1607 by the Virginia Company. Among the settlers was Robert Hunt, a chaplain who planted the Anglican Church in the New World. He first gave the Lord's Supper to the colonists under the protection of an old sail while the worshipers sat on logs. By 1611 Alexander Whitaker, a leading Puritan, had become the minister of the Anglican Church in Virginia. In 1624 the Virginia Company was dissolved; Virginia became a royal colony ruled by a governor. Though the Anglican Church remained the established church in the new colony, its influence waned until the arrival of James Blair in 1689. He founded the College of William and Mary in Williamsburg to provide a more literate training for pastors entering the ministry.

In time the Anglican Church also became the established church of Maryland, despite the opposition of Roman Catholics who had settled there in great numbers under the religious toleration of Lord Baltimore. The Anglicans also became the established church in New York by 1693, notwithstanding the opposition of the Dutch Calvinists who had originally settled New York as New Amsterdam. Similar acts were passed in the early eighteenth century, making the Anglican Church the established religion in North Carolina, South Carolina, and Georgia. Thus Anglicanism became the predominant denomination of the middle and southern states.

In the meantime, the situation in New England was distinctly different. Here the early colonists were Congregationalist-Puritans who held to a strong Calvinistic theology. The separatist congregation at Scrooby, England, migrated to America in August of 1620 on the *Mayflower*. Now known as the Pilgrims, they landed at Plymouth in New England rather than in Southern Virginia, which was their original goal. Before they ever landed, they drew up the Mayflower Compact as an instrument of government for the new colony. In reality, it was an extension of the covenant concept of covenant theology to the realm of civil government. With Elder Brewster as their spiritual leader and William Bradford as their first governor, the Pilgrim Fathers established strong settlements at both Plymouth and Salem, Massachusetts. The church became the dominant force in the spiritual and social life of these communities. John White, a Puritan pastor at Dorchester, England, led a settlement of Puritans to Salem, landing there in the fall of 1628. They were organized as the Massachusetts Bay Company; the right to vote was limited to church members. In essence, then, Congregationalism became the state religion of the new colony. The colonists rejected episcopacy as a form of government but upheld the principle of uniformity of faith. Between 1628 and 1640, over twenty thousand Puritans arrived in Massachusetts. The vast majority of their pastors were university graduates who had been educated at Cambridge, England during the height of Puritan influence there. These churches were therefore congregational in governmental policy and strongly Calvinistic in theology.

In time, similar colonies were established by the Puritans in Connecticut, by Thomas Hooker and John Davenport. They obtained land from the Indians by treaty and eventually established a commonwealth in 1639, based on the Bible. Again they limited voting rights to church members only. It should be observed that while the Pilgrim and Puritan fathers came to America for the purpose of religious freedom, they did not readily grant that same privilege to those who disagreed with them. In essence, they were fleeing from persecution and came to America to establish their own religious convictions, rather than to promote the religious freedom of all varying Protestant groups. This can be clearly evidenced from the Cambridge (Massachusetts) Synod of 1646 at which representatives of the four Puritan colonies adopted the Westminster Confession of Faith as an expression of their theology. This led to the development of the Cambridge Platform, adopted in 1648, declaring that each church was autonomous but related to the others for the purpose of fellowship. Each church was established by a church covenant linking the believers of one to the others in Christ as the head of the Church.

As early as 1710 thousands of Scotch-Irish Presbyterians migrated from Britain to America. Most were unhappy with the church situation in New England and moved to New Jersey and New York instead. Others became influential in the Pittsburgh area, and still others moved as far south as the Shenandoah Valley of Virginia. Francis Makemie became the father of American Presbyterianism when he organized the Presbytery of Philadelphia in 1706. By 1719 this synod also adopted the Westminster Confession as its doctrinal statement.

One of the trademarks of the early Calvinists in America was the establishment of colleges as educational centers for civic and religious leaders. Harvard was founded in 1636 to "advance learning and secure a literate ministry"; Yale College, in 1701 in Connecticut to provide a "liberal and religious education." In 1726 William Tennent, a Scotch-Irish Presbyterian, established his now famous "Log College" near Philadelphia to educate young men for the ministry. This school was later known as the College of New

Jersey and eventually as Princeton University. In the early educational systems of America, the Bible definitely had first place and classical training took second place, as an aid to further religious education. The Puritan interest in education can be traced directly to the influence of Calvin and Luther at the time of the Reformation.

PURITANISM

Puritanism was a reforming movement within the sixteenth-century Church of England, eventually fathering Presbyterians, Congregationalists, and Baptists. Theologically dependent upon continental Calvinism, the Puritans believed that the English Reformation under Henry VIII had stopped short of "purifying" the church of all Romish and Catholic influences. During the reign of Queen Elizabeth I (1557-1603) the Puritans tried to work within the Church of England to bring about a series of reforms that would remove all forms of compromise with Rome.[2] They attacked clerical garments, prayer books, bishops, wedding rings, candles, the sign of the cross, and even Christmas observance as unnecessary Romish "Popism." In short, they demanded a more complete reformation of the Church of England along Calvinistic and congregational lines.

Haller observes that the heart of Puritan unrest at this period was the criticism of the preaching in the Elizabethan court church, captured in the words of Richard Greenham, who lamented the number of ministers "whose knowledge is in swelling words and painted eloquence of human wisdom."[3] To the Puritan mind, the true ministry was not in the itch of ears but in the care of souls. Shelley states: "Sparks from the pulpits of these early Puritans, as much as any other single factor, ignited the movement that called England and America to spiritual awakening."[4]

Puritanism can be distinguished from the Anglicanism of its day by its insistence upon the Bible as the only basis of the Church's life and practice. This belief ignited controversy with the Anglicans and within various groups of Puritanism itself. The Puritans also maintained a strong belief in the sovereignty of Christ over nature and history. However, they grounded their belief in predestination on the experience of the believer and were much more active and less passive than the continental Calvinists. They believed that God had called them and that they must live for His glory. It is in this sense that Shelley observes that they prove to be the forerunners of later Evangelicals.[5] Thus they sought to preserve the priority of God and the responsibility of humanity. Emerson states: "Puritan doctrine was, to begin with, evangelical: the central point of the Puritan's life was supposed to be conversion."[6]

The ideals of Puritans were certainly exemplary. The Church and the commonwealth were to walk together harmoniously so that all of society and life would be devoted to God's glory. But their excessive emphasis on church discipline, with the exclusion of hypocrites from the membership and the limitation of the franchise to church members only, inevitably created a society wherein the saints were all-powerful and the unchurched were less than second-class citizens. The seeds of Puritan church decay lay in the fragmentation of society caused by the increase of individualism in the New World.[7]

SEPARATISM AND THE BAPTISTS

The Baptist movement in America began with Roger Williams (1603?–83). He was educated for the Anglican ministry at Cambridge, England, but soon adopted separatist views that led him from England to Boston and then Plymouth, Massachusetts. Opposed by the Puritan oligarchy, he was expelled from the colony because of his opposition to the state church and his insistence that political rulers had no power over a person's religion. In 1636 he made his now famous journey through the wilderness and was aided by some friendly Indians from whom he eventually purchased the tract of land that he named Providence (Rhode Island). In 1638 a Baptist church was founded at Providence and all of the members were rebaptized, including Williams himself. Another Baptist church was established in 1648 at Newport under the influence of Mrs. Anne Hutchison, who similarly was banned from the Massachusetts Colony because of religious meetings that she was holding in her home without church approval. The greatest contribution of the Baptists was their emphasis upon the separation of Church and State and the freedom of the individual believer's conscience. With their emphasis upon the priesthood of the believer, the Baptists developed a more individualistic emphasis on one's approach to salvation.[8]

A leading Baptist-separatist of the colonial period was Isaac Backus (1724–1806), who applied the principle of the liberty of the individual soul to matters of Church and State relations. He openly backed the Revolutionary War, preaching to the troops on numerous occasions. Theologically he was a follower of Jonathan Edwards and a defender of the New Light Revival, but politically he was an admirer of Thomas Jefferson's opposition to a religious establishment. McLoughlin observes that "to understand Backus is to understand the American Evangelical mentality which went through the Age of Reason, deism and rationalism, almost unscathed, to emerge with greater devotion than ever to revivalistic religion."[9]

It may well be said that Backus was the father of Baptist separatism. Goen states: "His career well typifies how the revivalistic piety of the Separates gradually infiltrated Baptist ranks."[10] In one ten-year stretch Backus traveled 14,691 miles and preached 2,412 sermons promoting the Baptist cause. His greatest contribution, however, was with his pen. He became the most prolific of all the Baptist writers of the period. His *History of New England with Particular Reference to the Denomination of Christians Called Baptists* is one of the most accurate and exact of all the histories of New England. In spite of opposition to his views by the Congregationalists, Backus continued to pour forth a steady stream of books and pamphlets promoting the cause of religious liberty and the separation of Church and State.

REVIVALISM

As time marched on in colonial America, the second and third generations of English settlers did not have the same enthusiasm for God that their fathers and grandfathers had shown. Woodbridge comments: "This gradual dilution of Puritan thought was matched by a progressive cooling of the religious fervor that had characterized many of the country's first settlers."[11] The unity of society based on common Calvinistic theology began to wane in spite of the brilliant theological treatises of Samuel Willard and Cotton Mather. It was not until the late 1720s that a great spiritual revival would shake colonial America. The "Great Awakening" was so extensive in its effects and consequences that it may unequivocally be stated that America would never be the same again! While Pietism on the Continent and Methodism in England were gaining in evangelical fervor, it was the Great Awakening that exploded the influence of revivalism on American life in the early eighteenth century.[12]

The revival movement had its beginning in 1726 in the Dutch Reformed congregation of Theodore Frelinghuysen in New Jersey. It stimulated a new interest in personal, heartfelt conversion. His work then influenced the Presbyterian pastors Gilbert and William Tennent.[13] With a strong hold in the Middle Colonies, the revival movement spread northward among the Puritan Congregationalists. In Northampton, Massachusetts, Jonathan Edwards (1703–58) had succeeded his grandfather Solomon Stoddard as the pastor of the local church. After his student days at Yale College, Edwards had a conversion experience much like that of John Wesley. He stated that there entered his soul "a sense of the glory of the divine being" while he was reading the Pauline ascription: "Now unto the King eternal, immortal, invisible, the only wise God, be honour and glory for ever and ever. Amen" (1 Tim. 1:17).[14] From this point on, Edwards began to preach the necessity of personal conversion and attempted to wed his newfound experience with Calvinistic orthodoxy. His powerful preaching and vivid imagery were so overwhelming that they resulted in an unusual number of conversions, serious confession of sin, and a general improvement in public morality.

When George Whitefield (1714–70) arrived in the colonies in 1738, he found much of the groundwork already laid for revival. He was readily welcomed by Edwards in the winter of 1740 and "touched off a powder keg" in New England that sent the blaze of revival through the colonies.[15] Their preaching was so powerful that men and women wilted in confession of sin before them. The revival had begun in 1734 in New England and reached its greatest crest by 1742, but its effects continued to influence American life greatly up until the time of the Revolutionary War. In spite of the acceptance of the revival among the laity, the established clergy voiced opposition to certain practices of the revival preachers. They charged them with uninhibited "enthusiasm" and causing divisions within the established churches. The faculty of Harvard went so far as to pass a public censure of Whitefield's preaching because of his "enthusiasm" and extemporaneous delivery and his itinerant ministry.[16] However, the ultimate effect of the revival was an increase of religious tolerance. Shelley notes: "Of equal importance was the tolerance that cut across denominational lines."[17] This attitude contributed to a national spirit of religious tolerance that would characterize an evangelical consensus that continues to our own day. The society of New England hovered between the old Puritan ideology and a new, still-developing theology of revivalism. The unity and purpose of the Puritan ideology lay in its ability to hold in proper tension, for its time and place, the centrifugal forces of Western culture: reason and emotion. It left American society flexible enough to encompass change and conservative enough to maintain continuity. The great heritage of the revival movement was undoubtedly the spiritual development of the soul of America. It is estimated that as many as one third of the adult population of colonial America were converted in the forty-year period from 1730 to 1770. Certainly America was ready for freedom when the Revolutionary War came upon the scene.

The major interruption to the revival movement came in the form of the French and Indian War and then the American Revolution. Woodbridge observes that "while New England Congregationalists, Pennsylvania Presbyterians, and Carolina Baptists argued about how men were freed from sin, colonists all across America spoke even more eagerly about being freed from parliament."[18] The Declaration of Independence would proclaim that "all Men are created equal, that they are endowed by their Creator with certain unalienable Rights." The renewed emphasis on individualism and the importance of people's taking responsibility to shape their future began to deemphasize the old Reformed theology that had so long controlled New England. The doctrines of total depravity and limited atonement were especially offensive to Americans who wanted a sense of shaping their own destiny. With the success of the Revolutionary War came a major advance in American religious development: complete religious freedom! By the time the war ended, the American Colonies were made up of several divergent religious groups. With the exception of Pennsylvania, where the Quaker William Penn had allowed religious freedom, most of America was still struggling with a state church. Since all these divergent groups contributed in one form or another to the success of the independence effort, the new Congress of the United States decided to allow total religious freedom throughout all the states.

DENOMINATIONALISM

With the rise of the new nation came a renewed emphasis on denominational distinctives and the establishment of great national churches.[19] The Anglican Church was especially in danger because of its strong dependence upon England. The First Amendment to the Constitution guaranteed separation of Church and State in those states where there had previously been an established church. The Methodists, led by Thomas Coke and Francis Asbury, created the Methodist Episcopal Church in 1784. The Anglicans set up the Protestant Episcopal Church in 1789. The Presbyterians created a national church and called a general assembly in the same year. The Dutch and German Reformed churches also formed national denominations, in 1792 and 1793. The way was being paved for a new wave of denominational distinction. By the early nineteenth century several major developments were well under way. The theological unity of Reformed evangelicalism was beginning to dissipate and would soon be replaced by strong influences from Arminian and Holiness theology. Evangelicalism was dominating American life less and cooperating with it more. Hence there began a century-long struggle with the matter of social identification and adaptability of the Church in society. There was at the same time an increasing "Americanization" of the Church, as the United States of America itself was seen as the agent for doing God's work in the world.

The Second Great Awakening began in the 1790s and continued into the early part of the nineteenth century. Timothy Dwight (1752–1817), grandson of Jonathan Edwards, led a great revival movement in New England as the new president of Yale College.

In the meantime, the Presbyterian evangelist James McGready brought an even more emotional revival to the Mid-South in the spectacular camp meetings in Kentucky and Tennessee. The frontier revivals emphasized the work of the Holy Spirit directly in the life of the believer.[20] The emphasis of the revival preachers of the Second Awakening leaned more strongly toward encouraging the listener to make a personal response to Christ. Several new schools were also formed at this time, such as Andover Theological Seminary (1808), in opposition to the rising tide of Unitarianism among the New England Congregationalists. By the end of the nineteenth century there would be significant changes in the methodology of revivalism through the influence of Charles Finney and ultimately Dwight L. Moody.[21]

Moody and Finney were much stronger in their proclamation of the love of God.[22] They urged their listeners to make an immediate and personal response to the Gospel apart from denominational considerations. They had great appeal to the masses of lower-class and average Americans who made up their audiences.

Of all the denominations, however, Shelley observes: "None surpass the Methodists and Baptists in their fire and forgiveness preaching. By their ceaseless seeking of souls, these two denominations quickly overtook what had once been the strong Colonial churches, Congregationalists and Episcopalians. Just before the Civil War the combined strength of Methodists and Baptists accounted for nearly seventy percent of the total number of Protestant communicants."[23] The impact of the revival would remain a major impulse in the development of nineteenth-century Evangelicalism and would pave the way for the rise of Fundamentalism.

PERFECTIONISM

The American revival movements of the nineteenth century were greatly influenced by the Methodist revivals under John Wesley in England. American Methodism was led by the efforts of Francis Asbury (1745–1816) and Peter Cartwright (1785–1872). By 1844 the Methodists had become the largest denomination in the United States.[24] The influence of Methodism in American life may be seen in the fact that it did more to popularize personal religion than any other ecclesiastical movement of its time. Because of Wesley's emphasis on personal holiness and sinless perfection,[25] Methodism became the lineal parent of the Holiness and Pentecostal movements that arose from its influence.

Charles G. Finney (1792-1875) became the leading promoter of the particular form of Arminian theology that came to be known as Perfectionism, or "Oberlin theology." Along with Asa Mahan, the first president of Oberlin College and author of *The Scripture Doctrine of Christian Perfection* (1839), Finney became the leader of the new "Holiness Movement." Though raised a Presbyterian, Finney strongly rejected his Calvinistic heritage for a proclamation of a message of personal decision to trust Christ as one's Savior. Though he was denounced by older men like Lyman Beecher, Charles Hodge, and Asahel Nettleton, Finney became the first professional evangelist and the father of modern evangelism.[26] In his day he ranked with Horace Greeley and Daniel Webster as an outstanding American of his time.

Finney's spectacular revivals in New York City in the 1830s attracted unprecedented interest in evangelistic crusades. In 1839 Phoebe Palmer and her sister Sarah Lankford began promoting the "Tuesday Holiness Meetings." The same year, Bostonian Timothy Merritt began publishing *The Guide to Christian Perfection*. The Holiness theologian and historian Vinson Synan notes that Mrs. Palmer also developed, prior to the Civil War, her "altar terminology" for leading believers into the "second blessing."[27] She became the first woman preacher of the Holiness Movement, conducting large revival meetings throughout the United States, Canada, and England. She also established the Five Points Mission in New York City in 1850. Thus the social consciousness of the evangelical revival within the Holiness Movement had already begun.[28] The establishment of the Salvation Army also typified the social reforming trend among Holiness advocates.

After the Civil War the Holiness Movement spread beyond the boundaries of the Methodist Church through the impetus of the National Holiness Association, founded in 1867 under the leadership of John Inskip. The movement grew rapidly until 1900. Until then it was strongly supported by many leading Methodist bishops. The major tenet of the movement, however, continued to be the teaching of entire sanctification as a second work of grace. By 1894 the Methodist Church officially rejected the Holiness Movement, and it began to fragment into various denominations (Nazarene, Pilgrim Holiness, Church of God, and others). In the meantime, the movement had strongly influenced the Keswick Conferences, which adopted the concept of the baptism of the Holy Spirit as an "endowment of power" for service and for an overcoming life of spiritual victory. However, with the influence of Moody, Torrey, and Simpson, the strict Holiness emphasis upon the "second blessing" began to dissipate. In the meantime, the more radical wing of the movement became known as the "fire-baptized holiness" believers; they followed the views of B. H. Irwin as demonstrated in the Cane-Ridge camp meetings.[29]

Weisberger quotes one version of a typical Methodist camp meeting in Alabama:

> Then he tried to argy wi' me—but bless the Lord!—he couldn't do that nother! Ha! Lord! I tuk him fust in the Old Testament— bless the Lord!—and I argyed him all thro' Kings—then I throwed him into Proverbs—and from that, here we had it up and down, Kleer down to the New Testament, and then I begun to see it work him! Then we got into Matthy, and from Matthy right straight along to Acts; and thar I throwed him! Yes L-O-R-D! and h-e-r-e he is![30]

The major positive contribution of the Holiness Movement was its emphasis on personal, practical, and devout Christian living, which would leave its imprint on American Evangelicalism in the decades ahead. This can be evidenced by the influential book *The Christian's Secret of a Happy Life*, written by Hannah Whitehall Smith in 1875. The Holiness Movement represents an intensification of Wesley's original teaching, rather than an alteration of it, and has continued as a powerful influence in American Evangelicalism ever since. Like dispensationalism, it has influenced many Evangelicals who have no lineal connection with the Methodist or Holiness movements themselves.

PENTECOSTALISM

The "second blessing" theology of the Holiness Movement ultimately grew into the Pentecostal expression under the teaching of

Charles F. Parham, a former Methodist, who himself had been influenced by the Holiness Movement. He began to teach that the baptism of the Holy Spirit was something more tangible than just the inward experience of the second blessing. Relying heavily upon the Book of Acts, he urged his students to seek a supernatural gift from the Holy Spirit. He reasoned that the same phenomena that characterized the early Church should characterize the modern Church. Students at his Bethel Healing School in Topeka, Kansas, began speaking in tongues early in 1901. Suddenly the Holiness Movement found an immediate and tangible evidence of its longed-for expression of the second blessing. Tongues-speaking became the major impulse of the Pentecostal Movement.[31]

In 1906 one of Parham's students, W. J. Seymour, received an invitation to speak at a Negro Holiness Church in Los Angeles. When his message and central proposition (that anyone who did not speak in tongues was not baptized with the Holy Spirit) did not receive favorable audience from the congregation, Seymour rented an old Methodist church on Azusa Street in Los Angeles. From this the now famous Azusa Street Mission became the world headquarters for the spread of the Pentecostal message and shook the Christian world in the early twentieth century. In reality, Parham and Seymour merely extended the doctrines of the Holiness Movement.[32]

The relationship of the Pentecostal Movement to that of the Fundamentalists was extremely ambiguous in light of the dispensational scheme adopted by most of the Fundamentalists and Evangelicals during the same period. In spite of the adoption by most Pentecostals of the dispensational scheme (which was diametrically opposed to their claim that the charismatic gifts had been restored to the Church), they ultimately ended in a bitter and disruptive break from the main body of Fundamentalists. The earliest and most extreme opposition to the Pentecostal Movement came from both the Fundamentalist and Holiness groups, who rejected tongues-speaking as being valid for the Church today. The break became formal in 1928 when the World's Christian Fundamentals Association disenfranchised the Pentecostals, charging them with promoting "fanatical and unscriptural emphases on tongues and healing." Pentecostal historian Vinson Synan notes: "As a rule, the Pentecostals were assigned to the lunatic fringe of

American religion and disowned by practically everybody."[33] Nevertheless, the spread of Pentecostalism in the twentieth century has been nothing short of phenomenal. The movement spread quickly in the South and West, as well as throughout various parts of Europe and South America (where three fourths of all Protestants are considered to be Pentecostal). Since World War II the Pentecostal Movement has taken a renewed form in the Charismatic Movement and has gained an even wider acceptance among the traditional main-line denominations.[34]

In more recent times moderate Evangelicals have been much more accepting of the Pentecostal denominations. Within the National Association of Evangelicals, since the 1940s it is proper to state that the Pentecostal Movement has occupied a legitimate place in the mainstream of American Evangelicalism. The movement has reaffirmed the importance of the Holy Spirit's ministry as a neglected doctrine in evangelical and nonevangelical churches alike. While Fundamentalists, as a group, violently reject the Pentecostal-Charismatic Movement because of its emphasis on the doctrine of tongues, it must, nevertheless, be recognized that the Pentecostal Movement is based upon an evangelical doctrinal foundation. To that foundation, however, the movement has added a stronger subjective religious experience than is accepted by most conservative Christians.[35]

MILLENNIALISM

Although the Puritans had been overwhelmingly premillennial in their earlier days, by the middle of the eighteenth century they began to give way to the rise of postmillennialism, which was spurred on by the views of Jonathan Edwards, America's leading theologian before the Revolutionary War. Premillennialism taught that Christ would return before the Millennial Kingdom in order to establish that kingdom upon the earth. By contrast, postmillennialism taught that Christ would return after the Millennial Kingdom was already established by the preaching of the Gospel and the work of the Church. Unlike either of these two views, amillennialism taught that there would be no literal one-thousand-year kingdom on the earth. This view sees the Church as the New Testament fulfillment of God's promises to the nation of Israel; therefore, as an eschatological system it sees no distinct future for Israel at all.

In light of the sweeping revival movements of the early nineteenth century, church leaders such as Lyman Beecher began to proclaim that "the millennium is at the door."

Throughout the nineteenth century, which may be viewed as the great century of evangelical accomplishment in the Western world, the postmillennial view gained further acceptance until the dawning of the disasters of the early twentieth century. In the meantime, premillennialists, according to Timothy Weber, began to associate the Pope's exile from Rome in 1798, at the hands of the French troops, as an exact fulfillment of the prophecies of Daniel.[36] These passages predicted that after 1,260 "days" the reign of the "Beast" would end and be followed shortly by the coming of the Son of Man. The premillennialists identified the Beast as the Roman Pope and converted the "days" into years. By dating the rise of the Papacy as A.D. 538, premillennialists could claim by simple arithmetic that the events in 1798 were a dramatic fulfillment of this prophecy.

Another faction, led by William Miller, a Baptist pastor from Vermont, calculated that the 2,300 "days" in Daniel 8:14 could also be dated from the proclamation to rebuild the Jerusalem Temple, which he believed to have been in 457 B.C. and, again by converting the days to years, he calculated Christ's coming to about 1843. This date was later revised to October 22, 1844. When the day of "Great Disappointment" came, many of Miller's followers refused to give up their view and wrote off the rest of Protestantism and Roman Catholicism as the "great whore" of biblical prophecy. Thus the Seventh-Day Adventist Movement began; it has grown to considerable size and influence.[37]

To say the least, premillennialism had fallen on hard times, but by 1875 a new kind of "dispensational" premillennialism emerged and gained a greater acceptance among Evangelicals than ever before.[38] The movement was promoted by the Plymouth Brethren as early as 1830 in Plymouth, England.[39] One of the leading teachers of the new futurist premillennialism (or dispensationalism) was John Nelson Darby (1800–82). His views strongly influenced William Kelly and the American Bible teacher C. I.

Scofield, whose premillennial ideas were incorporated into the now famous Scofield Reference Bible. They viewed dispensations in Scripture as periods of time in which God dealt differently with humankind in regard to His revealed truth. Thus human history could be divided into various epics or dispensations of time in which humanity fulfilled a basic stewardship of responsibility to God.

While these dispensations were divided differently by various writers, one thing became clear: dispensationalists made a definite distinction between Israel (God's earthly people) and the Church (His Heavenly people). The key phrase of the movement became "rightly dividing the word of truth." The present Gentile Era of the Church Age was looked upon as the "times of the Gentiles," in which Israel must suffer while it awaits the fulfillment of the biblical promises of a messianic kingdom. Dispensationalists viewed the Church as the "Great Parenthesis" that stood between the past and former dealings of God with Israel. This concept left the Church with no real earthly claim and may be seen as the major weakness in the dispensationalists' lack of social concern and involvement with the present world. The future for the Church was to look forward to the Rapture, a secret snatching away of the New Testament saints by Christ, prior to the Tribulation Period that would ensue on the earth.

In the meantime, the rise of theological Liberalism tended to force all conservative Evangelicals into a very close defensive alliance. Conservatives needed each other to win the battle against Liberalism, and in time the dispensational concept of the rise of apostasy at the end of the Church Age seemed to coincide with the rise of Liberalism in the American Church. Suddenly Evangelicalism had the weapon it needed to face the crisis of an ever-changing American public. "Modernism" was viewed as the "falling away" of the last days and, as such, became the brunt of an excessive attack by the new dispensational Fundamentalists.[40]

Conservative cooperation can be evidenced in the Bible Conference Movement, which began as early as 1875 with the organization of the Believers' Meeting for Bible Study, which later changed its name to the Niagara Bible Conference. These conferences provided a gathering place for conservative Evangelicals from a variety of denominations who "gathered by one spirit unto the name of the Lord, to worship in perfect sympathy and fellowship and in utter forgetfulness of all differences, before one Father."[41] In a short time the premillennialists overpowered the Bible Conference Movement and added the plank of premillennialism to the creed of faith that they held. In general, the Bible conferences upheld the inspiration of Scripture, the fall and sinfulness of humanity, justification by faith alone, the necessity of personal conversion, the importance of the work of the Holy Spirit, the inclusion of all true believers in the universal Church of Christ, and the reality of blessedness or damnation for eternity. These essentials were emphasized in light of the liberal restatement of traditional Christian beliefs.[42] Out of the Niagara Creed would grow the "fundamentals" of the faith held by conservatives in general in the early twentieth century. Eventually the first American Bible and Prophetic Conference was held in New York City, at Holy Trinity Episcopal Church in October 1878. Subsequent conferences were held in Chicago in 1886; in Allegheny, Pennsylvania, in 1895; in Boston in 1901; in Chicago again in 1914; and in Philadelphia and New York, both in 1918. These continued to emphasize the fundamentals or basics of the Christian faith.

Premillennial eschatology was also given a boost by evangelists D. L. Moody and R. A. Torrey. One Fundamentalist, William Bell Riley, called premillennialism "the sufficient if not solitary anecdote to the present apostasy."[43] Dispensational premillennialism was further spurred on by the efforts of C. H. Mackintosh, A. T. Pierson, A. B. Simpson, A. J. Gordon, J. Wilbur Chapman, Clarence Larkin, and Billy Sunday.[44] Soon Bible conferences were springing up all over America, promoting the new approach to biblical eschatology. These included the Boardwalk Bible Conference in Atlantic City, the Montrose summer gatherings in Pennsylvania, and the famous Bible conference at Winona Lake, Indiana. In Chicago the Moody Bible Institute was formed as an educational arm of dispensational and evangelistic endeavors. MBI has had a long and distinguished history of training thousands of pastors, missionaries, and Christian workers.[45] Dr. James M. Gray, who served as dean and president of Moody for thirty years (1904–34), testified that he became a premillennialist while attending the first Prophetic Conference in New York City in 1878.[46] Arno C. Gaebelein, editor of the premillennial *Our Hope* magazine, was also "converted" to premillennialism through the Niagara Bible Conference. In time, William Pettingill became dean of the Philadelphia School of the Bible, and Robert McQuilkin became president of Columbia Bible College in South Carolina. Both of these schools further spread the dispensational-premillennial approach to biblical eschatology.

The premillennial movement was also marked by a strong commitment to the inspiration of Scripture and the priesthood of the believer. Opposing higher criticism on the grounds that it denied a person's right to come to the Scripture and interpret it individually, premillennialists rejected it in the words of D. L. Moody, who said that it was "ruining revival work and emptying the churches."[47] The movement also emphasized a basic desire to return to the purity of the New Testament Church of the first century A.D. It maintained as well a strong supernaturalism that had characterized the earlier evangelical tradition. A survey of 236 theological professors from twenty-eight seminaries in eight denominations conducted by James Snowden, a postmillennialist theology professor from Western Theological Seminary, showed that there were only seven premillennialists serving on the faculties of these schools when the twentieth century dawned.[48] During the early years of this century, however, more and more "testimonies" were gleaned from postmillennialists who "converted" to the premillennial view in light of the "signs of the times." No correct evaluation of Fundamentalism can properly be made without a proper assessment of the development and impact of dispensationalism upon the eschatology of the Evangelical Movement at the turn of the century.

AMERICANIZATION OF EVANGELICALISM

The popularity and growth of the Bible Conference Movement must be seen in light of contemporary criticism and attacks upon the Bible that were being waged at the end of the nineteenth century. The development of evangelical Christianity in America had undergone a significant process of change by that time. The roots of American Evangelicalism can certainly be traced to the Puritan founding fathers in New England. Their love of Scripture and their strong adherence to doctrine and personal piety were still very much evident within the American evangelical tradition. The inclusion of (and to some extent rejection of) various elements of Pietism, Methodism, Revivalism, and Perfectionism had brought an emphasis upon practical, personal Christian living. Meanwhile, the excessive emotionalism and subjectivity of the Pentecostals had been rejected by the majority of Evangelicals in favor of the biblical commitment of the premillennialists. Thus the "Americanization" of Evangelicalism was well under way by the turn of the century.

The framework that would become the Fundamentalist Movement could already be traced to at least two nineteenth-century sources of conservativism: first, the old-school Presbyterians, centered at Princeton Theological Seminary; second, the premillennial eschatology of the Bible Conference and Bible school movements. Ever since its founding in 1812 Princeton Seminary had stood as a bastion of biblical orthodoxy in the Western world. Led by such great theologians and scholars as Archibald Alexander, Charles Hodge, and B. B. Warfield, the cornerstone of Princeton theology centered in the doctrine of the inspiration of Scripture.[49] This view was crystallized in the writings of Warfield, who asserted three foundational postulates: (1) the inspiration of Scripture is both plenary and verbal; that is, it extends to the very words of the Bible itself; (2) the Scriptures themselves teach their own inerrancy; (3) the inspiration of Scripture applies literally only to the "original autographs."

This case for biblical inerrancy was widely accepted by Evangelicals and became the foundation of the fundamentalist view of the Bible. J. Gresham Machen, himself an anti-premillennialist, was nevertheless a staunch defender of Princetonian orthodoxy and carried the campaign for biblical inerrancy into the fundamentalist controversy. Unable to sway the board of Princeton, Machen led a withdrawal of several faculty and students in the formation of Westminster Theological Seminary, which he founded in Philadelphia in 1929. In spite of his amillennial position, Machen became a strong associate of the Fundamentalists in their campaign to defeat Liberalism. Thus we must conclude that the ultimate and deciding factor in Fundamentalism was not eschatology. Rather, it was the doctrine of biblical inspiration and authority.

The additionally unique feature of American Evangelicalism

was its almost total acceptance of premillennial eschatology in the late nineteenth century. The historical premillennial position of Bible commentators such as Delitzsch, Godet, and Meyer encouraged a general expectation of Christ's future earthly reign. To this was added the dispensational emphasis of Darby and Scofield, and hence the Americanization of Evangelicalism was now complete. Evangelical historian Bruce Shelley correctly observes that "if the theology of the fundamentalists was oversimplified, that of the liberals was oversecularized. If the liberals had a point in insisting that Christianity's survival depended upon its speaking to modern men, fundamentalists were right in demanding that it declare the public message.[50]

To the evangelical mind, the rise of Liberalism represented a return to the rationalistic approach of deism, unitarianism, and higher criticism. In essence, it may clearly be said that two sides had formed in American Protestantism by the end of the nineteenth century. On the one side stood Liberalism, with its emphasis upon the natural, the rational, the explainable: on the other, Evangelicalism, with its emphasis upon the spiritual, the supernatural, and uncompromising faith in the Bible as the Word of God. It was out of the inevitable confrontation between these two movements that reactionary Evangelicalism (or Fundamentalism) would be born as the clearest and strongest expression of the American Church's commitment to the basic doctrines of the Bible. Rather than viewing the Fundamentalist Movement as a new aberration of American Christianity, history shows that it was the fullest possible expression of American Evangelicalism as it faced the challenge of the modern age.

4

❊❊❊

THE WAR WITH LIBERALISM: 1900–1930

The first three decades of the twentieth century are the most interesting and the most controversial in the war between Modernism and Fundamentalism. The rise of Modernism, which finds its roots in higher criticism, evolutionary philosophy, and rationalism, had grown until it was entrenched in the major denominations of that era. By the twenties Liberalism was "the acknowledged point of view in approximately half of the Protestant Theological Seminaries."[1]

HISTORY OF THE WAR

Although there was great concern among conservative theologians over the extent and impact of the liberal movement, the conservatives had made no unified, organized effort to combat its influence. It was during the first three decades of the twentieth century that they organized, articulated clearly the issues, and faced Liberalism in a head-on collision. This period of religious confrontation can be divided into three major sections: between the years 1900 and 1918 the controversy brewed; it exploded from 1918 to 1925, and then faded from 1925 to 1930. We shall attempt to examine each of these specific eras and identify the key events and people that give one perspective and understanding of Fundamentalism and Liberalism.

The Controversy Brews: 1900–1918

By 1900 Liberalism was well entrenched in the major denominations in America. The leaders of the movement had already defined their theological position and organized their movement. Up to this point, Fundamentalists had neither defended their position nor organized to combat the growing Modernism. To properly understand the growth of Liberalism, which climaxed in the 1920s, one must understand the tenor of the times. There were many factors in American culture that contributed to its growth:

"1. A method of inquiry and of judgement arose that discredited reliance upon authority and tradition.
2. Particular beliefs vanished before advancing knowledge of nature, of history, and of mind.
3. Men acquired increasing voluntary control over conditions and areas that religion traditionally assigned to superhuman powers. At the same time, there arose a sharper awareness that certain phases of life (e.g. "id") were beyond man's conscious control or the seeming guidance of a god.
4. The whole mental atmosphere changed as ancient fears, attitudes of submission, and reliance upon the dim or the imagined were supplanted by a self-confident realism. If men did not feel more at home in the here and now, at least they were newly disposed to making it a home."[2]

This atmosphere of rebellion and rejection of absolute authority and emphasis on humanity's rational capabilities allowed Liberalism to deny and criticize the traditional position of the Church.

The fact that Liberalism was gaining impetus forced Fundamentalism to react in an organized fashion. There were two events from 1900 to 1918 that gave birth to the organized reaction to Liberalism. First, in 1909 a group of scholars from around the world published for the first time the Fundamentalist position, in a series of twelve booklets, financed by Wyman and Milton Stewart, entitled *The Fundamentals: A Testimony of Truth.*

Started under the direction of Amzi Clarence Dixon (1854–1925) and later supervised by Reuben A. Torrey (1856–1928), dean of the Bible Institute of Los Angeles, these booklets were written by a group of Fundamentalists from throughout the English-speaking world. Included were such people as George F. Wright and Melvin G. Kyle, archaeologists; Philip Mauro, lawyer; James M. Gray, dean of the Moody Bible Institute; Robert E. Speer, a Presbyterian; Edgar Y. Mullins, a Southern Baptist; and Leander W. Munhall, a Methodist. Although these articles dealt with higher criticism and evolution, their major contribution was the identification of the "five points" that "were to become the *sine qua non* of Fundamentalism."[3] These five tenets were the infallibility of the Bible, Christ's virgin birth, His substitutionary atonement, His resurrection, and His second coming. These five doctrinal positions were so influential that in 1910 and 1914 the Northern Presbyterian delegates to the General Assembly addressed these five points.

These booklets were sent to pastors, evangelists, missionaries, professors, students, and personnel of the YMCA/YWCA throughout the world. There were as many as three million booklets distributed in this first organized and well-articulated response to the liberal movement. Some have identified the birth of Fundamentalism with these publications.

This first attempt to articulate in writing the position of Fundamentalism was highly credible. *The Fundamentals* provided "calm, well-reasoned and well-balanced testimony to Christian truth."[4] Many of the subsequent writings were emotional and hostile and thereby caused some to consider the term "Fundamentalist" a word of scorn.

It is interesting to note that in the writing of *The Fundamentals* there was great ecumenicity. The authors represented Presbyterian, Methodist, Baptist, and Episcopalian denominations, people of varying theological positions who were all committed to the basic fundamentals of historic Christianity. The Fundamentalist Movement later became fragmented and polarized, but in its embryonic days it joined together a broad spectrum of conservative leaders. The breadth of that spectrum will be explored in greater detail later in this chapter as we identify some of the prominent personalities of that era.

The second major publication of the early part of the twentieth century was the Scofield Reference Bible, edited by C. I. Scofield (1843–1921), a Congregationalist minister from Dallas, Texas. Published in 1909, amplified in 1919, and revised in 1966, the Scofield Bible became a major reference edition for preachers, teachers, and laypeople.[5]

An outstanding Bible expositor, Scofield became pastor of the First Congregational Church of Dallas, Texas. He had studied law and was a member of the Kansas Bar. His first book, *Rightly Dividing the Word of Truth*, was circulated throughout the world. In 1902 he resigned from his pastorate to give his time totally to the Reference Bible. He spent 1902 to 1909 preparing the work. He was strongly encouraged and influenced by Dwight L. Moody.

The Controversy Explodes: 1918–1925

By 1918 the Liberals and the Fundamentalists had clearly articulated their position and organized their movements. Exposed to external threats, the Fundamentalists had minimized their differences and maximized their areas of agreement. They had united around the five fundamentals and were now ready for a head-on collision with the liberal movement. There were a number of important events during this particular period, all of which brought Liberalism and Fundamentalism into direct confrontation. In May of 1918 the first major fundamentalist conference took place. The Philadelphia Prophetic Convention attracted some five thousand people. The earlier publication of *The Fundamentals* had paved the way for such a conference.

Though the conference was primarily devoted to millennial issues, W. B. Riley addressed the threat of Modernism to traditional Christianity. The pamphlet entitled *Light on Prophecy* was published by the conference. It discussed the return of Christ and included a "Statement of Belief" of "all of the traditional doctrines as well as a warning against the dangers inherent in a drift toward liberal theology."[6] As a result of the 1918 convention, the delegates decided to meet the next year at the Moody Bible Institute in Chicago.

Although attendance somewhat declined from the previous year, the participants issued a written publication entitled *God Has Spoken: 25 Addresses*. This publication again emphasized the five points of Fundamentalism. During the 1919 conference at the Moody Bible Institute the leaders of the new Fundamentalist Movement added a further dimension to their plan. They proposed a bold commitment to move on the offense against the liberal movement. They encouraged the establishment of Bible conferences and Bible schools, and encouraged their supporters to get involved in correcting the educational institutions that promoted theological error. They also decided to begin an organization that would withstand Modernism and evolution. That organization later became the World's Christian Fundamentals Association. Their offensive gained great support because of the charismatic personalities who led it. In 1922 they met with T. C. Horton at the Bible Institute of Los Angeles and discussed the issue of evolution. By 1922 the organization had published an official magazine entitled *Christian Fundamentals in Church and School*. The organization continued its annual meetings with such spectacular events as the 1923 convention at Fort Worth, where J. Frank Norris had a mock trial of several Texas colleges accused of teaching evolution, higher criticism, and rationalism. The fury of the movement reached its apex in 1925 with a full-fledged attack on Modernism within the denominations and evolution within the school systems. It climaxed with the Scopes trial when William Jennings Bryan became the public defender of the fundamentalist cause.

In 1923 the Baptist Bible Union was formulated. This was the synthesis of three groups: a group from the Northern Baptist Convention; the followers of J. Frank Norris, and a group led by T. T. Shields of Jarvis Street Baptist Church in Toronto, Canada. The meeting started in May 1923 in Kansas City, Missouri. T. T. Shields served as the only president of this organization. When the BBU ultimately faded, Robert Ketchum organized the General Association of Regular Baptist Churches out of its membership. At the peak of its influence it had 50,000 members.

The theological and emotional controversy from 1918 to 1925 can best be understood by two of the major confrontations: that between Harry Emerson Fosdick and Clarence E. Macartney, and that between William Jennings Bryan and Clarence Darrow. These two major battles identified the two most defined issues in the war: Modernism vs. Fundamentalism and evolution vs. supernaturalism. The two movements were at last coming into open, public, and violent conflict.

FOSDICK VS. MACARTNEY

In 1922, Harry Emerson Fosdick (1878–1969), a liberal Baptist pastor of a Presbyterian church in New York City, preached a sermon entitled "Shall the Fundamentalists Win?" He had intended this sermon as a plea for greater understanding and unity between Liberalism and Fundamentalism. Ivy Lee, a layman in his church, took that sermon and published and distributed it under the title "The New Knowledge and the Christian Faith." This became one of the most widely read sermons of the era, generating such controversy that it ultimately led to Fosdick's resignation from the Presbyterian Church three years later. In his message he accused Fundamentalism of being "illiberal and intolerant." He accused Fundamentalists of being anti-intellectual and unwilling to expand their minds to include the broad advancements in the area of scientific knowledge. "Now, there are multitudes of reverent Christians who have been unable to keep this knowledge in one compartment of their minds and the Christian faith in another."[7]

Fosdick identified three fundamentalist issues and issued a plea for more understanding and flexibility in regard to their definition and acceptance. He identified the Fundamentalist Movement as centered around the virgin birth, the inspiration of Scripture, and the second coming of Christ. He contended that one could be a genuine Christian and not hold to the limited moral definitions that Fundamentalists espoused. He appealed for a "spirit of tolerance and Christian liberty" and "clear insight into the main issues of modern Christianity and a sense of penitent shame that the Christian Church should be quarreling over little matters when the world is dying of great needs."[8] He made strong appeals for tolerance: "I plead this morning the cause of magnaminity and liberality and tolerance of spirit. . . . I would, if I could, reach their ears, say to the fundamentalists about the liberals what Gamaliel said to the Jews, 'refrain from these men, and let them alone: If this counsel or this work be of men, it will be overthrown; but if it is of God ye will not be able to overthrow them; lest haply ye be found even to be fighting against God.'"[9] He concluded his message with his strongest appeal: "God keep us always so and ever increasing areas of Christian fellowship; intellectually hospitable, open-minded, liberty-loving, fair, tolerant, not with the intolerance of indifference, as though we did not care about the faith, but because always our major emphasis is upon the weightier matters of the law."[10]

Even though Fosdick was a brilliant spokesman of the liberal cause, he failed to understand the importance of the fundamental issues. He even concluded in his sermon that "I do not believe for one moment that the Fundamentalists are going to succeed."[11] History has proved him wrong. In his message he attempted to minimize the cardinal doctrines of Fundamentalism and substitute for them the larger issues of social concern. He defined Christianity as something less than a commitment to truth. His ideology lacks a defined theological foundation.

Clarence E. Macartney (1879–1957), a Presbyterian minister from Philadelphia, responded to Fosdick's message in a sermon entitled "Shall Unbelief Win?" In his message he clearly identified the irreconcilable differences between traditional Christianity and Liberalism. He accused Liberalism of subjectivity and unscriptural ideas. Macartney also pursued this matter through the official channels of the Presbyterian Church. He brought the issue to a meeting of the Presbytery of Philadelphia and requested that the preaching of the First Presbyterian Church of New York City (Fosdick's church) conform to traditional orthodox Presbyterian doctrine.

Macartney, in presenting his case, quoted from a secular paper: "It is not exactly ethical for a vegetarian to accept employment from a meat packer and urge a diet of spinach upon all who come asking for meat. This is a land where anyone may worship God as he sees fit, but this does not mean that he can make people who disagree with him keep him in their house of worship."[12] The parallel was obvious. It was unethical for a liberal Baptist minister to preach in a Presbyterian church and espouse doctrine contrary to the tenets of the Presbyterian Church.

After two years of proceedings, the Judicial Commission of the General Assembly asked the Presbytery of New York to require Fosdick to become a Presbyterian minister. This would force him to conform to the Confession of Faith. Fosdick responded by resigning his position in the church. "In answer to [the Assembly's] proposal I must in all honesty set my long standing and assured conviction that creedal subscription to ancient confessions of faith is a practice dangerous to the welfare of the church and to the integrity of the individual conscience."[13]

SCOPES TRIAL

The second major controversy that brought Fundamentalism and Liberalism into direct confrontation was the Scopes trial in Dayton, Tennessee. It was called by many the trial of the century. It pitted the articulate public spokesman for Fundamentalism William Jennings Bryan against the equally brilliant Clarence Darrow. Although they came into direct confrontation at the Scopes trial, their animosity had been building for a number of years. Bryan, as the proponent of Fundamentalism, had taken the brunt of criticism from many churchmen, philosophers, and historians. Darrow had been one of the leading critics of Bryan, and on July 4, 1923, he published fifty-five questions about the Bible in the Chicago *Tribune,* addressing these questions specifically to Bryan. The fact that Bryan ignored these questions later became a basis of Darrow's cross-examination in the 1925 trial.[14] The trial in Tennessee was the ultimate opportunity for public confrontation. It was more than a confrontation of ideologies: it was a confrontation of personalities.

The trial centered around the defendant, John Thomas Scopes, who was a public school teacher in Tennessee. There was a law requiring that no one teach any hypothesis contrary to creationism in the public school system. Those who opposed the law encouraged Scopes to teach evolution and thereby challenge the state law. The trial started on July 10 in sweltering heat. It was a trial of national importance. Headlines of the Louisville, Kentucky, *Courier Journal* on July 21, 1925, read: "*3,000 AT TRIAL, GET THRILL!*" The town of Dayton became the center of national attention. Everyone from Fundamentalists to lemonade vendors was there, along with more than one hundred newspaper reporters. Judge T. Raulston presided over the court. The jury was selected. All twelve of the jurors were farmers.

The most important move of the trial came when Darrow

called Bryan to the stand as a defense witness. This move, with the subsequent examination of Bryan, proved disastrous for Bryan and Fundamentalism.

"Darrow had appeared in many trials in which more was at stake than this one. Scopes had little to lose. It was Bryan who would lose most in the end, for though he was not the accused and suffered no legal penalty, he lost a reputation, was humiliated in public, and was shown to be a man of clay even to his ardent supporters. Darrow's cross-examination and the scorn to which Bryan was subjected in the newspapers—especially by H. L. Mencken—broadcast to the nation that his time had passed. There was something cruel about the proceedings. Bryan appeared trapped, like a dumb animal. The truth was that he was too far removed from the modern world, from intellectual exercise, to put up a decent fight. He was used to popular adulation, and had grown flabby. Darrow, accustomed to adversity and fighting public opinion, had grown strong and hard."[15] Bryan also lost the respect of Fundamentalists when he subscribed to the idea of periods of time for creation rather than twenty-four-hour days. The following transcript became the crux of the trial.[16]

Darrow: Mr. Bryan, do you believe that the first woman was Eve?
  Bryan: Yes.
    D: Do you believe she was literally made out of Adam's rib?
    B: I do.
    D: Did you ever discover where Cain got his wife?
    B: No, sir; I leave the agnostics to hunt for her.
    D: You have never found out?
    B: I have never tried to find out.
    D: You have never tried to find out?
    B: No.
    D: The Bible says he got one, doesn't it? Were there other people on the earth at that time?
    B: I cannot say.
    D: You cannot say. Did that ever enter your consideration?
    B: Never bothered me.
    D: There were no others recorded, but Cain got a wife.
    B: That is what the Bible says.
    D: Where she came from you do not know. All right. Does

the statement, "The morning and the evening were the first day," and "The morning and the evening were the second day," mean anything to you?

B: I do not think it necessarily means a twenty-four-hour day.

D: You do not?

B: No.

D: What do you consider it to be?

B: I have not attempted to explain it. If you will take the second chapter—let me have the book. [Examines the Bible.] The fourth verse of the second chapter says: "These are the generations of the heavens and of the earth, when they were created in the day that the Lord God made the earth and the heavens." The word "day" there in the very next chapter is used to describe a period. I do not see that there is any necessity for construing the words, "the evening and the morning," as meaning necessarily a twenty-four-hour day, "in the day when the Lord made the heaven and the earth."

D: Then, when the Bible said, for instance, "and God called the firmament heaven. And the evening and the morning were the second day," that does not necessarily mean twenty-four hours?

B: I do not think it necessarily does.

D: Do you think it does or does not?

B: I know a great many think so.

D: What do you think?

B: I do not think it does.

D: You think those were not literal days?

B: I do not think they were twenty-four-hour days.

D: What do you think about it?

B: That is my opinion—I do not know that my opinion is better on that subject than those who think it does.

D: You do not think that?

B: No. But I think it would be just as easy for the kind of God we believe in to make the earth in six days as in six years or in 6,000,000 years or in 600,000,000 years. I do not think it important whether we believe one or the other.

D: Do you think those were literal days?

B: My impression is they were periods, but I would not attempt to argue as against anybody who wanted to believe in literal days.

D: Have you any idea of the length of the periods?

B: No; I don't.

D: Do you think the sun was made on the fourth day?

B: Yes.

D: And they had evening and morning without the sun?

B: I am simply saying it is a period.

D: They had evening and morning for four periods without the sun, do you think?

B: I believe in creation as there told, and if I am not able to explain it I will accept it. Then you can explain it to suit yourself.

D: Mr. Bryan, what I want to know is, do you believe the sun was made on the fourth day?

B: I believe just as it says there.

D: Do you believe the sun was made on the fourth day?

B: Read it.

D: I am very sorry; you have read it so many times you would know, but I will read it again:

"And God said, let there be lights in the firmament of the heaven, to divide the day from the night; and let them be for signs, and for seasons, and for days, and years. And let them be for lights in the firmament of the heaven, to give light upon the earth; and it was so. And God made two great lights; the greater light to rule the day, and the lesser light to rule the night; He made the stars also. And God set them in the firmament of the heaven, to give light upon the earth, and to rule over the day and over the night, and to divide the light from the darkness; and God saw that it was good. And the evening and the morning were the fourth day." Do you believe, whether it was a literal day or a period, the sun and the moon were not made until the fourth day?

B: I believe they were made in the order in which they were given there, and I think in the dispute with Gladstone and Haxley on that point—

D: Cannot you answer my question?

B: I prefer to agree with Gladstone.

D: I do not care about Gladstone.

B: Then prefer to agree with whomever you please.

D: Cannot you answer my question?

B: I have answered it. I believe that it was made on the fourth day, in the fourth day.

D: And they had the evening and the morning before that for three days or three periods. All right, that settles it.

The day after Darrow's examination of Bryan, the judge refused further questioning and ordered Bryan's testimony stricken from the record. Darrow responded by asking the jury to be brought in and instructed by the judge to return a guilty verdict in order to permit the defense to appeal to a higher court. This would make it a matter of constitutionality. The judge instructed the jury, and it in turn pronounced the defendant guilty of violating the state law by teaching evolution.

A few days after the trial, William Jennings Bryan died. Darrow's scorn of Bryan was evident in responding to this tragedy. "A man who for years had fought excessive drinking, now lies dead from indigestion caused by overeating."[17] Although Bryan was humiliated by Darrow and the media, he was an irreplaceable loss to the fundamentalist cause. His dynamic contribution to the movement was overshadowed by the results of the Scopes trial, which was an apparent public defeat for Fundamentalism. Most of the newspeople were influenced by Darrow and the way he handled the trial. In fact, when Scopes was fined and bail set at $500, the Baltimore *Sun* acted as the bondsman. Although William Jennings Bryan technically won the trial, the sway of public opinion went with Darrow. This caused many to falsely assume that Fundamentalism was now a dying phenomenon.

The Controversy Diminishes: 1925–1930

The Fundamentalist Movement had begun in the early part of the twentieth century. The issues were clearly defined through *The*

Fundamentals and propagated through the Scofield Reference Bible. The movement organized through the Philadelphia Prophetic Conference in 1918. William Jennings Bryan (1860–1925) became the articulate public spokesman who added evolution as another major issue in the controversy. Having articulated the issues, organized itself, and attacked Liberalism, the Fundamenalist Movement was brought to an abrupt halt in 1925 at the Scopes trial. In 1926 *Christian Century* published an article entitled "Vanishing Fundamentalism." In this article it was predicted that Fundamentalism would "be a disappearing quantity in American religious life, while our churches go on to larger issues, finding their controversies in realities that are pregnant and signficant for human welfare rather than in hollow and sterile dogmas which are irrelevant even if true."[18] Many assumed that Fundamentalism had been dealt the death blow and that soon the movement would be totally buried.

Although it did retreat somewhat from the public view, rigor mortis had not set in for Fundamentalism. Rather, the Scopes trial forced it to rebuild and become an underground movement. Instead of public controversy, the Fundamentalist Movement went back to the objectives that were clearly outlined in the 1919 meeting of the World's Christian Fundamentals Association. Fundamentalists recalled that at that Moody Bible Institute meeting they had committed themselves to more Bible conferences, Bible schools, and the building and establishing of new churches. It was to this goal that Fundamentalists now turned their energies.

After the Scopes trial, the 1926 meeting of the World's Christian Fundamental Association in Toronto had a noticeable drop in attendance. Over the next several years there were clear shifts in the purpose of the organization. Rather than being aggressive and confrontational, it became a more evangelistically oriented movement, involved in Bible conferences and evangelism. At the 1927 convention, attention was given to a Christian view of war and the issue of prohibition. It is interesting to note that in 1930 none of the speeches at the convention mentioned Modernism or evolution.[19] In the twelve years since its inception, the organization had lost the vitality and purpose for which it was originally founded.

Rather than fighting Modernism, it was now committed to building its own movements through churches, schools, and colleges.

This practice of withdrawal from Modernism and the consequent building of alternate organizations is clearly demonstrated in the controversy of the late twenties at Princeton Seminary, where J. Gresham Machen, Oswald T. Allis, and Robert Dick Wilson championed the cause of orthodoxy. These men were opposed to liberal trends in the school and the weak theological position of its president, J. Ross Stevenson.

The controversy climaxed at the 1929 meeting of the general assembly. Compromise proposals were offered to reorganize the administration of the seminary. The Fundamentalists refused to accept such compromise, and Machen, Allis, Wilson, and Van Til resigned from the faculty at Princeton. Shortly after the general assembly that same year, they organized Westminister Theological Seminary. In 1933 these Fundamentalists organized an independent foreign missions board, and in 1935 they left the church completely. This withdrawal and separatist position became a leading characteristic of the Fundamentalist Movement. Rather than fighting, its members decided to withdraw from the liberal seminaries and churches and establish their own seminaries and churches. This left the major denominations in control of the Liberals.[20]

PERSONALITIES OF THE WAR

In attempting to describe the era of 1900–30, it is impossible to conceptualize the confrontation fully without a detailed analysis of the personalities involved. The controversy of Modernism and Fundamentalism was much more than a confrontation of ideologies. In many respects it was a confrontation of charismatic personalities, climaxed by the Scopes trial in 1925. The trial became much more the confrontation of Darrow vs. Bryan rather than of evolution vs. supernaturalism. Often the ideas became subsumed within the personalities of the people who represented those ideas. To understand this era better, one must analyze some of the leading fundamentalist and liberal personalities.

Fundamentalist Personalities

J. FRANK NORRIS

J. Frank Norris (1877–1952) is one of the most controversial religious leaders of the twentieth century. He was a preacher, author, church builder, and political activist; his ministry was characterized by strong confrontation with sin and wrong. He was born on September 18, 1877, in Dadeville, Alabama, of a poor family, and at the age of eleven moved to Hubbard, Texas. He was converted during a revival service at the age of thirteen. He attended Baylor University, where the first indications of his charismatic leadership emerged. During a chapel service the president of the university lost his self-control, took a dog that students had planted in the auditorium as a prank, and threw it out the second-story window. Norris led a student revolt against the president's actions. After contacting the Society for the Prevention of Cruelty to Animals, the students pressured the university trustees into procuring the resignation of the president. After graduation from Baylor, Norris attended Southern Baptist Theological Seminary in Louisville, Kentucky. After graduation he was pastor of the McKinney Avenue Baptist Church in Dallas, until 1908. He also was business manager of the *Baptist Standard*. In 1909 he resigned his editorial post and assumed the pastorate of the First Baptist Church of Fort Worth, Texas. He served there for forty-three years.[21]

Norris has been described as a "fundamentalist, a sensationalist, a politician, and always a controversialist."[22] During the first three years of his pastorate in Fort Worth, everything went smoothly. However, in 1911 he went to Owensboro, Kentucky, where he was deeply influenced by a revival meeting. After that experience with revival, his ministry was never the same. Besides being pastor of the church in Fort Worth, Norris became pastor of Temple Baptist Church in Detroit in 1935. He served both of these congregations for sixteen years. He claimed that both churches had a combined membership of 25,000 people.[23] His ability as a church planter and a motivator is unquestioned. Although both his own churches grew during his ministry, he had continual controversies with the Southern Baptist Convention. This ultimately led to the establishment of his own fellowship in 1931. The group was named the "Premillennial, Fundamental, Missionary Fellowship"; it was later known as the "Premillennial Baptist Missionary Fellowship" and then the "World Baptist Fellowship." Norris strongly opposed Modernism and communism. The following excerpt from one of his messages illustrates his feelings:

> "These preachers who masquerade under the livery of heaven
> —I don't care how many degrees they have after their names—
> LLd's, DD's, Asses, they are infidels when they deny the word
> of God. . . . I have more respect for Tom Paine in his grave,
> and Bob Ingersoll—at least they had self-respect enough to stay
> out of the church and out of the pulpits—they were not like
> these little modernistic, lick-the-skillet, two-by-four aping, asi-
> nine preachers, who want to be in the priest's office so they can
> have a piece of bread, and play kite tail to the Communists. . . .
> Oh! some sister will say, 'I don't think that's the Christian
> spirit,' —Honey, you wouldn't know the Christian spirit, any
> more than a bull would know Shakespeare."[24]

J. Frank Norris was also a political activist. In 1928 he aggressively campaigned for Herbert Hoover for President. He spoke more than 119 times in thirty cities in three and one half months. As a result of his influence, Hoover was elected and Norris attended the inauguration. The list of national and international dignitaries with whom he corresponded is impressive. He had contacts with "Presidents Hoover, Roosevelt, Truman, and Eisenhower, and while overseas he held interviews with such foreign dignitaries as David Lloyd George, Winston Churchill, The Grand Mufti of Jerusalem, the Lord Mayor of London, and Benito Mussolini, and Pius XII."[25] He was so successful as a preacher politician that the Texas legislature introduced a bill in 1929 prohibiting ministers from becoming governor of Texas. This was a direct assault on the influence of Norris.

The preaching style and methods of Norris were sensational. He created great interest and generated a great following. His sermon titles included such subjects as "Shall Uncle Sam be Made an Ass Again?" and "If Jim Jeffries, the Chicago Cubs, and Theodore Roosevelt Can't Come Back, Who Can?" He had a dynamic pulpit mannerism; "with the newspaper in one hand and a Bible in the other, he roamed the platform, gesturing with conviction, shouting to emphasize a point, and weeping—on occasion—to move the emotions of his listeners. Then frequently he would leap from the pulpit platform to the level of the congregation, there concluding his discourse by inviting members of the congregation to join with him in an act of dedication."[26] During his controversy over evolution he brought monkeys and apes to his church auditorium to introduce his people to the relatives of those who accepted Darwin's thesis. The church in Fort Worth grew from 1,200 members and an average attendance of 500 in 1909 to 12,000 members and an average attendance of 5,200 in 1928. In Detroit he began with 800 members in 1934 and in 1943 had increased to 8,597 members.[27]

Norris' life was filled with problems and tragedies. In January 1912 the church in Fort Worth was burned. Norris was accused of arson but was acquitted in April of that same year. On July 12, 1926, he received a threatening telephone call from D. E. Chipps, who was a friend of the city's mayor. Mayor Meacham had been the center of Norris' current attack. When Chipps entered Norris' study there were harsh words spoken, and then Norris shot and killed Chipps. Many historians feel that this was the turning point in the ministry of Norris. Although he was indicted for murder, he was later found not guilty by the jury. Two years after this incident the entire church building burned to the ground again. The pressure of the trial and the strain of rebuilding the church had a profound effect on Norris.

Perhaps the greatest contribution of J. Frank Norris was his training of young preachers. In 1939 he organized the Bible Baptist Seminary in Fort Worth. Attendance at the seminary grew by the forties to a high of 305. G. Beauchamp Vick, Norris' assistant at Temple Baptist in Detroit, was appointed president of the seminary in 1948. By 1950, however, a growing number of people in the World Baptist Fellowship were concerned about the administration of the seminary. Vick resigned in 1950. As a result, the Baptist Bible Fellowship was formed, and in September of 1950 it organized its own school, Baptist Bible College of Springfield, Missouri. More than one hundred pastors formulated this new fellowship. It was the Baptist Bible Fellowship that played a dominant role in the church planting movement of the fifties and sixties.

J. Frank Norris lived a stormy, controversial life. He lived, worked, and preached in the midst of trouble and opposition. He died surrounded by a crumbling empire of past glory. Yet his legacy lives on. Hundreds of preachers have been inspired by his example. Hundreds of churches have been started through his influence. He remains the epitome of an independent, fundamental Baptist. He describes his life in a sermon preached on September 21, 1930, in his twenty-third year in Fort Worth.

> Take the denominational machine—the Baptists are one thing and the machine is another. Most of their machinery is in the junk heap.
> If I had been willing to bow down to the unscriptural demands of the denominational Hamans there would never have been any *trouble*.
> If I had never exposed evolution in Baylor University that forced seven evolution professors to resign, there would have been no *trouble*.
> If I had meekly and subserviently put on their post-millennial program of institutionalism there would have been no *trouble*.[28]

CLARENCE E. MACARTNEY

Clarence E. Macartney (1879–1957) was born in Northwood, Ohio, on September 18, 1879. He attended the University of Denver and graduated from the University of Wisconsin in 1901. While at the University of Wisconsin he became one of the leading debators in the university. He finally attended Princeton Theological Seminary, where he received a master of arts degree. He was pastor at three churches: the First Presbyterian Church of Paterson, New Jersey (1905–14), the Arch Street Presbyterian Church of Philadelphia (1914–27), and the First Presbyterian Church of Pittsburgh (1927–53).[29]

He differed from many of the other fundamentalist leaders in his eschatology: he rejected the premillennial, imminent return of Christ. He remained faithful to his theology throughout his life, his orthodoxy unchanged in spite of the wars, the depression, and liberal theology.

The most stirring controversy of his life occurred when he responded to Harry Emerson Fosdick's famous sermon "Shall the Fundamentalists Win?" His response and ultimate pressure on the General Assembly of the Presbyterian Church brought about the resignation of Fosdick. Macartney was the undisputed leader of the fundamentalist Presbyterian movement, but although he forced the ultimate resignation of Fosdick, the public reacted against him strongly and favored Fosdick.

J. GRESHAM MACHEN

J. Gresham Machen (1881–1937) was born of wealthy parents on July 28, 1881, in Baltimore, Maryland. He entered Johns Hopkins University when he was seventeen and then enrolled in Princeton Theological Seminary in 1902. He was deeply influenced at Princeton by Benjamin Breckinridge Warfield. He also studied in Germany under Bauer, Bousset, and Herrmann. Upon returning to America he served as a member of the faculty at Princeton Seminary.

His opponents characterized him as an "adamant, impatient, censorious, frequently bitter, ultraconservative leader." His friends described him as "a scholarly defender of Biblical faith, whose sincerity, courage, integrity, and completeness of dedication 'sometimes evoked heroic responses.'"[30]

During the 1920s there was a tremendous controversy at Princeton that polarized the entire faculty and student body (see earlier, under "The Controversy Diminishes: 1925–1930"). It was suggested that the seminary reorganize to resolve the problem. Machen responded in 1929 by forming Westminster Theological Seminary with three other faculty members, Robert Dick Wilson, Oswald T. Allis, and Cornelius Van Til.[31] In conjunction with the formation of the seminary, Machen also formed a new Presbyterian movement. It was organized as the Independent Board for Presbyterian Foreign Missions, later to become the Presbyterian Church of America and ultimately the Orthodox Presbyterian Church. As time passed, Machen became more separatist, and in 1937, in a further division, Carl McIntire, J. Oliver Buswell, president of Wheaton, and Allan A. MacRae joined together to form the Bible Presbyterian Synod. Machen thereby found himself alienated from the movement that he had started, and one month later he died.

Machen contributed academic and intellectual credibility to

the Fundamentalist Movement, in sharp contrast to the emotionalism and sensationalism of J. Frank Norris. Throughout his life he maintained a strong opposition to Modernism and Liberalism and a strong commitment to the truth of God's Word. The following quotations illustrate this.

> Modern liberalism in the Church, whatever judgment may be passed upon it, is at any rate no longer merely an academic matter. It is no longer a matter merely of theological seminaries or universities. On the contrary its attack upon the fundamentals of the Christian faith is being carried on vigorously by Sunday-School "lesson-helps," by the pulpit, and by the religious press. If such an attack be unjustified, the remedy is not to be found, as some devout persons have suggested, in the abolition of theological seminaries, or the abandonment of scientific theology, but rather in a more earnest search after truth and a more loyal devotion to it when once it is found.[32]

He was strong and unchanged in his attack against Liberalism. Yet he provided intellectual credence to his opposition.

> Two lines of criticism, then, are possible with respect to the liberal attempt at reconciling science and Christianity. Modern liberalism may be criticized (1) on the ground that it is un-Christian and (2) on the ground that it is unscientific. We shall concern ourselves here chiefly with the former line of criticism; we shall be interested in showing that despite the liberal use of traditional phraseology modern liberalism not only is a different religion from Christianity but belongs in a totally different class of religions. But in showing that the liberal attempt at rescuing Christianity is false we are not showing that there is no way of rescuing Christianity at all; on the contrary, it may appear incidentally, even in the present little book, that it is not the Christianity of the New Testament which is in conflict with science, but the supposed Christianity of the modern liberal Church, and that the real city of God, and that city alone, has defences which are capable of warding off the assaults of modern unbelief. However, our immediate concern is with the other side of the problem; our principal concern just now is to show that the liberal attempt at reconciling Christianity with modern science has really relinquished everything distinctive of Chris-

tianity, so that what remains is in essentials only that same indefinite type of religious aspiration which was in the world before Christianity came upon the scene. In trying to remove from Christianity everything that could possibly be objected to in the name of science, in trying to bribe off the enemy by those concessions which the enemy most desires, the apologist has really abandoned what he started out to defend. Here as in many other departments of life it appears that the things that are sometimes thought to be hardest to defend are also the things that are most worth defending.[33]

WILLIAM BELL RILEY

William Bell Riley (1861–1947) was born in Green County, Indiana, on March 22, 1861. He graduated from Hanover College in Indiana and from Southern Baptist Theological Seminary in Louisville, Kentucky. His most prominent pastorate was the First Baptist Church in Minneapolis, where he served for forty-five years (1897–1942). Besides his pastorate, he founded three schools, the Northwestern Bible and Missionary Training School, the Northwestern Evangelical Seminary, and Northwestern College. Prior to his death, he passed the leadership of these schools to Billy Graham. He wrote more than sixty books and published many articles. Upon his death he left "a heritage that probably made him the most important fundamentalist clergyman of his generation."[34] He was one of the founders of the World's Christian Fundamentals Association and its leader for some eleven years. In his first message to that association he stated, "The hour has struck for the rise of a new Protestantism . . . this organization is of more importance than the nailing of the 95 Theses."[35] He also joined with Norris and Shields in establishing the Baptist Bible Union in 1923.

During his pastorate he spent four months each year engaged in revivalist work throughout the country. Businesslike and quiet in his approach to the ministry, he was a sharp contrast to Billy Sunday and other fiery preachers, yet he had tremendous success in his meetings. For example, there were 352 individuals converted in Fort Worth, Texas, in one of his meetings. He was strong in his opposition to evolution and formed the Anti-Evolution League of Minnesota. He championed anti-evolution legislation and spoke extensively on this issue throughout the state of Minnesota. He also sought to make the Northern Baptist Convention more conservative. Disillusioned with his attempts in that area, he devoted his energies to the Baptist Bible Union. He also sought to bring unity among Fundamentalists by the establishment of the World's Christian Fundamentals Association. He was a man of many talents: he was pastor of "a large downtown church that had just completed a half-million-dollar building program, was president of a growing Bible school, preaching in cities far removed from Minneapolis, debater on a popular lecture circuit, editor of several religious publications, would-be reformer of his denominational family, vice-president of the Baptist Bible Union of which he was a charter member, and president, executive secretary, and chairman of the conference committee of the WCFA."[36] At his death there were two thousand alumni of the three institutions he had founded. No fewer than 70 percent of the 125 ministers in Baptist churches in Minnesota were trained in his schools. Despite his constant desire for unity within Fundamentalism, that unity quickly dissipated at his death. The Fundamentalists in Minnesota ultimately divided into six different groups after his death.[37]

T. T. SHIELDS

T. T. Shields (1873–1955) was born in England in 1873. He received no formal educational training. His most prominent pastorate was the Jarvis Street Church in Toronto, of which he was pastor from 1910 to 1955. Although his ministry centered in Canada, he had great influence over the American Fundamentalist Movement. He came to prominence as a Fundamentalist over his opposition to Modernism at McMaster University, Ontario, which was the convention school of Canada. During the 1920s he became heavily involved in American Fundamentalism and helped start the Baptist Bible Union. He was its president for seven years.

In 1922 Shields started the *Gospel Witness,* using this publication to expose and confront Modernism and Romanism. He strongly opposed Romanism and expressed great concern over its growing influence in politics. That same year he started Toronto Baptist Seminary. In 1927 he assumed the leadership of Des Moines University, which was controlled by the Baptist Bible

Union. When the school was closed down by a student riot two years later, Shields withdrew from his predominant public role in American Fundamentalism.

He spent the thirties and forties building the Jarvis Street Church. In 1948 he joined the International Council of Christian Churches and became close friends with Carl McIntire.[38] He wrote of his own life:

> I had a stormy life. . . . I have been zealous for the Gospel. . . . I regret nothing of my contention for the faith, save that I have not striven more heroically and continuously for the glory of the Gospel. . . . Preaching is the biggest business I know. . . . I am a soldier in the field. . . . I will have no compromise with the enemy.[39]

J. C. MASSEE

Jasper Cortenus Massee (1871–1965) of Georgia was an unusual Fundamentalist in that he was both liked and despised by his fundamentalist colleagues. He was hailed as a champion of the fundamentalist cause and later viewed as an apostate and categorized with Fosdick. He attended Mercer University and then Southern Baptist Theological Seminary. He served numerous churches in both the North and South as pastor. Although he gave credence to the five points of Fundamentalism, he differed with the view of inerrancy. He was consumed by the call for evangelism and so spent little time in the pulpit attacking the Liberalism and Modernism of his era. It was during his tenure at Brooklyn in 1920 that he began expressing concern for the liberal tendencies within the Northern Baptist Convention. He presided at a conference on "Fundamentals of our Baptist Faith" at Delaware Avenue Baptist Church, Buffalo, New York, in 1920. This convention led to the formation of the Fundamentalist Federation, of which Massee was president.[40] Massee attempted to maintain a middle-of-the-road position and ultimately lost the confidence of both the Fundamentalists and the Liberals. The Fundamentalists, in rebellion against Massee's leadership, founded the Baptist Bible Union in 1923. Finally, by the late twenties, Massee withdrew from the fundamentalist controversy. "I left the fundamentalists to save my own

spirit, it became so self-righteous, so critical, so un-Christian, so destructive, so incapable of being fair that I had to go elsewhere for spiritual nourishment." Shortly after his departure from Fundamentalism he commented, "I do not believe in the wisdom or the righteousness of denunciation, misinterpretation, the imputing of motives and the widespread directing of suspicion toward men who declare their conservatism and their faithful adherence to the Word and to the Christ of God."[41] While many of his friends advocated the formation of a new denomination, Massee tenaciously attempted to hold together the denomination to which he was loyal.

JOHN R. STRATON

John Roach Straton (1875–1929) was born in Evansville, Indiana. He attended Mercer University, but because he could not pass the language requirements, never graduated. He attended Southern Baptist Theological Seminary, again not graduating. Although he was a pastor in four American cities—Chicago, Baltimore, Norfolk, and New York—his most prominent pastorate was at Calvary Baptist Church in New York City from 1918 to 1929. He came to national prominence in 1923 at the annual meeting of the Northern Baptist Convention in Atlantic City. He openly protested the keynote speaker and implied that he denied the virgin birth and second coming of Christ. He later defended his activity in the *Watchman Examiner*. He was overruled at the convention, to the cheers of the delegates, and ultimately withdrew his New York City church from the convention in 1926.

Straton was a very close friend of J. Frank Norris and even had Norris preach evangelistic services in his New York City church; when Norris was indicted for murder, Straton stood by his friend. Straton's church was the first in New York to go on the radio. Later in his life he bought a hotel at Greenwood Lake, New York, where he founded a summer Bible conference.

On December 20, 1923, Straton had an open debate in his church, with Charles Francis Potter, a Unitarian minister, over the issue of the infallibility of Scripture. The debate ended in a vote of two to one in favor of Potter and against Straton. Following that debate and the resignation of seventeen deacons, Straton increased his attacks on Liberalism. On January 28, 1924, in Carnegie Hall, he debated Potter again on the issue of evolution. This debate ended in a unanimous decision in favor of Straton; the radio audience, however, voted 57 percent to 43 percent in favor of Potter. A third debate was inaugurated on March 22, 1924, on the virgin birth of Christ; the verdict was a two-to-one vote in favor of Potter. The fourth debate was held on April 28, 1924, on the deity of Christ; Straton won this with a unanimous vote. The fifth debate was to have been on the return of Jesus Christ, but never materialized.[42]

WILLIAM JENNINGS BRYAN

William Jennings Bryan (1860–1925) was born in Salem, Illinois, on March 19, 1860. He graduated from Illinois College and attended Union College of Law in Chicago. He moved to Lincoln, Nebraska, where he won election to Congress on the Democratic Party ticket. After serving two terms he was not reelected. He was the champion of tariff and monetary reforms. He continued to stump for his economic reforms and in 1896, at the age of thirty-six, became the Democratic nominee for the presidency.

He lost to William McKinley by a narrow margin. He opposed McKinley again in 1900, running on an anti-imperialist platform. Again he was defeated. However, he was nominated by the Democratic Party in 1908 for a third attempt for the presidency. He lost this time to William Howard Taft. Bryan was influential in the nomination of Woodrow Wilson in 1912.

When Wilson assumed the presidency, he appointed Bryan as Secretary of State. Bryan was actively involved in the development of the Federal Reserve Act. He retired from government in 1915 after only twenty-seven months of service. During the last ten years of his life, his time was devoted more to religion than to politics. He became the antagonist of evolution and the national spokesman of Fundamentalism.[43]

Bryan's rise through the political machinery was due in part to his exceptional gift of oratory. In his acceptance speech in 1896 he stated:

> Our campaign has not for its object the reconstruction of society.
> We cannot ensure to the vicious the fruits of a virtuous life; we

would not invade the home of the provident in order to supply the wants of the spendthrift; we do not propose to transfer the rewards of industry to the lap of indolence. Property is and will remain the stimulus to endeavor and the compensation for toil. We believe, as asserted in the Declaration of Independence, that all men are created equal; but that does not mean that all men are or can be equal in possessions, in ability, or in merit; it simply means that all shall stand equal before the law. . . .[44]

When Bryan entered the arena of Fundamentalism, he brought with him his national prominence. He gave the fundamentalist cause public credibility. He enjoyed his alliance with religion and became the most renowned spokesman of its cause. In his lecture "The Prince of Peace" he states:

I am interested in the science of government, but I am more interested in religion. . . . I enjoy making a political speech . . . but I would rather speak on religion than on politics. I commenced speaking on the stump when I was only twenty, but I commenced speaking in the church six years earlier—and I shall be in the church even after I am out of politics.[45]

The greatest tragedy of his life was the humiliation of the Scopes trial in 1925. However, in the total perspective of his contribution to politics and Fundamentalism, Bryan remains one of America's most prominent sons. When President Franklin D. Roosevelt unveiled the Bryan Memorial in Washington, D.C., on May 3, 1934, he quoted the words of Bryan's speech to the Democratic Convention in 1904:

You may dispute over whether I have fought a good fight; you may dispute over whether I have finished my course; but you cannot deny that I have kept the faith.[46]

Liberal Personalities

The mounting forces of Liberalism also had their charismatic and persuasive personalities. Although Liberalism depended more on its articulated ideologies, it was publicly represented by some very influential people.

HARRY EMERSON FOSDICK

Harry Emerson Fosdick (1878–1969) was born in Buffalo, New York, on May 24, 1878. He attended Colgate University, where he revolted against the orthodox teachings of his youth. At Colgate he was influenced by William Newton Clarke. He transferred to Union Seminary and Columbia University. At Union he was influenced by the importance of a social consciousness toward the problems of society. He was challenged by the influence of Rauschenbusch, who was the pioneer champion of the social gospel. His preaching reflected his interest in social problems, and he utilized the Bible and extrabiblical sources in dealing with problems of society.

Fosdick's liberal theology has been well defined in his sermons and in his writings. In the introduction to one of his books he wrote: "Obviously, any idea of inspiration which implies equal value to the teachings of Scripture, or inerrancy in its statements, or conclusive infallibility in its ideas, is irreconcilable with such facts as this book presents."[47]

From 1904 to 1915 Fosdick was pastor at the Baptist Church at Montclair, New Jersey. From 1919 to 1925 he supplied the pulpit of the First Presbyterian Church in New York. After his famous sermon in May 1922, "Shall the Fundamentalists Win?" he was forced to resign from the Presbyterian Church. From 1925 to 1930 he served at Park Avenue Baptist. In 1930 a new church was erected and paid for by John D. Rockefeller: the Riverside Church in Morningside Heights in Manhattan. The church cost $10 million to build and provided the public forum for Harry Emerson Fosdick. His pulpit ministry was so impressive that the National Broadcasting Company allowed him free time on Sunday afternoon for the broadcast of the "National Vespers." Fosdick retired from Union Seminary and Riverside Church in 1946. He championed two basic responses to the common charges against Liberalism. "The first and central response was that modernistic liberalism not only is Christian but also is actually closer than its rivals to the genius of Christianity. The second was that unless Christianity can present people with a liberal opinion, it cannot function in the modern world and probably cannot survive there."[48]

SHAILER MATTHEWS

Second to Fosdick was the influence of Shailer Matthews (1863–1941), dean of the divinity school at the University of Chicago. Matthews wrote *The Fate of Modernism,* published in 1924. This book has been called "the most important liberal work of the 1920s and [it] made his very phraseology common coin among adherents and opponents of modernism."[49] He contended that Christianity was a basic set of convictions and a governing method. "The basic Christian convictions were humanity's need for salvation from sin and death; the love, fatherliness, and forgiving nature of God the creator; Christ as 'the revelation and human experience of God effecting salvation'; good will as essential to the nature of God and as the foundation for human betterment; the persistence of individual human lives after death; and the centrality of the Bible as the record of God's revelation and as a guide for religious life. The 'governing method' of Christianity had been associated throughout the ages with a spirit of cultural awareness of which the twentieth-century modernist was simply the most recent heir."[50]

Shailer Matthews proposed that the Christian community must expand to allow differences of opinion. In his writings entitled *The Affirmations of Faith* he proposed certain affirmations that all modernists can accept. They are:

I believe in God, eminent in the forces and processes of nature, revealed in Jesus Christ and human history as Love.

I believe in Jesus Christ, who by his teaching, life, death and resurrection, revealed God as Savior.

I believe in the Holy Spirit, the God of love experienced in human life.

I believe in the Bible, when interpreted historically, as the product and the trustworthy record of the progressive revelation of God through a developing religious experience.

I believe that humanity without God is incapable of full moral life and liable to suffering because of its sin and weakness.

I believe in prayer as a means of gaining help from God in every need and in every intelligent effort to establish and give justice in human relations.

I believe in freely forgiving those who trespass against me, and in good will rather than acquisitiveness, coercion, and war as the divinely established law of human relations.

I believe in the need and the reality of God's forgiveness of sins, that is, the transformation of human lives by fellowship with God from subjection to outgrown goods to the practice of the love exemplified in Jesus Christ.

I believe in the practicability of the teaching of Jesus in social life.

I believe in the continuance of individual personality beyond death; and that the future life will be one of growth and joy in proportion to its fellowship with God and its moral likeness to Jesus Christ.

I believe in the church as the community of those who in different conditions and ages loyally further the religion of Jesus Christ.

I believe that all things work together for good to those who love God and in their lives express the sacrificial good will of Jesus Christ.

I believe in the ultimate triumph of love and justice because I believe in the God revealed in Jesus Christ.[51]

This list of modernistic affirmations gives undue emphasis to God's love to the exclusion of His wrath and judgment. There is no mention of the judgment of sin and the literal fires of hell. The inerrancy of Scripture is eliminated, and Scripture is made subject to human interpretation.

WALTER RAUSCHENBUSCH

Walter Rauschenbusch (1861–1918), professor of Church History at Rochester Seminary, is best known as the champion of the social gospel. His most prominent work was *A Theology for the Social Gospel*, published in 1917. He also published *The New Evangelism* in 1904, in which he dealt with many of the social issues to be confronted by the Gospel and the Church. He claimed that the social revolution was the most permanent problem of his time. He talked about inequality, human nature, inequity, corruption, and moral decay. In his call for a more modernized gospel, he claimed, "When all other departments of life and thought are silently changing, it is impossible for religion to remain unaffected. The Gospel, to have power over an age, must be the highest expression of the moral and religious truths held by that age. If it lags behind and presents outgrown conceptions of life and duty, it is no longer in the full sense the Gospel. Christianity itself lifts the minds of men to demand a better expression of Christianity. If the official wardens of the Gospel from selfish motives or from conservative veneration for old statements refuse to let the spirit of Christ flow into the larger vessels of thought and feeling which God himself has prepared for it, they are warned by finding men turn from their message as sapless and powerless."[52]

Conclusion

During the War with Liberalism in the first three decades of the twentieth century, several characteristics of Fundamentalism can be observed. These developing qualities ultimately became the foundational distinctions of the emerging movement in subsequent decades.

First, the Fundamentalists displayed an uncompromising commitment to truth. From their perspective, the War with Liberalism was in reality a war of truth against error. With regard to the five fundamentals, there could be no tolerance or dialogue. Denial of any of these doctrinal tenets was in essence the embracing of error.

Second, the Fundamentalists displayed an attitude of separatism. They felt it was hopeless to continue their fight within the Liberal denominations and their representative schools. This period of religious history could be described as the "Great Exodus."

Third, the Fundamentalists began building their own independent empires. Free from denominational pressure and control, they did "their own thing." They devoted their energies to church building. They were experts in utilizing the media (both radio and printed page), and they started their own doctrinally pure institutions of higher education.

Fourth, by the end of the twenties the movement became polarized and fragmented. The Fundamentalists' independent spirit polarized the movement around different personalities and organizations. The movement lost its unity and cooperation. Consequently, some anticipated the demise of the Fundamentalist Movement. But it was a force that could not be silenced. The strength of commitment characteristic of Fundamentalists can best be understood in the words of Billy Sunday, the great evangelist of that era:

> I'm against sin. I'll kick it as long as I've got a foot, and I'll fight it as long as I've got a fist. I'll butt it as long as I've got a head. I'll bite it as long as I've got a tooth. And when I'm old and fistless and footless and toothless, I'll gum it till I go home to Glory and it goes home to perdition.[53]

5

✦✦✦

THE AFTERMATH:
Fundamentalism Survives:
1930–1980

The war had ended. Liberalism and Fundamentalism had battled
in open confrontation. Neither side had gained a clear-cut victory.
The Liberalism that had been entrenched in the major denominations was still entrenched, and the onslaughts of Fundamentalism
had not uprooted its influential position. Neither had Liberalism
obliterated Fundamentalism. Protestantism had become polarized
around both extremes. The conflict had no sooner abated in the
late 1920s than the nation's attention was turned to the Great
Depression. In order to fully conceptualize the aftermath of the
war, one must study the influence and progress of three separate
impulses: Fundamentalism, Liberalism, and Evangelicalism. It is
the history of these three movements from 1930 to 1980 that char-
acterizes the progress of Protestantism in America. To comprehend
better the role and growth of Fundamentalism, one must be cog-
nizant of both the role and growth of Liberalism and Evangelicalism.

In describing the ensuing events of these five decades, it is impossible to segregate movements, people, and organizations from
their relationship to each other. History is the synthesis, integration, and confrontation of all of these elements. In describing individuals and organizations there will be some overlapping. Many organizations grew out of parent institutions in reaction against the
direction of these. In dealing with the history of this era, one must
examine the decades by identifying the important movements, or-

ganizations, and people of that decade, as well as the critical issues and how they affected the growth of Fundamentalism.

1930–1940

During the 1930s the established denominations experienced a major decline in their growth and influence. Membership in the Northern Presbyterian and Protestant Episcopal denominations declined 5.0 and 6.7 percent respectively between 1926 and 1936. During this period many of the foreign missionaries returned home because of lack of support. Contributions in all areas declined.[1] Using these statistics, church historians incorrectly assumed that the Protestant religious movement was on the decline and headed toward a depression of its own. Most historians have ignored the response of Fundamentalism in light of this decline. The Fundamentalists of this period retreated and redirected their efforts toward building churches and propagating the Gospel. They recognized that it was impossible to uproot Liberalism from the denominations and consequently concentrated their efforts on building their own churches, schools, and organizations. The thirties became an important time of growth and expansion for the Fundamentalist Movement.

One of the important contributions to the influence and growth of the movement was the development and expansion of Bible institutes. This concept was originally pioneered by A. B. Simpson of the Christian and Missionary Alliance, who started the Missionary Training Institute in New York City in 1882. Dwight L. Moody was another pioneer, who founded the Moody Bible Institute of Chicago in 1886. According to the *Sunday School Times*, a fundamentalist paper, by 1930 there were more than fifty Bible schools throughout the country.[2] These institutes grew in numbers and influence because Fundamentalists mistrusted the major educational institutions of that era. The battles over Liberalism and evolution grew out of the fact that both of these ideologies were taught in many of the schools in the twenties. These new schools became substitutes for the denominational schools that had digressed into Liberalism and Darwinianism.

The most influential institute of this time was the Moody Bible

Institute in Chicago. Its influence extended far beyond the geographical confines of Chicago. Besides training missionaries, pastors, and Christian workers, the institute hosted Bible conferences, printed Christian literature, and conducted a radio ministry. During 1936, for example, Moody Bible Institute conducted 500 Bible conferences in churches across the country. By 1937 it had more than 15,000 people involved in its correspondence school. WMBI, its radio station, had transcribed programs to 187 stations by 1942. Its publication, *Moody Monthly*, increased from 13,000 subscribers in 1939 to 40,000 in the early 1940s.

The Moody Bible Institute, unlike other institutes of its time, extended its influence nationally. There were also many other Bible institutes, including Philadelphia School of the Bible, Bible Institute of Los Angeles (BIOLA), Providence (Rhode Island) Bible Institute, Columbia Bible College, Denver Bible Institute, and Northwestern Bible and Missionary Training School—each of which had great influence in its particular geographical location. William Bell Riley, who founded Northwestern Bible and Missionary Training School, had 75 pastors statewide who had attended his school. BIOLA had 180 Christian workers in California by 1939.[3]

The growth of educational institutions also centered around the building of liberal arts colleges. During the thirties three major fundamentalist schools were emerging: Wheaton College in Chicago; Bob Jones College in Cleveland, Tennessee; and Gordon College of Missions and Theology in Boston. Wheaton College was founded in 1857 but experienced its phenomenal growth under the leadership of J. Oliver Buswell, who was president from 1926 to 1940. Wheaton's enrollment grew from 400 in 1926 to over 1,100 in 1941. Wheaton's commitment was, and is, to high academic standards, and throughout the years Wheaton College has been known as the "Harvard of the Bible Belt."[4] It has produced such noteworthy leaders as Carl H. Henry and Billy Graham.

Bob Jones College was formed in 1926 at St. Andrews Bay, Florida. After the stock market crash of 1929, when the college assets were liquidated, the school moved to Cleveland, Tennessee. In 1947 the university was transferred to Greenville, South Carolina. Bob Jones was one of the leading evangelists of his era. In the midst of highly successful evangelistic campaigns he felt that he must build a school that would provide a sound educational background and yet would have a definite religious and cultural emphasis. "When people think of this school," he said, "they must think of the Bible and of the fundamentals that are accepted by all orthodox, Bible-believing Christians, and not of some particular doctrine."[5]

The purpose and intent of Bob Jones University was clearly outlined in "A Tribute and a Pledge," a message prepared by Dr. Bob Jones, Jr., and read at the funeral of his father. "As long as it please God and the Board of Trustees that we shall be entrusted with the administrative responsibility of this university, Bob III, and I shall continue unyielding in our warfare against Anti-Christ and shall undertake to assure that Bob Jones University shall remain a lighthouse of God's Truth amid the lengthening shadows of a great apostasy. We shall, in the words of our charter:

"Conduct an institution of learning for the general education of youth in the essentials of culture and in the arts and sciences, giving special emphasis to the Christian religion and the ethics revealed in the Holy Scriptures, combating all atheistic, agnostic, pagan and so-called scientific adulterations of the gospel, unqualifiedly affirming and teaching the inspiration of the Bible (both Old and New Testaments); the creation of man by the direct act of God; the incarnation and the virgin birth of our Lord and Saviour, Jesus Christ; His identification as the Son of God; His vicarious atonement for the sins of mankind by the shedding of His blood on the cross; the resurrection of His body from the tomb; His power to save men from sin; the New Birth through the regeneration by the Holy Spirit; and the gift of eternal Life by the grace of God."[6]

Bob Jones University has led the way among Fundamentalists in standing for biblical truth while providing quality education for its students.

The second major area of influence and growth for the Fundamentalist Movement in the 1930s was the development of alternate organizations to the major denominations. The influence of the charismatic leaders of the 1920s, such as Riley, Norris, and Shields, faded somewhat in the thirties. This gave birth to numerous fundamentalist church organizations. The Fundamentalists had been rejected by the major denominations and had concluded that it was impossible to salvage those denominations from within. They left the denominations and began their own organizations. This trait of separatism became a major characteristic of the Fundamentalist Movement. Later, in the forties and fifties, separatism became an issue of equal importance to the earlier issue of Liberalism. Several new groups came into prominence during this time.

General Association of Regular Baptists

The General Association of Regular Baptists was the outgrowth of the Baptist Bible Union, which held its last meeting in Chicago in May of 1932. The meeting was poorly attended, and none of the original founders (Norris, Shields, and Riley) were there. A new group met in Buffalo, New York, in 1933 and organized the GARBC, with Harry G. Hamilton, pastor of First Baptist Church in Buffalo, as the first president. The intent of the GARBC was to formulate an association of churches and not a convention. At this particular meeting five objectives were listed.

1. An association of churches.
2. Separation from Northern Baptist work of any kind.
3. Conformity to the London Confession of Faith (1689) and the New Hampshire Confession of Faith.
4. The promotion of the spirit of missions among pastors.
5. Helping churches find sound pastors.[7]

One of the foremost leaders of the GARBC was Robert T. Ketcham (1889–1978). In 1932 he became pastor of Central Baptist Church in Gary, Indiana. In 1933 he was elected vice-president of the GARBC; and in 1934, president, serving in that capacity for a number of years. In 1938 he became editor of *The Baptist Bulletin* and served as consultant to the GARBC. In his presidential address he stated that the purpose of the GARBC was threefold: "(1) To provide a haven of Fundamental Fellowship, (2) To promote Independent, Orthodox, Baptist Missions, and (3) To disseminate authentic information concerning conditions in the Northern Baptist Convention."[8] It was at this conference that the

GARBC adopted its policy relating to the establishment of approved schools. It decided that no school or organization would have direct contact with the association. Each organization and school desiring the approval of the GARBC would submit annually for that approval. This permitted the GARBC to withdraw its approval at any time when a school or organization departed from the tenets of the organization.

In 1934 a Council of Fourteen was established to oversee the directives given at the annual meetings. The members of this committee were elected by the assembly at large. Five mission boards were approved: Baptist Mid Missions; the Association of Baptists for World Evangelism; Fellowship of Baptists for Home Missions; Hiawatha Independent Baptist Missions; and Evangelical Baptist Missions. At that time two seminaries were approved: Los Angeles Baptist Seminary and Grand Rapids Baptist Seminary. There were six approved colleges: Western Baptist Bible College, Salem, Oregon; Faith Baptist Bible College, Iowa; Grand Rapids Baptist Bible College, Michigan; Cedarville College, Ohio; Baptist Bible College, Pennsylvania; and Los Angeles Baptist College, California. In 1942, when the American Council of Christian Churches was established, Ketcham assumed a leading role in that organization as well, and in 1944 he became its president. In 1950 the GARBC expanded its influence by the establishment of the Regular Baptist Press through which it would disseminate its printed material.

One of the major confrontations of the GARBC centered around J. Frank Norris and the Temple Baptist Church in Detroit, Michigan. When Norris assumed the pastorate in Michigan in 1937, he immediately applied for admission into the GARBC. Norris and the church were denied admission on the basis that the church itself had not voted to enter the fellowship. Norris responded in 1938 by sending a letter to Ketcham, accusing him of numerous things: "Your feet will be held to the fire in this one issue.

- You have been hollering and squawking about me trying to crucify you. You have crucified yourself.
- Everyone is laughing at you—lifelong friends—men who have known you are pitying you.
- You were fired at Waterloo [*from the GARBC*] and they let you down easy by discontinuing the office. They did like I

saw a crowd do to a smart alec at a country dance when I
was a boy. They slipped the chair out from under him
and his caboose hit the floor.
- You have ruined the GARB."[9]

Following the letter, Norris attacked Ketcham in print in his
paper, the *Fundamentalist*. The GARBC quickly arose to the defense of Ketcham, and the ensuing months were months of great
trial for Ketcham as Norris continued his attack. Norris was never
admitted to the GARBC and his attacks on Ketcham were instru-
mental in developing greater unity among GARBC members.

Ketcham had an overwhelming influence on the leadership and
growth of the GARBC. At Ketcham's memorial service, Dr. Joseph
M. Stowell said, "I suppose that more than any other one man, Dr.
Ketcham was responsible for the building of our Association. Now
with more than fifteen hundred churches, it was his life and his
heart in the latter years of his life. He gave his very best for it. He
guided its direction and established its structure and was used of
God to maintain its position, which still continues to this very
hour."[10] His outstanding leadership cannot be overestimated; he
was one of the leading Fundamentalists of that era.

The Independent Fundamental
Churches of America

The Independent Fundamental Churches of America began in
February of 1930 when William McCarrell, pastor of the Cicero
Bible Church in Cicero, Illinois, met with thirty-nine men. They
were interested in uniting with the American Conference of Un-
denominational Churches and adopting a new name. The people attending this first gathering of the IFCA included twelve Congregationalists, three Presbyterians, nineteen Independents, one
Baptist, and four nondenominational persons. The organization
grew as quickly as did the GARBC. In 1935 there were 38 churches
in the IFCA with a total membership of 550, and by 1940 this
figure had grown to 75 churches. In the 1969–70 directory 560
churches were listed, with a total membership of 75,000. There
were also 340 churches whose pastors were listed as members of

the IFCA. The movement was led in the early years by men such as M. R. DeHaan, W. L. Pettingill, J. F. Walvoord, and J. O. Buswell, Jr. The official publication of the IFCA is *The Voice*.[11]

World Baptist Fellowship

Founded originally by the efforts of J. Frank Norris, the World Baptist Fellowship became closely intwined with the Bible Baptist Seminary in Fort Worth, Texas, moving into its facilities in 1952 after Norris' death. The name of the school was officially changed to the Arlington Baptist Schools, which included a junior liberal arts curriculum as well as the seminary program. This group represents such outstanding churches as the Dayton Baptist Temple (Ohio), pastored by Gerald Fleming and Massilon Baptist Temple (Ohio), pastored by Bruce Cummons. The latter also sponsors the Massilon Baptist College. The president of the Arlington School is Wayne Martin, who recently succeeded Earl Oldham, and the president of the fellowship is Raymond Barber. The majority of the 1,000 W.B.F. churches are in Texas, Florida, and the Midwest. They promote aggressive evangelism and a strong church planting program through their schools and their official publication, *The Fundamentalist*.

American Baptist Association

The American Baptist Association began in 1925 as a result of the influence of J. M. Pendleton and John R. Graves.[12] Graves (1820–93) was a leading southern preacher known for establishing the "Landmark Controversy," advocating the return of churches to "old landmarks." In evaluating this position, Baptist historians Bush and Nettles state: "Those distinguishing marks by which Graves sought to identify the true church included an emphasis on the local congregation (with a corresponding denial of the current existence of a universal church) and the necessity of a properly authorized administrator of the ordinances before they could be considered validly performed. Graves also emphasized his belief that the Great Commission promised there would be a succession of true churches from Christ to the present day. The name may have varied through the years, but Graves identified these churches as Baptist churches. No baptism could be accepted if it was not performed by an authorized Baptist preacher, and the Lord's Supper was to be taken only by members of the local Baptist Church where it was served."[13]

J. M. Pendleton (1811–91), who also influenced the American Baptist Association, was the great advocate of plenary verbal inspiration of Scripture. This was clearly outlined in his *Christian Doctrines*, published in 1878.

The American Baptist Association was founded on these landmark principles. It was distinguished from all other Baptist groups by the following criteria:

1. John the Baptist's baptism was truly Christian.
2. Jesus established the Church from John's converts.
3. Churches of like faith and practice have been existing ever since—so we really have a Baptist perpetuity.
4. There has been a line (though not necessarily a strict succession) of true churches from the time of Christ to ours.
5. Jesus gave the two ordinances (baptism and the Lord's table) to the church He founded and to no other. Any other practice is alien.[14]

The influence of the theological positions of the American Baptist Association has extended far beyond the limits of its own organization. Landmarkism has affected Baptists of every distinction and variety.

Grace Brethren

The Grace Brethren movement began in the late thirties as a reaction to the liberalism at Ashland Theological Seminary. In 1937, under the leadership of such men as Alva McClain, Herman A. Hoyt, and L. S. Bauman, Grace Theological Seminary was founded in Winona Lake, Indiana. Although there was no official split with the Ashland group, there developed around the new seminary and its supporting pastors a movement that would eventually grow larger than the one they had left.

Today the Grace Brethren have over 300 churches with about 40,000 members. They have an aggressive missions program and their mission points around the world include over 100,000 converts. The seminary has about 500 students, and Grace College now has an enrollment of 1,000. They have represented fundamentalist scholarship with the writings of such men as Homer A. Kent, Jr.; John J. Davis; and John C. Whitcomb. While not a large group, their commitment to an academic defense of fundamentalist beliefs has caused them to have a great influence in the training of conservative leaders.

Radio Ministries

During the thirties the influence of Fundamentalism was greatly extended through the popularity of radio preaching. Charles E. Fuller, pastor of Calvary Church of Los Angeles, spoke weekly on the "Old-Fashioned Revival Hour." The program began in 1925 and by the late 1930s was the most popular religious program on the air. In 1933 Charles Fuller resigned his church to work full-time with the radio ministry. In 1939 he was heard on 152 stations and by 1942 on 456 stations.[15]

The "Old-Fashioned Revival Hour" program had a powerful influence nationwide. The following excerpt from "Washington Day-by-Day," which appeared in three hundred newspapers, indicates the impact of Charles Fuller.

> In a world with war and crime, writing the annals of greed and violence in the blood of countless victims, it is restful to hear an old-fashioned preacher preach old-time religion in the good old-fashioned way. Coming out of California every Sunday evening, this Gospel hour of the radio breaks through the din and clamor of swing-whoopee, croonings, and news broadcasts to almost startle a weary world with its unretouched truths.
>
> This earnest, pleading Baptist preacher who exhorts a bizarre world in a manner simple and devoid of sophism is the Rev. Charles E. Fuller. His millions of devoted listeners contribute money for buying radio time on several hundred stations—a whole hour each week—indubitably a stupendous sum.
>
> The radio sets of blasé Washingtonians pick Evangelist Fuller's

soul-searching messages from the gentle autumn breezes that
blow out of the night across the Potomac lush-lands and over the
low-hung islands which dot historic Chesapeake Bay. The
congregation's singing such time-tried hymns as "There Is A
Fountain Filled With Blood," "Let The Lower Lights Be
Burning," and "Sweet Hour of Prayer," comes like a ground
swell from a new and better world, and by the air waves
reaches comforting hands across all the North American
continent and to the islands of the sea, bringing the new-old
story of religion to the weary heart not only here in sophisticated
Washington but to mansions and hovels, homes and brothels,
prisons and cocktail lounges the country over. It steals into
rooms made restless by the unquiet slumber of sick life, hovers
over the cabins in the cotton, and filters into the lumbermen's
camp in the great North woods.[16]

Fuller's highly popular program was the means by which Jerry
Falwell came to know Christ as personal Savior. This program
served as the model for one of the key methods used by Fundamentalism. In the following years many other preachers and evangelists utilized the airwaves to propagate the message of the Gospel. The "Old-Fashioned Revival Hour" was the forerunner for
later religious radio programs.

The voice of Fundamentalism that had occupied the national
media in the twenties was gaining national attention once again
through radio. Although the liberal denominations chose to ignore
Fundamentalism, and although the national media were consumed
with the depression and war, Fundamentalism made great inroads
with the grassroots of America by ministering to humanity's needs
through radio. M. R. DeHaan's program "Radio Bible Class" and
Donald Gray Barnhouse's "Bible Study Hour" and the influence of
Moody Bible Institute's syndicated programs all contributed to the
growing movement of Fundamentalism. The broadcasts of Oliver
B. Greene, J. Vernon McGee, and Theodore Epp would also later
extend the influence of conservative Christianity over the airwaves.

The Sword of the Lord

John R. Rice has been one of the leaders of the Fundamentalist
Movement and is respected as one of its foremost writers. Much of

his influence in the Fundamentalist Movement came through *The Sword of the Lord*. Rice began *The Sword of the Lord* paper on September 28, 1934. Five thousand copies were issued at its first printing. Since its inception, its purpose has remained constant: "An independent religious weekly, standing for the verbal inspiration of the Bible, the deity of Christ, His blood atonement, salvation by faith, New Testament soul winning and the premillennial return of Christ. Opposes modernism, worldliness and formalism." The circulation grew from 7,200 per week in 1934 to 32,800 in 1944 and 106,592 in 1956. *The Sword of the Lord* has had extensive influence, especially in molding and directing the stand for Fundamentalism among preachers. Because it contains sermons, this newspaper has been popular among fundamentalist preachers. Many people have spoken highly of *The Sword of the Lord,* including Dr. Hyman J. Appleman, evangelist E. J. Daniels, Dr. Robert G. Lee, and Dr. Oswald J. Smith. Dr. Robert G. Lee has written, "*The Sword of the Lord* deserves a great increase in the number of subscriptions. When a weekly magazine of such evangelistic fervor and faithfulness to the Word of God is published, it should be read by millions. The bright fire of the ably edited paper that stands for 'the faith once delivered to the saints'—that makes prayerful efforts to win the lost and to build them up in the most holy faith—will be made the brighter and the more far-reaching by a great increase in the number of subscriptions."[17]

Dr. Rice traveled to some twenty-five *Sword of the Lord* conferences each year. He wrote more than 185 books and pamphlets, with 52 million copies in print in 38 languages. In the April 21, 1978, issue of *The Sword of the Lord* it was reported, "We have already had this year 197 letters from people saved through our literature. We have had about 19,000 such letters from those saved through sermons in *The Sword of the Lord* and the literature which we promote."

Because of Dr. Rice's challenge to pastors and churches regarding soul-winning and, in particular, his challenge to churches to baptize more than two hundred persons annually, hundreds of churches have accelerated their evangelistic efforts. No man has had a more wholesome impact on doctrinal points within Fundamentalism. He has been the "guardian of the faith once delivered."

As the most prolific writer among fundamentalist preachers, Dr. Rice exerted an extensive influence on conservatives of all kinds.

The extensive influence of this paper will certainly continue. Dr. Curtis Hutson, pastor, evangelist, author, and prominent soul winner, is now the editor of *The Sword of the Lord.* Under his capable leadership, this newspaper will continue to lead the way among the ranks of Fundamentalism.

1940–1950

The decade of the forties started with the formation of two very important organizations: the American Council of Christian Churches and the National Association of Evangelicals. The formation of these organizations gave birth to the controversy between Fundamentalism and Evangelicalism.

American Council of Christian Churches

In September 1941 the American Council of Christian Churches (ACCC) was organized to "dispute the claim of the Federal Council to speak for all Protestants."[18] The ACCC was formulated under the leadership of Carl McIntire, who continued for many years to exert his influence over the organization. He started the *Christian Beacon* and Faith Theological Seminary in Philadelphia. In 1948 McIntire founded the International Council of Christian Churches (ICCC) to oppose the influence of the World Council of Churches. When the ACCC and ICCC were founded, they both had the support of the GARBC and the IFCA. Ultimately, the IFCA broke from McIntire and his group. McIntire lost control of the ACCC in 1970, and in 1971 most of the faculty of the seminary left to organize Biblical Theological Seminary in Hatfield, Pennsylvania.

Much of McIntire's efforts were directed against the World Council of Churches. His famous book *Modern Tower of Babel* was written immediately after the 1948 First Assembly of the World Council of Churches and after the First Plenary Congress of the International Council of Churches. His later book *Servants of Apostasy* was written in 1954, after the Second Assembly of the World Council. McIntire operated under the belief that there were two great movements in the twentieth century. "The first is the Ecumenical Movement, represented in the World Council of Churches and the International Missionary Council. The second is the Twentieth Century Reformation movement, represented in the International Council of Christian Churches and its related organizations."[19]

National Association of Evangelicals

The second major organization founded in the forties was the National Association of Evangelicals (NAE). On April 7, 1942, in Chicago, one hundred and fifty delegates assembled for the National Conference for United Action among Evangelicals. This conference has since been declared the birthplace of the National Association of Evangelicals. Four key individuals presented messages at the conference: Dr. Harold John Ockenga, pastor of Park Street Church in Boston, Massachusetts; Dr. William Ward Ayer, pastor of Calvary Baptist Church, New York City; Dr. Stephen W. Paine, president of Houghton College; and Dr. Robert G. Lee, pastor of Bellevue Baptist Church in Memphis, Tennessee.

The NAE grew out of New England Fellowship, which was formed in 1929 to deal with "(1) evangelism, (2) evangelicals' relation to government, (3) national and local use of radio, (4) public relations, (5) the preservation of separation of church and state, (6) Christian education and (7) the guarantee of freedom for home and foreign missionary endeavor."[20]

According to Bruce Shelley there were three major reasons for the development of the NAE. First, the Evangelicals of that era were dissatisfied with all previous attempts at Christian unity. They were critical of the Federal Council of Churches of Christ for its liberal stance and infiltration by the social gospel. On the other hand, they were not satisfied with Carl McIntire and his American Council of Christian Churches. They felt that such an organization was too critical and that its only point of cooperation was in criticism of other people. It is interesting to note that McIntire was afforded the opportunity of addressing the NAE at its inception, but he declined the invitation. The second major reason for the NAE was a feeling of loneliness among conservative Christians. This was articulated by Dr. Ockenga in one of the keynote messages at the St. Louis annual conference. The third factor that aided in the formulation of the NAE was "the firm conviction that a positive witness could be given by united evangelicals."[21]

Harold J. Ockenga was one of the leaders involved in the rise of Evangelicalism and neo-Evangelicalism. The term "neo-Evangelicalism" was coined by Ockenga himself in 1947. He felt that the term "evangelical" was being misused to describe Fundamentalists. Since he did not want identification with Fundamentalism, he coined the term "neo-Evangelicalism" and emphasized that the New Evangelicals were willing to "handle the societal problems that fundamentalism had evaded."[22] The Evangelicals agreed with the orthodox theological position of Fundamentalists, but objected to their methodology and attitudes.

Fundamentalists were suspicious of anyone who did not take the fundamentalist position. "Their suspicion gave way to criticism, and criticism led to attack—even against brethren committed to some of the same truths and principles they themselves held. These attacks drove away some of the men who ideologically belonged to the fundamentalist group. Unjust accusations and misrepresentations were made with no retractions when called to the attention of those who made them."[23]

Ockenga also objected to the strategy of the Fundamentalists. He felt that Fundamentalism promoted a purist church and a separatist theology. He concluded that the history of Fundamentalism was a history of splitting and separating, e.g., the formation of Westminster Theological Seminary in 1929 as a reaction to Princeton; the formation of Faith Theological Seminary as a reaction to Westminster; the division of Faith Theological Seminary; the founding of Covenant Theological Seminary; and finally the breaking away from Faith Theological Seminary to form Biblical Theological Seminary.

Lastly, Ockenga objected to the theological persuasion of Fundamentalists on eschatology. He rebelled against their concept that world conditions would deteriorate until the return of Christ and that the Gospel was the only effective answer for the individual. He claimed that Fundamentalists ignored efforts for world peace and against racial conflict and the importance of the United Nations. He felt that the Fundamentalist Movement failed to conquer and address the social issues and problems of that day.[24]

The purpose of the NAE was to "experience revival of Christianity in a secular world, to recapture the denominational leadership from the inside by infiltration instead of a frontal attack, to achieve respectability for orthodoxy, and to attain social reform."[25] The NAE helped organize the National Religious Broadcasters, the Evangelical Foreign Missions Association, the World Evangelical Fellowship, the National Sunday School Association, and the magazine *Christianity Today*. There were a number of important leaders in the NAE, including Wilbur Smith, Carl F. H. Henry, Edward Carnell, and Harold Lindsell.

The NAE quickly experienced growth and soon had 29,000 churches connected with it. It claimed to represent 2.5 million Christians. During this period of growth, Dr. Clyde Taylor, who served as head of the office of public affairs for the NAE, executive secretary for Evangelical Foreign Missions Association, and ultimately as the general director of NAE, provided the dynamic leadership that helped the association transcend the various denominational walls and barriers that separated Christians in the 1940s. By 1972, thirty-four complete denominations were in the NAE, along with churches from twenty-six other denominations.

Conservative Baptist Association of America

The Conservative Baptist Association (CBA) of America was formed in 1947, comprised of a group of churches that were dissatisfied with the American Baptist Convention. They objected to the fact that the American Baptist Convention would not require creedal tests for its membership. The purpose of the newly formed association was to provide "a back-to-the-Bible fellowship of autonomous churches, dedicated to soulwinning, missions, church planting and the defense of the faith and . . . opposed to mod-

ernism, all forms of theological inclusivism and ecumenicalism."[26] During the forties one of the leading writers of CBA was Chester E. Tulga, who provided the publication of "Case" books: *Against the Social Gospel, Against the National Council of Churches, Against Modernism in Evangelism, For the Virgin Birth, For Jesus the Messiah, For the Atonement, For Dispensationalism, For the Resurrection, For Holiness in These Times, For Separation,* and *For the Independence of the Local Church.*

The Conservative Baptist Association of America was formed under the leadership of B. Myron Cedarholm. Connected closely with the association was the Conservative Baptist Foreign Missions Society. In 1950 the Conservative Baptist Home Missions Society was established. In 1961 the Conservative Baptist Association claimed a membership of 1,300 churches.[27]

While McIntire and other Fundamentalist leaders were forging their alliances, there were also reform movements among the main-line denominations. One of the strongest occurred within the Methodist Church in reaction to the liberal controversy of the 1920s. In January 1940 the Southern Methodist Church was formulated. It operates the Southern Methodist College in Orangeburg, South Carolina. The American Association of Bible-Believing Methodists in Maryland was formed, and the Evangelical Methodist Church was started in 1946 in Memphis, Tennessee. The Evangelical Methodist Church operates three colleges, including Azusa Pacific College (California), John Wesley College (North Carolina), and Zennard College (Iowa).[28]

Word of Life

The foremost fundamentalist youth leader is Jack Wyrtzen, a successful businessman and dance band leader before his conversion. Wyrtzen surrendered to full-time service in 1935. He began with a Bible study in his home that led to the founding of Word of Life.

During the thirties he held rallies and banquets. In October 1941, in New York City, he began a rally and radio ministry. The rallies grew. In 1942 they were running 3,000. On April 1, 1944, there were 20,000 at one rally, with 10,000 outside. In 1947 the success of his rallies led to the purchase of an island in Schroon Lake, New York, to start a camping ministry. This was expanded later to include an adult inn, a Ranch, and a junior high camp.

Today Word of Life continues its dynamic ministry. It operates camps in many foreign countries, a Bible institute, and a nationwide club program for churches. Throughout the years Wyrtzen has maintained a balanced ministry. He has avoided the negativism of extreme separatism, but has not drifted into theological tolerance or compromised important personal standards. He exemplifies the position of main-line Fundamentalism.

1950–1960

Baptist Bible Fellowship

The 1950s began with one of the most important events in the history of Fundamentalism. On May 22, 1950, a group of pastors met together to formulate what was to ultimately become the Baptist Bible Fellowship (BBF). Historians have tended to minimize and overlook this vital event. The birth of the Baptist Bible Fellowship gave new impetus to the Independent Baptist church planting movement. Although the fellowship pastors were not involved directly in national ecclesiastical controversy, they devoted their time and energies to building some of the largest, and greatest, churches in America. Their influence on and contribution to America's religious heritage cannot be minimized or overlooked.

Much of the vision and momentum of the Baptist Bible Fellowship came from the leadership of J. Frank Norris. During the late forties, many of the preachers who followed Norris' leadership began to experience disillusionment with some of his attitudes and activities. This disillusionment ultimately bred discontent, until in 1950 there was a severe split among the World Baptist Fellowship. In a taped interview, G. Beauchamp Vick, Norris' associate at Temple Baptist Church and later its pastor, made the following comment concerning Norris: "Now he has helped a great many preachers. I mean, I thank the Lord for the association that I had with him. I learned a lot of things to do, and I learned a great many things not to do. But he did help a lot of young preachers, and he was almost the idol of many young preachers in the South. But on the other hand, he left behind him a trail of broken preachers, some of whom left the ministry because of his treatment of them."[29] The unrest climaxed with some questionable dealings with regard to Norris' seminary. In 1950 Vick, who had been appointed president of the seminary, was dismissed by Norris without the approval of the college trustees. The result was that a number of men, including Vick, John W. Rawlings, Noel Smith, W. E. Dowell, Wendell Zimmerman, Fred Donnelson, R. O. Woodworth, and Scottie Alexander, left the World Baptist Fellowship and formed the Baptist Bible Fellowship.

On June 23, 1950, the first issue of its publication, the *Baptist Bible Tribune,* defined the reasons for the split with Norris and the purposes for the new organization: "Our faith and practice is the historic Baptist faith and practice. We believe in an infallible Bible, in the virgin birth, in the substitutionary death of the Saviour, in His physical resurrection, in His physical ascension, in His literal, Premillennial return to the earth. We believe that the fundamental basis of the fellowship of apostolic churches was not educational but missionary. We believe in every kind and form of evangelism which is effective in bringing men and women to Christ. We are in every practical way against the Modernism now rampant in the Northern and Southern Baptist Conventions. For that we have no apology."

On June 29 papers were taken out to open a new school, in Springfield, Missouri, under the auspices of High Street Baptist Church. The new school experienced phenomenal growth: it began with 150 students in 1950, and by 1970 more than 2,000 were enrolled.

The Baptist Bible Fellowship also inaugurated the *Baptist Bible Tribune,* edited by Noel Smith. This served as the official publication for the newly formed BBF. Smith devoted his energies to such matters as error among Southern Baptists, dealing with communism, the National and World councils of churches, and modernism. Through the years he also dealt with the issues of Billy Graham's evangelism and other separatist controversies. The greatest contribution of the fellowship has been in the building of aggressive, independent, soul-winning Baptist churches. Its pastors have been responsible for the founding and building of some of the largest churches in America, including Landmark Baptist Temple in Cincinnati, Ohio, with John W. Rawlings; Canton Baptist Temple in Canton, Ohio, with Harold Henniger; Akron Baptist Temple in Akron, Ohio, with Dallas and Charles Billington; Temple Baptist in Detroit, with G. B. Vick; Indianapolis Baptist Temple, with Greg Dixon; Thomas Road Baptist Church in Lynchburg, Virginia, with Jerry Falwell; and many other dynamic, growing churches. There are now over 3,500 churches in the fellowship, representing between 2 and 3 million people, making the Baptist Bible Fellowship the largest independent fundamentalist Baptist organization in the United States. Today its outstanding pastors include men like Truman Dollar, A. V. Henderson, Jerry Prevo, and Ray Batema. The Baptist Bible Fellowship left behind it the World Baptist Fellowship (WBF). After the split, the WBF retained national prominence and influence through the Arlington Baptist Schools, which are an outgrowth of the seminary at Norris' church. Over the years this group has remained true to its fundamentalist heritage.

Baptist Missionary Association

The Baptist Missionary Association (BMA) was organized in 1950 by 822 people representing 465 churches. All of these churches once belonged to the American Baptist Association but broke away from that association. The BMA is characterized mainly by the influence of Landmarkism. It claims to be "only a fellowship of local churches." It prides itself in being in historic succession to apostolic principles and practices—a succession, however, "based on principles, not popes."[30] By the early 1970s it represented 1,425 churches with 194,000 members.

The Rise of and Reaction to Billy Graham

The separatism of the developing Fundamentalist Movement climaxed in the 1950s with the confrontation involving Billy Graham and cooperative evangelism. Billy Graham came to prominence in the 1940s and by the early 1950s became a national figure. After graduating from Wheaton College, he was pastor of a church in Western Springs, Illinois. In 1945 he was asked by Torrey Johnson to join Youth for Christ, which he did, becoming a full-time representative for Y.F.C. In 1947 Dr. W. B. Riley asked him to be his successor as president of Northwestern Schools. In the same year Billy Graham became the first vice-president of Youth for Christ International. Commensurate with his travels for Youth for Christ, between 1947 and 1949 he held two- and three-week revivals in various cities in the United States.

The most prominent event in the life of Billy Graham was his 1949 Los Angeles crusade. He was invited to hold a three-week tent crusade in Los Angeles, which was sponsored by pastors, Youth for Christ, and various other Christian organizations. By the end of the third week more than 1,500 people had been converted, and the committee extended the meetings. William Randolph Hearst, the newspaper publisher, instructed editors nationwide to give Graham wide coverage in the newspaper. At the same time as this national coverage country singer Stuart Hamblen was converted. By the sixth week of the crusade the Associated Press picked up the story, and Billy Graham was compared to Billy Sunday. There were many other dramatic conversions of famous figures. By the end of the crusade 2,703 people had made decisions for Christ, and Graham's ministry was nationally launched. In the early fifties, Graham held crusades across the United States and in other parts of the world. He was friendly with both the Evangelical Movement and the Fundamentalist Movement.

The rift with Fundamentalists came in 1957 at the New York City crusade. When Graham was originally invited to New York, a number of modernist preachers were invited to serve on the executive committee. Evangelist Jack Wyrtzen, James E. Bennett, and numerous fundamentalist leaders drew up a petition and requested that all cooperating ministers sign a doctrinal statement. This doctrinal statement read: "We recommend to the committee of 100 that we associate ourselves with the evangelist (Dr. Graham) in presenting to the public the best doctrinal faith upon which the crusade will speak to the hearts and minds of our cities —that this include the Bible as inspired of God and the only infallible rule of our faith and practice, the deity and virgin birth of our

Lord Jesus Christ, the vicarious and substitutionary atonement wrought by Him on the cross, His bodily resurrection from the dead and the salvation which is ours by faith in Him alone."[31] As a result of this move by Wyrtzen, twenty-six liberal ministers withdrew their support from the crusade, declining to sign the doctrinal statement.

In reality, Graham had received two invitations to hold a crusade in New York. One had come from a group of fundamentalist leaders under the auspices of Jack Wyrtzen, and the other invitation had come from the Protestant Council of New York City. Because of the controversy over the doctrinal statement, Graham accepted the invitation from the Protestant Council and thereby forced the issue and split with Fundamentalism.

Throughout the late 1950s and early 1960s the issue of ecumenical evangelism became central within the Fundamentalist Movement. Further discussion in this book will be devoted to the pros and cons of this issue and to the personalities involved in articulating and defining further the position of Fundamentalism. The issue with Graham solidified the separatist element within Fundamentalism.

The direction of Graham's decision affected all parts of the Fundamentalist Movement. The reactions varied from deep concern to harsh public rebuttal. Dr. Charles J. Woodbridge warned, "If you persist in making common cause with those who deny the Word of God, and thus in minimizing the sharp line of distinction between those who are loyal and disloyal to the Scriptures, it is my strong opinion that the verdict of church history will be that you will be known as the greatest divider of the Church of Christ in the twentieth century."[32] Dr. Smith, editor of the *Baptist Bible Tribune*, wrote: "1. I have criticized him for praising the Roman Catholic Church all over the world. 2. I have criticized him for refusing a revival unless all the Modernists in town were invited to publicly cooperate, making no public difference between those who believe in Christianity and those who reject it. 3. I have criticized him for having no real enemies but the Christian people who were responsible for his conversion, for his education, and for the opportunity that came to him to be what he is. 4. I have criticized him for refusing to stand up like a man and defend, or apologize for, statements he has made in all parts of the world. 5. I have criticized him for all the encouragement he has given to the creation of the one-world church. And I have criticized him for saying in Honolulu that "as far as truth is concerned, you can accept the Bible's account of the Garden of Eden literally or figuratively."[33]

Dr. John R. Rice wrote in *The Sword of the Lord* on December 4, 1964: "We should love Modernists. We should love the infidels, but we ought not to call them Christians and we ought not to condone their rejection of Jesus Christ and their continuing on unconverted."[34]

William E. Ashbrook wrote: "Billy Graham represents the most appalling enigma of our time, that he should on the one hand preach the gospel of Christ's saving grace which fundamentalists hold dear, and that he should on the other hand berate the consistent and long-time exponents of that gospel with charges of bitterness, hypocrisy, and lack of concern for the souls of men. He finds the sweetest fellowship with, and constantly seeks out the company and favors of men who hate the gospel he preaches, and who repudiate the virgin-born, crucified, and risen Son of God which he proclaims! No other such phenomena have appeared in this confused age."[35]

Southwide Baptist Fellowship

One of the prominent fundamentalist influences in the Southeast is the Southwide Baptist Fellowship. It was founded on March 20, 1956, with 147 charter members at Highland Park Baptist Church in Chattanooga, Tennessee. This organization was designed to provide fellowship for pastors of fundamentalist Baptist convictions. The early members of this group included Lee Roberson, John R. Rice, Harold B. Sightler, J. R. Faulkner, Wayne Van Gelderen, Norman G. Lemmons, Gene Arnold, Bob Gray, Bob Bevington, and John R. Waters. Yearly meetings include inspirational messages with a strong emphasis on evangelistic church building. By the early sixties the membership of the SBF had grown to 1,100, and by the early seventies, to nearly 2,000.

One of the leaders of this fellowship has been Lee Roberson of Highland Park Baptist Church in Chattanooga, Tennessee. He is pastor of the 33,000-member Highland Park Baptist Church and is founder of Tennessee Temple Schools. Currently Tennessee Temple University includes a Bible school, a liberal arts college, and a seminary. Their combined total enrollment is over 5,000.

Anti-Communist Crusades

While Fundamentalists dealt with the ecumenical evangelism issue of the 1950s, there was also a growing interest in anti-communist activities spearheaded by Carl McIntire and Billy James Hargis. Many different Fundamentalists united under the anti-communist banner. Hargis founded the Christian Crusade in 1948 in Tulsa, Oklahoma. Its stated purpose was to fight communism and religious apostasy. Hargis used letters, pamphlets, newsletters, magazines, newspapers, radio, and television in his crusade against communism. He came to national prominence in 1953 when he led a project of the International Council of Christian Churches headed by Carl McIntire. During that time he made strong efforts to infiltrate the Russian satellite countries with the Gospel. He used more than a million gas-filled balloons, each six feet in diameter, to carry portions of the Bible behind the iron curtain. This was known as the "balloon project" and gained great attention in the right-wing Fundamentalist Movement.[36] During the 1950s he traveled extensively and spoke at rallies and in churches. His radio network expanded, carrying his daily fifteen-minute program on hundreds of stations. He attacked the United Nations and the National Council of Churches in his *Christian Crusade Magazine,* blamed the civil rights movement on the communists, and blasted the postal zip code system as a communist plot!

In the early 1960s Hargis came into direct confrontation with the U. S. Air Force. A writer for an Air Force manual was asked to cover the subject of communism and asked his pastor to help with resource material. The pastor suggested he contact Billy James Hargis. Hargis responded by printing a pamphlet entitled "Apostate Clergymen Battle for God-hating Communist China." Hargis' attack continued against the National Council of Churches. He received attention from *The Saturday Evening Post* and other national magazines. In the late sixties he moved from downtown Tulsa into a beautiful and spacious building in the suburbs and named it the Cathedral of the Christian Crusade. He was also heavily involved in fighting to keep sex education classes out of the public schools; he published a booklet entitled "Is the Little Red School-House the Proper Place to Teach Raw Sex?" Hargis became increasingly involved in the political atmosphere of the country. His crusade finally deteriorated when his character became marred by serious moral accusations.

During the turbulent forties and fifties there were few preachers or evangelists who remained unbloodied from ecclesiastical conflict. Some were involved in combating liberalism, some neo-Evangelicalism, some ecumenical evangelism, and some communism. While it was necessary to maintain the fundamentalist position, one evangelist who remained especially well balanced throughout these controversies was Dr. B. R. Lakin. In 1939 Dr. Lakin became the associate pastor of Cadle Tabernacle in Indianapolis, Indiana. He shared the pastorate until 1942, when, after the death of Dr. Cadle, he became the full-time pastor. He was the speaker on the "Nation's Family Prayer Period," a radio program that originated from the Cadle Tabernacle and was ultimately carried nationwide by the Mutual Broadcasting Corporation. His messages are fervent and dynamic and carry with them the air of the great preachers of the past. Lakin has not limited himself to the confines of any fundamentalist mini-movement. He remains a prophet of God, free to move by the leading of God himself.[37]

1960–1980

Charismatic Movement

Beyond Fundamentalism, one of the fastest-growing movements of the sixties and seventies was the Charismatic Movement. According to a *Christianity Today* Gallup poll, "19 percent of all adult Americans (over 29 million) consider themselves to be Pentecostal or Charismatic Christians."[38] In studying this movement, it is important to distinguish between Pentecostalism and the Charismatic Movement. Pentecostalism began around 1900 with an emphasis on speaking in tongues as evidence of the baptism of the Holy Spirit.

It is represented by denominations such as the Church of God in Christ, Assemblies of God, United Pentecostal Church, Pentecostal Holiness Church, Foursquare Gospel Church, and the Church of God. (It is interesting to note that, while the Charismatic Movement has been experiencing phenomenal growth, the traditional Pentecostal denominations have been experiencing a decline.)

In 1960 Dennis Bennett, who was then rector of St. Mark's Episcopal Church in Van Nuys, California, reported his experience of the baptism with the Holy Spirit and the gift of speaking in tongues. This particular event marked the beginning of the modern Charismatic Movement.[39] This new movement, also termed neo-Pentecostalism, has received notable attention and has made inroads worldwide. It is much more contemporary in outlook and life-style than traditional Pentecostalism. It emphasizes an experience that supersedes all denominational theology. It also emphasizes outward evidence of the baptism with the Holy Spirit with the accompanying experience of speaking in tongues. The leaders of this new movement clearly identify the source of its phenomenal growth as "the effects of 25 years of Oral Roberts, Full Gospel Businessmen, the television ministries of CBN and PTL, and the evangelistic fervor of Pentecostal churches."[40]

The Charismatic Movement of the sixties and seventies is a uniquely diverse movement. The 29 million Pentecostal Charismatics include almost equal percentages of Roman Catholics, Baptists, Methodists, and Lutheran denominations. Approximately one third of all Charismatics are Catholic and two thirds are Protestant. Of the total number who describe themselves as Charismatics, it is interesting to note that only 5 million claim to have spoken in tongues. The traditional Pentecostal movement as represented by the Pentecostal churches includes only one third of all Charismatics.

Because of its unique diversity and ecumenical nature, it is very difficult to make general statements about such a cosmopolitan movement. The following chart from *Christianity Today* includes some interesting facts related to the new Charismatic Movement.[41]

As we have traced the history of Liberalism, Evangelicalism, and Fundamentalism, it is difficult to ascertain the exact place of the Charismatic Movement in relation to the other three in the

Beliefs and Practices	% of General Public who are:	% of Pentecostal/ Charismatics who are:	% of Tongues Speakers who are:	% of Conversionalists who are:	% of Orthodox Evangelicals who are:
1. Catholics	30	27	14	11	9
2. Protestants	58	67	86	89	91
3. Who hold the Bible as Word of God and not mistaken in its statements and teachings	42	52	86	79	100
4. Hold Jesus Christ to be divine	83	92	100	99	100
5. Hold the only hope for heaven is through personal faith in Jesus Christ	45	59	85	85	100
6. Hold the devil is a personal being and influences others	34	45	67	67	70
7. Contribute 10% of income to religious causes	16	29	63	52	50
8. Contribute 5% or more to religious causes	29	47	71	70	70
9. Read the Bible once weekly or more	30	49	77	87	88
10. Attend church at least weekly	36	49	76	85	83
11. Talk about faith at least weekly	21	30	49	51	43
12. Members of a church	67	77	86	93	94
13. Do volunteer work for church	40	55	63	80	80
14. Hold the Bible to be most important religious authority	39	44	56	57	62
15. Set priority on winning the world for Christ	26	33	42	54	51
16. Approve of sexual relations before marriage	41	38	19	16	11
17. Use alcoholic beverages	66	57	29	30	33

twentieth century. Whereas 100 percent of orthodox Evangelicals accept the Bible as being inerrant, God's Word, only 52 percent of Pentecostal Charismatics hold that same belief; however, 92 percent of them believe that Jesus Christ is divine. While 62 percent of orthodox Evangelicals believe that the Bible is the most important religious authority, only 44 percent of Pentecostal Charismatics accept this. It is interesting to note that 11 percent of orthodox Evangelicals approve of sexual relations before marriage, but 38 percent of Pentecostal Charismatics approve of such sexual relationships. This percentage is only 3 percent beneath that of the general public.

Statistics such as these show why it is difficult to categorize the Charismatic Movement. It is obvious that there are some Fundamentalists who are charismatic in their convictions. Dr. Kenneth Kantzer states: "Only 50 percent of the entire group hold clearly to an evangelical view of salvation; less than half accept a personal devil. Only half accept an inerrant Bible, and less than half the Bible's supreme authority; many do not have a traditional orthodox view of the person of Christ."[42]

In light of these interesting statistics, most Fundamentalists would not accept the Charismatic Movement as a legitimate representation of Fundamentalism. In his book *The Charismatics*, John MacArthur, Jr., identifies numerous problems that the Charismatic Movement must face:

1. *The issue of revelation.* Charismatics claim that God is giving them new revelation as they prophesy under the inspiration of the spirit.
2. *The issue of interpretation.* Growing out of their approach to "new revelation," Charismatics get strange meanings out of Scripture with an *ad lib* "this-is-what-it-means-to-me" approach.
3. *The issue of authority.* The Charismatic emphasis on experience relegates Scripture to a secondary status of authority.
4. *The issue of Apostolic uniqueness.* Charismatics insist that the miraculous manifestations of the first century should be normative for today.
5. *The issue of historical transition.* Charismatic interpretation of

Acts 2, 8, 10, and 19 uses specially selected historical events to build a theology of the Holy Spirit.

6. *The issue of spiritual gifts.* Today's Charismatics run a course perilously close to the church at Corinth, where spiritual gifts were counterfeited and practicers of pagan ecstacies ran amuck.

7. *The issue of Spirit baptism.* Charismatics insist every believer needs a second work of grace called "the baptism of the Holy Spirit."

8. *The issue of Healing.* Charismatics confuse the biblical doctrine of healing by insisting that the gift of healing is still in use today.

9. *The issue of Tongues.* Charismatics claim that the ecstatic prayer language practiced in private is the same kind of tongues described in Scripture.

10. *The issue of Spirituality.* True spirituality, say the Charismatics, can be ours through the baptism of the Spirit; but Scripture teaches us to "walk in the Spirit," who already dwells in every Christian.[43]

Since Fundamentalism and Evangelicalism are founded upon a strong doctrinal commitment to the inerrancy of God's Word, it is impossible to place much of the Charismatic Movement within their camps. Although there are many Charismatics who are fundamentalist and evangelical in their doctrine, Russell Spintler, Assemblies of God minister and associate dean of Fuller Theological Seminary, states that the "Charismatic movement as a whole is doctrinally unpredictable."[44] The Charismatic Movement is an entity within itself that deserves further study and that is here to stay and will continue to have a profound effect upon American society.

There are a number of important lessons that Fundamentalists can learn from the phenomenal growth of the Charismatic Movement. First, it is important to cultivate a dynamic and intimate relationship with God. The Charismatic Movement has experienced tremendous growth because of the emptiness of dead orthodoxy. People desire a relationship with God, a relationship that integrates the intellectual, the spiritual, and the emotional aspects of life. Although the Charismatics have a tendency to overemphasize the emotional, many Evangelicals have a tendency to overemphasize the intellectual. Our worship of God must be intimate and dynamic. Second, the Charismatic Movement has placed great emphasis on love and unity. Their attitude is that doctrine is not all that important, but what is important is that we learn to love each other and that we learn to grow in a spirit of Christian unity. Fundamentalists must constantly remind themselves that in their militant stand for truth they must also display the love of God. It is this warm display of love that attracts people to the Charismatic Movement. It must be a warm display of love within Fundamentalism and its churches that attracts the unsaved world to Christ.

Southern Baptist Convention

One cannot describe the Fundamentalist Movement without studying the 13.3 million–member Southern Baptist Convention. This is the largest Protestant religious group in the nation. While Fundamentalism was waging its war with Evangelicalism and defining its separatism, the Southern Baptist Convention was experiencing some serious repercussions itself.

In the late 1960s many Fundamentalists advocated the withdrawal of conservative pastors from the Southern Baptist Convention. Their contention was that the convention had digressed and, like the major denominations of the twenties, was beyond reconciliation.

The Southern Baptist Convention had a growing unrest among its conservative leaders that was accented in 1970 by the publication of the *Broadman Commentary*. This commentary advocated liberal interpretations in the early chapters of Genesis. The publication of this commentary identified the major issue within the convention: the inerrancy of Scripture.

Conservative leaders began to organize their efforts. In the mid-1970s the Baptist Faith and Message Fellowship was formulated by such men as Charles Stanley and Adrian Rogers. Their goal was to vote into the presidency of the Southern Baptist Convention a person who was a strong defender of biblical inerrancy. The president of the convention exerts influence in that he appoints the resolutions committee and the fifty-two-member committee on committees. The latter nominates a committee on boards that ultimately places the board members on the Southern Baptist agencies and institutions. The conservatives felt that if they had control of the presidency, they could nominate to the boards of the seminaries people who advocated inerrancy. The feeling among the conservative element was that the seminaries were filled with faculty members who had very weak position on the subject of biblical inerrancy.

The two major leaders of the conservative movement were Judge Paul Pressler, a Texas appeals court judge from Houston, and Paige Patterson, president of the Criswell Center for Biblical Studies. In 1979, at the Houston convention, Adrian Rogers was voted into the presidency on the first ballot—the first time in 120 years that someone had been elected on the first ballot. His presidency was one of initial tranquillity and later strong reaction against Patterson and Pressler. At the 1980 convention in St. Louis, Bailey Smith was elected president on the first ballot. A resolution related to biblical inerrancy was passed that required conformity by the faculty members and professional staff of the seminaries and various institutions. Other resolutions passed were related to abortion, voluntary prayer in the schools, endorsement of Christian politics, anti-ERA, and a commendation to the Baylor University president for opposing Baylor women students who wanted to pose for *Playboy* magazine.[45]

The controversy over inerrancy and over concern for the seminaries will continue in the Southern Baptist Convention; however, with the renewed efforts of the conservatives within the convention, there seems at this time to be a rainbow of hope. The process of change will be strongly felt, since the roots of inerrancy have extensive influence within the convention.[46]

Secondary Separation

Although not a movement or formal organization, two issues emerged in the sixties that had a great impact on Fundamentalism. After the separation of the Evangelical and Fundamentalist movements, the issue of secondary separation became a prevalent discussion among Fundamentalists in the sixties and seventies. A *secondary separatist* "would be one who would not cooperate with (1) apostates; or (2) evangelical believers who aid and abet apostates by their continued organizational or cooperative alignment with them; or, as employed by some (3) fundamentalists who fellowship with those in the previous category."[47] This issue clearly divided the fundamentalist camp. The marks of a true Fundamentalist were extended beyond doctrine and belief to personal and public associations. For example, if a fundamentalist pastor had a Southern Baptist preacher in his church to speak, one who was actively involved in the cooperative program, that fundamentalist preacher would no longer be considered a true Fundamentalist because he would be associating with another preacher who had questionable associations. The *degree* of one's separatism became a hotly debated issue in many fundamentalist circles.

The Super Church

The 1960s and 1970s were also the age of the super church. Many fundamentalist churches grew to mammoth proportions. They ministered to thousands of people and developed large professional staffs to serve those people. The three churches described in this section are representative of a widespread super church movement.[48]

In 1942 the Highland Park Baptist Church in Chattanooga, Tennessee, called Dr. Lee Roberson as its pastor. In those days the Sunday school averaged 470 people. Currently the church has 11,000 in attendance on an average Sunday and a total membership of 33,000. Through the dynamic influence of Dr. Roberson, this ministry is making an impact all around the world.

One of the most influential ministries of the Highland Park church is the Tennessee Temple School system, with an enrollment of over 5,000 students. This university system includes a Bible school, a four-year liberal arts college, a graduate school, and a seminary. Since the founding of these schools in 1946, thousands of students have been trained and sent out worldwide to spread the Gospel message.

The Highland Park Baptist Church sponsors many other projects, including seventy mission outreach chapels and the printing of an evangelistic newspaper, *The Evangelist,* with over 57,000 subscribers. Dr. Roberson also hosts the oldest live daily radio broadcast in the nation, which has been on the air for nearly forty years.

The First Baptist Church of Hammond, Indiana, is one of the unusual churches of our time. Under the leadership of Dr. Jack Hyles, it has been acclaimed many times over in recent years as "America's fastest-growing Sunday school." In 1959 Hyles came to Hammond after pastoring and attending school in east Texas. At that time the First Baptist Church was averaging about 700 in attendance. Ten years later the church was averaging close to 4,000. Today, with an average attendance of 15,000, the First Baptist Church in Hammond is continuing to win souls and preach the fundamentals of the Christian faith.

Hyles is a firm believer in simplification of organization and promotes a dynamic soul-winning evangelism program. He feels that the main task of the pastor is to win souls and that each church member should be trained to do the same. He also hosts an outstanding Pastors' Conference every year, training thousands of pastors annually in pastoral leadership and soul-winning efforts.

The First Baptist Church is also well known for its bus ministry. On an average Sunday 150 buses bring people to the First Baptist Church to hear the preaching of the Word of God. The Sunday morning program includes thirteen separate preaching services, with crowds ranging from 200 to 5,000. Its all-time high Sunday school attendance was over 100,000, and the church once baptized 960 converts in one day!

The Landmark Baptist Temple in Cincinnati, Ohio, has a long tradition of leadership among Fundamentalists. The main facilities of the church are located just fourteen miles north of downtown Cincinnati, and for many decades it had maintained a dynamic influence through its ministry in that metropolitan area. In 1951 Dr. John Rawlings took over the pastorate of what was to become the Landmark Baptist Temple. The Sunday school was then averaging about 900; today, with a membership of 18,000, the church must hold nine separate services in locations scattered throughout the Cincinnati area, including two congregations in northern Kentucky, in order to accommodate the crowd.

Dr. John Rawlings has been recognized as one of the leading voices in the Fundamentalist Movement. For many years Dr. Rawlings traveled with his well-known Landmark Quartet, holding evangelistic rallies in some forty states. Dr. Rawlings is also heard on his radio broadcast "The Landmark Hour" across the Eastern Seaboard every day. Throughout his ministry he has always been a man ahead of his time. He has also been a strong promoter of the evangelistic church program of confrontational preaching and personal soul-winning.

6

****

THE RESURGENCE OF
FUNDAMENTALISM

Humpty Dumpty sat on a Wall
Humpty Dumpty had a great fall
All the king's horses and all the king's men
Couldn't put Humpty together again.

The condition of Fundamentalism by the end of the 1970s was similar to the condition of Humpty Dumpty. During the War with Liberalism it was a cohesive unified movement, but since that embryonic display of cooperation it has been characterized by a long history of separatism. By the late seventies there were so many broken pieces and independent organisms that it seemed impossible to put Humpty together again.

By 1976 the Fundamentalist Movement was so fragmented and diversified that it was impossible to describe it, categorize it, or even understand it. Each leader of the movement was defining Fundamentalism and its position in the light of his own environment and contacts. Was it possible for such a scattered movement to unite? To the surprise of both the Evangelicals and the society at large, it did unite and exerted a political influence that shocked the entire nation. Humpty Dumpty was together again!

In the 1920s, during the Modernist-Fundamentalist controversy, the leaders of the Fundamentalist Movement were very diversified and yet displayed their ability to present a unified front.

The unifying factor of the Fundamentalist Movement of the twenties was the realization of an external threat—the threat of Liberalism. Regardless of their denominational background or personal preferences, most Fundamentalists united around the banner of opposition to Liberalism. They were willing to adjust to personality differences and to minimize secondary theological interpretations and separatist preferences in order to fight Liberalism. The importance of this cooperative opposition far exceeded the importance of their individual differences. In 1979 and 1980 this tendency reemerged among Fundamentalists. Alarmed by the increasing humanism and secularism of American society, they united against the external threat of moral decay. Denominational tags, personalities, and personal preferences were all set aside for the cause of rebuilding a morally sound American society.

Jerry Falwell, in an interview with *Eternity*, clearly identified the issues and concerns that brought together the fragmented elements of Fundamentalism. He stated:

> Back in the sixties I was criticizing pastors who were taking time out of their pulpit to involve themselves in the Civil Rights Movement or any other political venture. I said you're wasting your time from what you're called to do. Now I find myself doing the same thing and for the same reasons they did. Things began to happen. The invasion of humanism into the public school system began to alarm us back in the sixties. Then the Roe vs. Wade Supreme Court decision of 1973 and abortion on demand shook me up. Then adding to that gradual regulation of various things it became very apparent the federal government was going in the wrong direction and if allowed would be harassing non-public schools, of which I have one of 16,000 right now. So step by step we became convinced we must get involved if we're going to continue what we're doing inside the church building.[1]

The growing concern over the threat of humanism and secularism quickly spread to the grass roots of conservative America through the efforts of influential preachers such as Dr. Greg Dixon, pastor of Indianapolis Baptist Temple and one of the leading Baptist Bible Fellowship preachers; Dr. James Kennedy, television preacher and pastor of Coral Ridge Presbyterian Church in Fort

Lauderdale, Florida; Dr. Charles Stanley, television preacher and pastor of First Baptist Church in Atlanta, Georgia; Dr. Curtis Hatson, editor of *The Sword of the Lord;* and Dr. Tim La Haye, noted author, family seminar speaker, and for many years pastor of Scott Memorial Baptist Church in San Diego, California. These men and thousands of others defined the issues, informed their people, registered over 4 million new voters, and attacked the political system.

One liberal congressman, who was defeated by a conservative candidate in the 1980 election, commented: "These people are organized and ready to take over the Congress and even the Presidency if they can. We'd better begin to fight force with force before this militant minority takes over."[2]

Fundamentalism was back, and according to Martin E. Marty it was "back with a vengeance."[3] To understand this resurgence properly, one must carefully analyze the status and position of both Fundamentalism and Evangelicalism. The condition of both these movements in the late seventies was the consummation of three decades of independent growth. During this time Fundamentalism tended to react and head more and more to the right while Evangelicalism tended to drift more and more to the left.

To understand the phenomenal resurgence of Fundamentalism, one must study the nature and extent of its separatist beliefs, which were clearly revealed regarding ecumenical evangelism, New Evangelicalism, and associational separation.

REACTIONARY FUNDAMENTALISM

The predominant characteristic of Fundamentalism in the last thirty years has been its strong commitment to separatism. This characteristic emerged after the War with Liberalism. In the 1920s Fundamentalists encouraged absolute and total withdrawal from the liberal denominations. They considered suspect those who maintained their connections with Liberalism. A true Fundamentalist was a true separatist. It was the issue of separation that forced Fundamentalism to become an independent religious movement. It was also the issue of separation that caused that independent movement to divide and subdivide within itself.

Ecclesiastical Separation and
Ecumenical Evangelism

The issue of Billy Graham and ecumenical evangelism was the first separatist conflict that divided Fundamentalism and Evangelicalism and solidified the concept of separatism. Fundamentalists insist that Billy Graham began as an outspoken Fundamentalist. In 1948 in *The Pilot,* Northwestern's magazine, Graham declared that he took a "militant stand against Modernism in every form."[4] Graham also had close connections with John R. Rice and served as a member of the cooperating board of *The Sword of the Lord.* He also had close associations with Bob Jones University, where he received an honorary doctorate. The objections of Fundamentalists to Billy Graham centered around a number of incidents:

1957. At the New York Crusade, Graham cooperated with notable Liberals, such as Henry P. Van Dusen, president of Union Theological Seminary.

1958. The San Francisco Crusade was co-chaired by Carl Howie, who propagated liberal ideas regarding the creation and Noah's flood.

1961. Graham attended the World Council of Churches conference in New Delhi.

1963. Bishop Gerald Kennedy was one of the leading proponents of the Los Angeles Crusade. Kennedy was a Methodist Liberal.

1965. Graham preached at a Roman Catholic institution, Belmont Abbey.

1966. Graham preached at the National Council of Churches meeting in Miami.

1968. Graham received an honorary doctorate from Belmont Abbey.

1969. At the U. S. Congress on Evangelism, sponsored by Graham, the morning devotions were brought by a Roman Catholic priest.

1971. A Catholic priest cooperated in the Oakland Crusade.

1973. Graham preached at Leighton Ford's "Reachout" and

was positive about his opportunity to preach in the Catholic cathedral and participate in a funeral mass.[5]

In dealing with the issue of ecumenical evangelism, two terms became the watchwords of Fundamentalism: "compromise" and "apostasy." Those who were involved in ecumenical evangelism were accused of being compromisers and guilty of the sin of apostasy. Apostasy is a direct repudiation of divine truth to which one has been clearly exposed and which one has professed. Unger defines apostasy as "the act of a professed Christian who knowingly and deliberately rejects revealed Truth regarding the deity of Christ (I John 4:1–3) and redemption through His atoning sacrifice (Philippians 3:18, II Peter 2:1)."[6]

The scriptural basis for separation centered around the issue of fidelity to apostolic doctrine. Many key passages of Scripture were utilized in demanding separation from apostates, or those who had turned from the truth of apostolic doctrine. A key passage is:

> I beseech you, brethren, mark them which cause divisions and offences contrary to the doctrine which ye had learned; and avoid them. For they that are such serve not our Lord Jesus Christ, but their own belly; and by good words and fair speeches deceive the hearts of the simple [Rom. 16:17–18].

From this passage come two important separatist principles. First Christians are to "mark them which cause divisions and offences contrary to the doctrine which ye have learned." From this Fundamentalists have felt compelled to identify people, organizations, and churches that have turned from the truth of biblical doctrine. The second aspect of this verse teaches Christians to "avoid them." This implies withdrawal from all association with those who deny the basic doctrines of Scripture.

The most critical passage related to the Fundamentalist-separatist issue is perhaps 2 Corinthians 6:14–18. This passage encourages separation from unbelievers and implies that rebuke is part of the responsibility of true Christians. "If there come any unto you, and bring not this doctrine, receive him not into your house, neither bid him God speed: For he that biddeth him God speed is partaker of his evil deeds" (2 John 10–11). Lloyd-Jones clearly identifies the doctrine of Christ as the central basis for Christian fellowship. He writes: "My contention is that the teaching of the New Testament is quite clear about this, that there is an absolute foundation, an irreducible minimum, without which the term 'Christian' is meaningless, and without subscribing to which a man is not a Christian. That is 'the foundation of the apostles and prophets'—the doctrine concerning 'Jesus Christ and Him crucified,' and 'justification by faith only.' The passages we have considered teach that apart from that there is no such thing as fellowship, no basis of unity at all. . . . In the same way the idea that you can evangelize together without bringing doctrine into it is surely the height of folly. If you call upon me to come to Christ certain questions at once inevitably arise: Who is He? Why should one come to Him? How does one come to Him? Why is He called the Saviour? How does He save? From what does He save?"[7]

The British pastor further summarized the fundamentalist position regarding Christian unity and ecumenical evangelism. He concluded:

1. Unity must never be isolated or regarded as something in and of itself.
2. It is equally clear that the question of unity must never be put first. We must never start with it, but always remember the order clearly so stated in Acts 2:42, where fellowship follows doctrine. . . .
3. We must never start with the visible church or with an institution, but rather with the truth which alone creates unity. . . .
4. The starting-point in considering the question of unity must always be regeneration and belief of truth. Nothing else produces unity, and, as we have seen clearly, it is impossible apart from this.
5. An appearance or a facade of unity based on everything else, and at the expense of these two criteria, or which ignores them, is clearly a fraud and a lie. . . . To give the impression that they are "one" simply because of a common outward organization is not only to mislead "the world" which is outside the Church but to be guilty of a lie.
6. To do anything which supports or encourages such an impression or appearance of unity is surely dishonest and sinful. Truth

and untruth cannot be reconciled, and the difference between them cannot be patched over. . . .

7. To regard a church, or a council of churches, as a forum in which fundamental matters can be debated and discussed, or as an opportunity for witness-bearing, is sheer confusion and muddled thinking. . . .

8. Unity must obviously never be thought of primarily in numerical terms, but always in terms of life. Nothing is so opposed to biblical teaching as the modern idea that numbers and powerful organization alone count. . . .

9. The greatest need of the hour is a new baptism and outpouring of the Holy Spirit in renewal and revival. Nothing else throughout the centuries has ever given the Church true authority and made her, and her message, mighty. . . . The ultimate question facing us these days is whether our faith is in men and their power to organize, or the truth of God in Jesus Christ and the power of the Holy Spirit. . . .[8]

The most comprehensive defense of ecumenical evangelism was written by Robert O. Ferm, who was dean of students at Houghton College in New York. He concluded in his book: "Having examined the policy of Billy Graham from the perspective of history and the Scriptures, it has been shown that he is neither out of harmony with the major evangelists, nor is his policy contrary to the Scriptures. He has not conducted his crusades with the attitude of an opportunist, doing evil that good may come, but he has sought for both message and method in the Scriptures."[9] He began his defense by appealing to the ministry of Jesus. He establishes the fact that Jesus worshiped in the synagogue and visited and preached there on numerous occasions. He emphasizes the relationship of Jesus Christ to "publicans and sinners." He further analyzes the ministry of the apostles and in particular the ministry of Paul. Paul, in the tradition of Jesus, continued his relationship with the synagogue and utilized it as a public place in which to preach the Gospel. Ferm deals with 2 Corinthians 6 and implies that that passage deals with "idolaters, pagans and immoral people."[10] He implies that it does not refer to fellowship with other churches. Ferm goes on to examine the evangelistic ministries of Edwards, Whitfield, Wesley, Finney, Moody, and Sunday. He concludes that the methodologies of these men were no different than the methodologies of Billy Graham and "Cooperative Evangelism."

He chastises the Church for not having a more positive attitude in the matter of ecumenicism, stating: "Negative separation is withdrawal from the very territory where the impact of a Christian witness is most needed. Each of the major evangelists has left the pattern of positive aggression. They did not withdraw from humanity and establish a monastic type of Christianity. They went forth with the confidence that their message had the power that could turn the world upside down."[11] Ferm further appeals for Christian unity and cooperation: "Most important of all, these are days when Christians should join hands in prayer for every fruitful work of making Christ known. It is a time when we should unite in prayer of thanksgiving and praise, of asking God's guiding and sustaining hand to rest on all who are preaching the unsearchable riches of His grace. Let us uphold and not hinder!"[12]

Gary G. Cohen, formerly of Faith Theological Seminary in Philadelphia, wrote a response to Ferm's defense of ecumenical evangelism.[13] He isolated the ten arguments used by Ferm to defend Cooperative Evangelism. These ten arguments were:

1. Christ instructed the twelve and the seventy to lodge with anyone who was willing to have them.
2. The Lord accepted the cooperation of any who did not oppose Him.
3. The Lord attended the Temple, which was dominated by those who erred.
4. The Lord attended the synagogue, which was dominated by those who erred.
5. The Lord engaged in religious contact and conversation with religious rejects.
6. Judge not that ye be not judged.
7. The Lord did not make an issue out of theological error.
8. The Lord stressed fellowship, not separation.
9. The Lord's method was to proclaim the Truth and to ignore error.
10. The Lord was never concerned with sponsorship.

After a careful point-by-point biblical analysis, Cohen concluded that "New Evangelicalism and its evangelical method, Cooperative (with the liberal neo-orthodox theologians) Evangelism, are not supported by the words and deeds of the Saviour, but rather they are boldly and clearly refuted by Christ. Thus the ten arguments for Cooperative Evangelism here analyzed actually provide a clear claim on every true Christian's conscience for biblical separation from all heretics and apostates in doing the work of the Lord. Let us constantly remember that 'God's work must be done God's way.'"[14]

The Graham issue continued to be controversial through the late fifties and sixties. A broad range of fundamentalist leaders wrote and spoke against ecumenical evangelism. Bob Jones University produced a printed packet of various materials outlining the issue in detail. Ian Paisley, the famous Presbyterian preacher of Northern Ireland, wrote a book entitled *Billy Graham and the Church of Rome,* tracing the history of Graham's "soft" approach to Roman Catholics.[15] Some of the attacks went beyond theological and scriptural issues, and some Fundamentalists attacked the content, style, and motive of Graham's preaching.[16] Many of the attacks were highly critical and some of them were quite unfounded. In their fervor to discredit Graham, some Fundamentalists misquoted and misinterpreted some of Graham's statements entirely out of their original context.

Rise of the "New Evangelicalism"

Although many of the Fundamentalists devoted their attacks to Billy Graham and his ecumenical evangelism, there was a much wider issue at stake: the New Evangelical Movement. Some Fundamentalists began to see the problem as more comprehensive than as simply that of one major evangelist. They observed that the whole foundation and thrust of New Evangelicalism was a threat to the traditional Fundamentalist position. The term "New Evangelicalism" was coined in 1947 by Harold J. Ockenga. Ockenga clearly identified the purpose of this new movement that he so zealously propagated. It was "to experience revival of Christianity in a secular world, to recapture the denominational leadership from the inside by infiltration instead of frontal attack, to achieve respectability for orthodoxy, and to attain social reforms."[17] The New Evangelical Movement was, in many ways, a reaction to what was considered the offensively critical attitude of Fundamentalism. This new movement claimed to be orthodox and fundamentalist. Ockenga states: "Doctrinally, the Fundamentalists are right, and I wish to be always classified as one." He goes on to discuss the inspiration of Scripture and the deity of Christ and concludes that "these beliefs identify me as a Fundamentalist."[18]

However, the Fundamentalists quickly attacked the New Evangelical Movement and its attitude of toleration. Dr. Charles Woodbridge wrote: "The new Evangelicalism advocates *toleration* of error. It is following the downward path of *accommodation* to error, *cooperation* with error, *contamination* by error, and ultimate *capitulation* to error."[19] Woodbridge, who championed the attack against New Evangelicalism, was vocal and open in his demands for separation from this subtly destructive movement. "The new Evangelicalism is a theological and moral compromise of the deadliest sort. It is an insidious attack upon the Word of God. No more subtle menace has confronted the church of Christ since the Protestant Reformation in the days of Luther and Calvin." He then enumerated seven basic reasons for his opposition to the compromise of New Evangelicalism:

> First, because it originated not outside evangelical circles as an attack from without but within these circles as a form of theological erosion.
>
> Second, because it is in some instances championed by men who for years have been known as Bible-believing Evangelicals.
>
> Third, because it is not a clearly defined system of alien theology which Bible believers may refute point by point. Discernment is needed to detect its insidious nature.
>
> Fourth, because it emphasizes love at the expense of doctrine and stresses societal aspects of the Gospel.
>
> Fifth, because it courts and caters to the theological intelligentsia of the liberal camp and implies that those who do not share its views are unenlightened. Pastors who have had little formal academic training may find this frustrating.
>
> Sixth, because many Christians are being brainwashed by its false but appealing views. As a result, a doctrinal and ethical letdown is discernible in many areas of church life.
>
> Seventh, because the camel's nose of the New Evangelicalism

is already in the Christian tent. The camel is pushing hard to get its entire body in.[20]

Fundamentalists were critical of the New Evangelical Movement in several areas. First, New Evangelicalism was described as a movement that attempted to walk down the center line of the religious marketplace. It was described as having an open appeal to both the liberal element of the Church and the orthodox element of the Church. Some called the movement the "New Neutralism." Ashbrook wrote: "New Evangelicalism, beyond question, is seeking middle ground with respect to the theological controversies of our day. Such neutrality represents a position difficult to maintain in any age, but in a day like ours when the battle is so clearly pitched between Christ and anti-Christ, it is an impossible position. In the realm of things moral and spiritual one must be either right or wrong. In the great fight of faith there is no middle ground on which the neutralist can complacently stand for long, and pronounce his anathemas or his benedictions, as the case may be, upon both sides. He is bound to wind up ere long in one camp or the other, and in a day when God is judging compromise in no uncertain terms, he is most likely to wind up in the wrong camp."[21]

This characteristic of neutralism was evidenced by the attitude of the Evangelical Movement toward Liberalism. According to Woodbridge, the New Evangelicals were openly tolerant of German Liberalism and neo-orthodoxy. He quotes the president of Fuller Theological Seminary, David Hubbard, who in his inaugural address stated: "The seminary should systematically inculcate in its students a theology of mutual tolerance and forgiveness towards those who, by reason of their particular doctrinal convictions, stand heretically over against the confessional lines set down by the first Christian community."[22]

The second major criticism of the New Evangelicals was of their overemphasis on intellectualism. Fundamentalists accused them of portraying Fundamentalism as a grossly anti-intellectual movement. Ockenga claimed that "the New Evangelical showed a willingness to face today's intellectual and societal problems. The intellectual climate of orthodoxy changed. . . . It asked for a reexamination and restatement of the questions of revelation and inspiration. It asked for a return to theological dialogue that expressed a willingness to recognize the honesty and Christianity of those who held views other than its own."[23] In terming the Fundamentalist Movement anti- or subintellectual, the Evangelicals made a grievous error. The Fundamentalist Movement has always been action-oriented and production-oriented. While Evangelicals were stroking one another's intellectual egos, the Fundamentalists were building churches and infiltrating the grass roots of America. In responding to this harsh judgment of fundamentalist anti-intellectualism, Woodbridge states: "To mature believers such an attack is puerile, pusillanimous, and irrelevant!"[24]

The third major criticism of the New Evangelical Movement was of its lack of separatism. The New Evangelicals were clearly committed to the philosophy of infiltration. They felt that a mood of understanding and tolerance would inevitably change those who questioned the basic tenets of orthodoxy. Fundamentalists reacted strongly. Their reaction grew out of the results of the War with Liberalism. It had been clearly demonstrated in the twenties that infiltration within the denomination could never resolve the problem of Liberalism. The results of the War with Liberalism produced the separatist movement. The attitude of the New Evangelicals was a return to the confusion of the twenties. They were reliving the failure of infiltration. For this reason Fundamentalists strongly opposed the methodology of New Evangelicals.

The last major difference between Fundamentalism and New Evangelicalism was in the area of the Christian's response to the social gospel. Ockenga accused the Fundamentalists of "a basic indifference to human suffering and a silence concerning social injustices. . . ."[25] New Evangelicals strongly believe that "faith must be related to the societal problems of race, class, war, delinquency, divorce, immorality, and use of liquor and drugs."[26] A careful study will, however, reveal that the Evangelicals were no more successful than the Fundamentalists in changing society.

The self-justifying treatises of the Evangelicals and the negative responses of the Fundamentalists polarized both groups. There were numerous appeals for unity, but that unity never came. Both sides showed a high level of commitment to their position. The Fundamentalists were proud of their stand on their position. The Evangelicals were filled with pride about their new credibility. Woodbridge wrote: "Perhaps the Spirit of God will graciously intervene, convict the New Evangelicals of their error, woo and persuade them to restore the ancient landmarks which their attitudes have jeopardized, and bring them back to a position where genuine evangelical unity may be attained, a unity based upon the inerrant verbally inspired, uncompromising, holy, and challenging Word of God."[27] The attitude of the New Evangelicals was just as strong in their condemnation of the Fundamentalists. Ockenga said: "Nevertheless, as a movement, fundamentalism failed. . . . The movement was unable to crack social problems. The influence of fundamentalism was reduced to inconsequential splinter groups that had no great social prophetic message."[28]

One must remember that genuine Christian people were struggling on both sides of this issue. In attempts to achieve a biblical perspective, perhaps the words of Jesus should be considered: "And John answered and said, Master, we saw one casting out devils in thy name; and we forbade him, because he followeth not with us. And Jesus said unto him, Forbid him not: for he that is not against us is for us" (Luke 9:49–50).

Personal Separation:
Long Hair, Short Skirts,
and Wire-rimmed Glasses!

The issues related to ecclesiastical separation and ecumenical evangelism continued to be major controversies in the early sixties. However, the Fundamentalist Movement can be characterized in the late sixties and early seventies by the renewed emphasis upon personal separation in reaction to the "Hippie," or Student Revolution, movement. Quebedeaux emphasizes the point that separatist Fundamentalism has a strong commitment to personal separation: "With respect to personal ethics (there is no social ethic) in Separatist Fundamentalism negativism prevails. Cultural taboos are applied rigorously in the fight against worldliness which is looked upon as the fruit of apostasy—no drinking, no smoking, no social dancing, no gambling, no attendance at the theater, and the like."[29] The banner of Fundamentalism became: We don't smoke, and we don't chew, and we don't go with girls who do!

The Fundamentalist Movement in the sixties and seventies

remained committed to personal separation. Jerry Falwell, in his famous article "Let's Hang Together (or We Shall Surely All Hang Separately)," reaffirms the commitment of Fundamentalism to a separatist life-style. "Here at Liberty Baptist College, for example, we require our faculty and students to abstain from the use of alcoholic beverages and tobacco. We do not permit indulgence in illegal drugs. We forbid attendance at dances or the Hollywood theater. We take a strong stand against pre-marital and extra-marital sex. As separatists, we feel we can support our position in all these matters with Scripture. In other words, fundamentalists and separatists take a position for the inerrant Word of God and all it has to say, and against worldliness and carnal living which damages the testimony of the believer and the church."[30]

Developing a comprehensive list of the personal separation issues is almost impossible. Every individual preacher, church, and group within Fundamentalism had its own list of do's and don'ts. These issues on personal separation then became the criteria by which to judge a true Fundamentalist. During the early seventies a Christian with long hair and sideburns was immediately relegated to the ranks of Evangelicalism. The great foundational issues of doctrine almost became secondary to the primary issues of personal separation. Often the Fundamentalist Movement was ridiculed because of its weak biblical defense of its separatist position.

Fundamentalist preachers, in their emotional defense of separatism, frequently actually used some ludicrous reasons, such as saying: "If God wanted us to smoke, He would have made us with a smokestack!" In their reaction to the hippie culture, some pastors preached constantly on long hair, sideburns, beards, flare-bottomed pants, high-heeled boots, wire-rimmed glasses, silk shirts, and so on. Others made a major issue out of women wearing slacks. Very few Fundamentalists, however, have taken a strong stand on such matters as health and fitness, contemporary television programming, the harmful effects of "junk" food, and excessive materialism. Few scholars attempted to make a legitimate apologetic for personal separation. However, there are numerous biblical principles that relate to this area of personal Christian living. Separation from the world and unto God is a biblical principle (Rom. 12:1-2). In his epistle to the Church at Corinth, Paul established these principles in dealing with the separation issues.

THE MASTERY TEST. "All things are lawful unto me, but all things are not expedient: all things are lawful for me, but I will not be brought under the power of any" (1 Cor. 6:12). The Bible clearly teaches that Christians are to be Spirit-controlled (Eph. 5:18). When something else is controlling our lives, then we are not Spirit-controlled. Paul's philosophy is that nothing other than God should control his life. When we are faced with an issue, we must ask, "Will this thing control me?" This test could be applied to such modern-day issues as alcohol, cigarette smoking, drugs, and television.

THE TEMPLE TEST. "What? know ye not that your body is the temple of the Holy Ghost which is in you, which ye have of God, and ye are not your own? For ye are bought with a price: therefore glorify God in your body, and in your spirit, which are God's" (1 Cor. 6:19-20). Our bodies belong to God. When we mistreat our bodies, we are destroying God's property. To do that is a violation of the above verses. This principle would apply to such areas as overeating, lack of exercise, and such drugs as would adversely affect our physical well-being.

THE STUMBLING BLOCK TEST. "Wherefore, if meat make my brother to offend, I will eat no flesh while the world standeth, lest I make my brother to offend" (1 Cor. 8:13). As part of Christ's body, we have an obligation to live for each other. Paul is teaching that we must set an example. If what we are doing hurts a weaker brother or sister, we must change. As part of the body of Christ, we have an obligation to those who are younger and eager to mature. Any practice or habit that would hinder their growth ought to be avoided.

THE SOUL-WINNING TEST. "For though I be free from all men, yet have I made myself servant unto all, that I might gain the more" (1 Cor. 9:19). Beyond our responsibility to each other, we have a responsibility to win the lost. Paul is willing to change in order to reach more people. He does not want to be involved in anything that will harm or limit his outreach. In determining right from wrong, we must be conscious of this relationship. If something hinders us from preaching the Gospel, then we must eliminate it. The soul-winning test asks the question "Will it help or hurt me in reaching the lost?"

THE GLORIFICATION TEST. "Whether therefore ye eat, or drink, or whatsoever ye do, do all to the glory of God" (1 Cor. 10:31). Humankind's supreme purpose is to bring glory to God. All that we do and say must be for that purpose. Any area of our life that inhibits our ability to glorify God is wrong.

In an age of changing values, there is an absolute. It is the Bible. The principles are eternal—only the circumstances change. The following principles can be utilized in achieving a balanced biblical concept of personal separation:

1. Will this issue control me?   yes no
2. Will this issue hurt my body?   yes no
3. Will this issue cause a weaker brother or sister to
   stumble?   yes no
4. Will this issue hurt me in reaching other people?   yes no
5. Will this issue detract from glorifying God?   yes no

During this time of strong emphasis on personal separation, Fundamentalism became even more fragmented, and those who were the most separated were considered the most fundamental. The outside world began to judge Fundamentalism by these external criteria. As a result, many people came to the conclusion that Fundamentalists had lost their love for each other, for other Christian believers, and for the world at large. In describing the separatist Fundamentalist Movement, Quebedeaux assesses one of its major weaknesses: "And human love—not to mention Christ's love—appears to have no real importance in that school of thought."[81] While this is certainly an overstatement, it nevertheless touches a vital issue we Fundamentalists must face.

The issue of personal separation is of critical importance in conformity to the image of Christ. However, one must never develop an attitude of spiritual superiority and utilize only external criteria as the basis for judgment of other Christians. Rules and regulations alone, though needed, do not totally express one's spirituality. The mandate of Scripture has always been the same: "Speak the truth in love." Fundamentalists have often gone to such extremes for truth that in so doing they have neglected a necessary expression of love.

This issue of secondary separation has been clearly debated by John R. Rice in The Sword of the Lord and by Bob Jones University. Bob Jones, Jr., insisted that Rice was guilty of violating separatist principles by printing messages from Southern Baptist preachers in his newspaper. In the late 1960s the publications of fundamentalist churches began dealing with the compromise of other fundamental preachers. (The issue was based on whom the person had invited to preach, with whom he had eaten lunch, and whom he had asked to sing.) The ultimate end of this issue was total isolation from everyone and everything. This issue eventually led to another major split in Fundamentalism; the result was the formation of a highly purist and absolutely separated segment within Fundamentalism. The dangerous conclusion of this new drift can be seen in the following diagram.

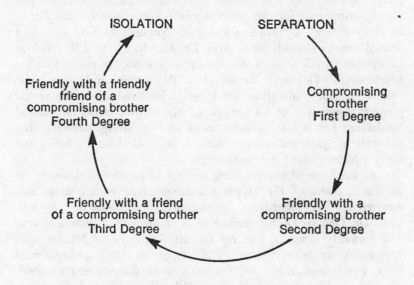

ISOLATION   SEPARATION

Friendly with a friendly
friend of a
compromising brother
Fourth Degree

Compromising
brother
First Degree

Friendly with a friend
of a compromising brother
Third Degree

Friendly with a
compromising brother
Second Degree

SEPARATION–ISOLATION CYCLE

Associational Separation: The Quest for Absolute Purity

The hotly debated issues of personal separation were paralleled by the concept of associational separation. In the quest for a pure

Church, the Fundamentalist Movement established a long list of legalistic requirements. Those who failed to live up to each of these requirements were considered suspect and bent toward the Evangelical Movement. As more and more lists became apparent, the Hyper-Fundamentalists began attacking and criticizing other Fundamentalists for their failure to conform to their personal preferences and standards.[32] True Fundamentalists were now judged by their associations, whether personal or organizational. Any Fundamentalist who ate with, talked to, or in any way associated with a questionable individual such as an Evangelical was not considered a true Fundamentalist.

The most recent controversy has been over the ministry of Jerry Falwell, who was labeled a "Pseudo-Fundamentalist." The pseudo-arguments for this position can be seen in *An Open Letter to Jerry Falwell* by evangelist David Sproul.[33] In this pamphlet Sproul attacks Falwell for inviting Dr. Harold Lindsell to speak at Liberty Baptist Seminary on the inerrancy issue. He then identifies Lindsell with Ockenga, Carnell, Van Til, Ramm, and others who "led the second generation into heresy where they deny the verbal plenary inspiration of all Scripture." He further criticizes Falwell for having Dr. W. A. Criswell speak at Lynchburg, claiming that Criswell is "perhaps second only to Billy Graham in being the biggest Judas-goat of the century."[34]

As the issue of associational separation continued through the seventies, many of the Hyper-Fundamentalists issued statements and wrote letters identifying the so-called compromise of Jerry Falwell. Dr. George Dollar, author of *A History of Fundamentalism* and formerly dean of Central Baptist Seminary in Minneapolis, Minnesota, wrote on September 20, 1979: "In this most significant hour, Fundamentalists need the sharpest of discernment and witness on Biblical separation. Jerry Falwell has sinned grievously against this and continues to sin. . . . In his choice of staff, his support of the California Graduate School of Theology (so-called), his weak-kneed faculty in his schools, and his invitations to leading lights (or dark beacons) of compromise, Falwell has become the leading TV bishop of Compromise, Inc."[35]

On January 9, 1978, the South Carolina Baptist Fellowship passed a resolution identifying what they called the pseudo-neo-fundamentalist movement.

Whereas, we define Pseudo-neo-fundamentalism as the following:

a. One who claims to be fundamental and associates with fundamentalists while at the same time shares the platform of Neo-Evangelical groups, thus incurring identification with them.

b. One who emphasizes numbers above faithfulness, using carnal means as "clowns," etc. to accomplish such. This obsession with bigness gives the erroneous belief that the end justifies the means. He equates numbers as an evidence of revival and bigness as a sign of success along with a substitution of worldly means to get results instead of prayer.

c. One who professes to believe in separation, but preaches in liberal-connected churches without any witness against the support of evil.

d. One who has an unscriptural belief in national conversion by repentence and faith in our Lord Jesus Christ.

e. One who popularizes the pulpit and the Christian witness by use of popular celebrities to draw a crowd irrespective of whether they are neo-evangelical, liberal, liberal connected, or an un-orthodox group.

f. One who adapts mod-tunes and worldly music to the Gospel.

g. One who pursues the idea of the "Super-church" to the point of destroying smaller fundamental works, and substituting a Radio or TV fellowship for a local fundamental church.

h. One who is unwilling to be bound by Scriptural limitations by saying "Whatever will get a crowd I will do it," or "I'll do as I please."

i. One who is always critical of those who insist on true fundamentalism by claiming the biblical fundamentalist is "nit-picking" and divisive among the brethren.[36]

The Fundamental Baptist Fellowship in June 1978 passed the following resolutions, which represent the vote of two hundred Christian workers and pastors: "The Fundamental Baptist Fellowship recognizes the danger of the movement known as pseudo-fundamentalism, sees it as new evangelicalism in embryonic form, and calls upon all local Bible-believing churches to reject pseudo-fundamental activities as those of the Jerry Falwell ministries."[37]

The drift of Fundamentalism in the seventies has been toward further polarization. The Hyper-Fundamentalists, in their sharp, open attacks on other Fundamentalists, have created a group within a group, calling themselves the only true Fundamentalists, and have spent their energies in criticism of other people. This direction is dangerous and only serves to hurt the cause of true Fundamentalism, leaving in its place a critical, cynical, and divisive atmosphere. The following cycle illustrates the condition of extreme Fundamentalism in the late seventies.

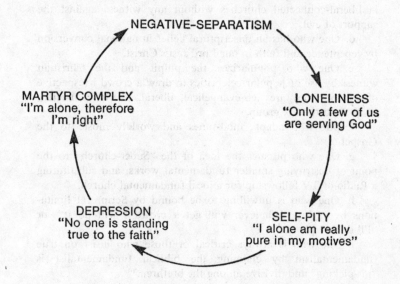

HYPER-FUNDAMENTALIST COMPLEX

NEGATIVE-SEPARATISM

MARTYR COMPLEX
"I'm alone, therefore
I'm right"

LONELINESS
"Only a few of us
are serving God"

DEPRESSION
"No one is standing
true to the faith"

SELF-PITY
"I alone am really
pure in my motives"

Since Hyper-Fundamentalists have spoken out loud and long, it would be easy to assume that they possess great strength and influence. Despite their claim to be the only true Fundamentalists, they represent little more than a tangential element of Fundamentalism. There are thousands of pastors who do not agree with their conclusions. It was these pastors by the thousands who rallied together to combine their influence during the last election. Most studies of the Fundamentalist Movement are woefully lacking in any real appreciation of the great independent pastors such as Jack Hyles, Lee Roberson, John Rawlings, Harold Henniger, Truman

Dollar, A. V. Henderson, Bob Gray, Bob and Raymond Barber, and many more. The Baptist Bible Fellowship, the General Association of Regular Baptist Churches, the Independent Fundamental Churches of America, the World Baptist Fellowship, and others are totally left out of most surveys of contemporary Fundamentalism. While we appreciate the concern of the extreme Fundamentalists over keeping the Church on the right track, we must not allow them to categorize and label everyone to death. The real fundamentalist majority must lead the movement in the 1980s and thereby prevent the tendency to react to the extreme right.

DRIFTING EVANGELICALISM

While Fundamentalism was struggling over separatism, Evangelicalism was subtly drifting in another direction. This occurred during the sixties and seventies. By the late seventies the Evangelical Movement had become almost as complex and diversified as the Fundamentalist Movement. In fact, Robert E. Webber indicates that there are at least fourteen different subcultural evangelical groups. He concludes: "I think we will have to argue that the movement as a historical event is too complex and dynamic to be fully explained by neat categories, no matter how helpful they may be."[38]

The Evangelical Movement, as represented by the NAE, began in the early 1940s. It began as a movement strongly committed to the fundamentals and the inspiration and inerrancy of scripture. Evangelicalism was a reaction to the attitude of Fundamentalism, not to its doctrine. Edward John Carnell, one of the leaders of the Evangelical Movement, identified the fundamentalist attitude as "the quest for negative status, the elevation of minor issues to a place of major importance, the use of social mores as a norm of virtue, the toleration of one's own prejudices but not the prejudices of others, the confusion of the church with a denomination, and the avoidance of prophetic scrutiny by using the Word of God as an instrument of self-scrutiny but not self-criticism."[39]

The early-1940s brand of Evangelicalism was in reality Fundamentalism with a new name. There were no real doctrinal distinctions between the two. By 1947, however, the two movements were clearly separate entities. This was the year that Harold J. Ockenga coined the term "the new evangelicalism." As this movement flourished in the fifties and sixties, its characteristics began to emerge. It clearly moved from its roots within Fundamentalism. Richard Quebedeaux identifies these characteristics:

> First, there is emerging a fresh understanding of the reliability and authority of scripture. . . . The old concepts of infallibility and inerrancy are being reinterpreted to the point that a number of Evangelical scholars are saying that the *teaching* of scripture (i.e., matters of faith and practice) rather than the text itself is without error. . . . Second, the New Evangelicals are again emphasizing the necessity of meaningful sanctification following regeneration (or the new birth). . . . Third, there is in the New Evangelicalism a marked aversion to Dispensationalism and its inherent apocalyptic speculations. . . . Fourth, the New Evangelicals are, in fact, displaying a fresh interest in the social dimension of the Gospel. . . . Fifth, the New Evangelicalism has reopened dialogue with mainstream Ecumenical Liberalism and has begun to converse with representatives of other religious traditions and even Marxists.[40]

The most prominent characteristic is that of tolerance. The Evangelicals' acceptance of doctrinal and individual differences become the catalyst that started their drift to the left.

The New Evangelicals had reacted against Establishment Evangelicalism. However, the atmosphere of tolerance was breeding another reactionary movement: a reaction, not against Fundamentalism or Evangelicalism, but against New Evangelicalism. Quebedeaux calls this new segment of Evangelicalism the "Young Evangelicals." Carl F. Henry gives the best description of the Young Evangelicals:

1. An interest in human beings not simply as souls to be saved, but as whole persons.
2. More active involvement by evangelical Christians in sociopolitical affairs.
3. An honest look at many churches' idolatry of nationalism.
4. Adoption of new forms of worship.
5. An end to judging spiritual commitment by such externals as

dress, hair style, and other participation in cultural trends, including rock music.

6. A new spirit with regard to ecumenical or nonecumenical attitudes.

7. Bold and, if need be, costly involvement in the revolutionary struggles of our day, and finally

8. A reappraisal of life's values.[41]

Quebedeaux implies that this new movement is a synthesis of new evangelical thought with the social-political concerns of the sixties. It attempts to relate its theology to the problems of society. This movement represents a drastic shift to the left. One must remember, however, that the Young Evangelicals do not represent the entire Evangelical Movement. The mainstream of Evangelicalism still remains true to its basic doctrinal foundation.

The latest step in the evangelical drift to the left can be observed in Quebedeaux's book *The Worldly Evangelicals*. He identifies two major groups of contemporary Evangelicals: the evangelical right and center and the young-evangelical left. The evangelical right and center are those who have maintained their doctrinal commitment to the inerrancy of Scripture. The evangelical left, although still a minority, represents a radical alternate to the traditional Evangelical Movement. Quebedeaux describes them:

Evangelicals of the left range from moderate Republicans to democratic socialists, if not Marxists. Most affirm the nuclear family but are at the same time open to alternative domestic lifestyles, from extended families to communes. Just about all of the left evangelicals are feminists and support the ordination of women, egalitarian marriage, and the use of inclusive language. The old evangelical taboos against alcohol, tobacco, social dancing, and the like are almost universally condemned (as binding, at least). Biblical criticism, used constructively and devoutly, is employed by a great many evangelical students and scholars of the left. They recognize the marks of cultural conditioning on Scripture, and their study of the Bible is informed by their knowledge of the natural, social, and behavioral sciences.[42]

The evangelical left is an extreme reaction to fundamentalist separatism. Tolerance is practiced to the maximum. Its members accept new concepts in the sexual realm; masturbation is acceptable, pornography "does not warrant undue concern," and some evangelicals "now regard oral sex as mere petting, not intercourse."[43] They go beyond dialogue and cooperation with liberal clergy. They accept those clergy on an equal basis as brothers and sisters in Christ. Quebedeaux concludes: "Obviously, Protestant liberals and Evangelicals are moving closer together, aided, as we have noted previously, by the increasing popularity among both groupings of relational theology and the charismatic renewal movement."[44]

In May of 1977 forty-five Evangelicals met in Chicago and issued the "Chicago Call." This document represents the doctrinal position and the attitude of the left. Robert Webber, an organizer of the meeting, states its purpose. "In the same way that our current evangelical fathers, Billy Gráham, Harold Ockenga, Harold Lindsell, C. F. H. Henry and others, grew beyond the borders of fundamentalism, so we, following their example, have continued to look beyond present limitations toward a more inclusive and ultimately more historic Christianity." One of the participants who did not sign the call objected on the following criteria. "He saw the call as leaning toward Roman theology in certain of its statements. . . . He also felt that certain aspects of the Call, in particular the section on a 'Call to Sacramental Integrity,' leaned toward Eastern church orthodoxy. . . . He felt that the Call tended to be soft on Scripture. . . ."[45]

Although Webber indicates that participants in the Call are the historic descendants of Fundamentalism and Evangelicalism, he is far from the truth. The evangelical left is so removed from orthodox roots that it is naïve even to retain the term "evangelical." These young and worldly Evangelicals may in reality be young and worldly Liberals. Robert S. Ellwood, Jr., from the University of Southern California, asks a valid question in evaluating the new drift. Is it "really something new *within* evangelicalism, or is it the shaky, searching first steps of a reborn liberalism?"[46] Ernest D. Pickering, a reputable Fundamentalist, gives his evaluation: "Early new evangelicals began to compromise on vital issues. The fruit of their compromise is now seen in the more blatant deviations of the young evangelicals. Believers are being misled. Local churches are being disrupted. Formerly strong schools are being weakened. The path to a complete apostasy is being prepared."[47]

The current slide toward Liberalism is openly admitted by the evangelical left. Quebedeaux indicates, "Now, however, the evangelical left provides a better option for evangelicals who may still *believe* like evangelicals, but wish to *behave* like liberals. Furthermore, among this group there may be an increasingly large number of people who really *have* moved beyond evangelical belief toward liberalism. In other words, they have rejected the evangelical position intellectually (though they may not admit or even recognize it), but they still have an emotional attachment to the movement in which they were converted and nurtured."[48] Traditional Evangelicals must resist the worldly Evangelicals and thus prevent the evangelical movement from further progression to the left. Evangelicalism faces the same challenge as Fundamentalism. Neither movement should surrender its direction and future to an extreme tangential element.

FUNDAMENTALISM AND EVANGELICALISM: A COMPARISON

By 1980 Fundamentalism had reacted to the right toward separatism and Evangelicalism had drifted to the left toward Liberalism. It is against the background of these extreme elements that Fundamentalism is resurging in the eighties. Having analyzed the history of both these movements, it is interesting to compare them.

The essential unity of theology between Fundamentalism and Evangelicalism has already been substantiated. It is obvious that there is very little doctrinal difference between these two movements. The ability to identify a contrast between the two groups must center on the extremities of both groups. Evangelicalism out of control ultimately leads to what Quebedeaux has termed "worldly Evangelicals." With its emphasis on dialogue with socialism and communism and its strong commitment to the integration of Christianity with existing cultures, the left wing of Evangelicalism comes very close to moderate Liberalism. The conservative theologian Francis Schaeffer has observed that there is virtually no difference any more between the right wing of Liberalism and the left wing of Evangelicalism. Both are given to an extremely subjectivistic approach to the formulation of doctrine. Schaeffer has also raised a warning flag to the Charismatic Movement that it is in danger of moving in the same direction.[49]

At the same time, Fundamentalism taken to the extreme leads to hyperseparatism. It is characterized by ultra-absolutism and severe rejection of any person, group, or movement that does not completely agree with it in all matters. As the British theologian James Barr has observed, there is no real, essential difference between conservative Evangelicals and most Fundamentalists. We believe that it is this observation that must form the basis for mutual understanding between Evangelicals and Fundamentalists. While some differences of attitude and methodology do exist between the two groups, it is more obvious that the extreme differences can be enunciated between the ultra-left-wing Evangelicals and the Hyper-Fundamentalists.

WORLDLY EVANGELICALS	HYPER-FUNDAMENTALISTS
Tolerance	Intolerance
Relativism	Absolutism
Compromise	Militancy
Flexibility	Inflexibility
Conformity	Separatism
Strong social emphasis	Weak social emphasis
Infiltration	Confrontation
Dialogue	Proclamation
Political liberalism	Political conservatism
Leadership by professors	Leadership by pastors
Being pro para-church	Being pro local church
Tendency to split to left	Tendency to split to right

Dr. Charles Woodbridge, a former professor at Fuller Theological Seminary, was the first Fundamentalist to point out that the basic tenet of "New Evangelicalism" was tolerance toward Liberalism and unbelief. It is this attitude that concerns and upsets

Fundamentalists and Hyper-Fundamentalists alike. It is one thing to tolerate a difference of opinion; it is another thing for Fundamentalists to tolerate inclusion of Christ-denying, Bible-deprecating unbelief. While Fundamentalists correctly criticize the tolerant mentality of worldly Evangelicalism, the Evangelicals have been equally justified in their criticism of the complete intolerant mentality of Hyper-Fundamentalists. This attitude has caused some extreme right-wing religionists to categorize anyone who disagrees with them in any way at all as a "liberal." Thus it is not unusual to find such conservative schools as Moody Bible Institute or Dallas Theological Seminary referred to as liberal or even neo-orthodox. Any thinking Christian realizes that such designations are totally erroneous.

Left-wing Evangelicalism is extremely relativistic in its approach to truth, whereas Hyper-Fundamentalism is overtly absolutist. To be sure, Fundamentalists and Evangelicals alike believe in absolutes, hence the "fundamentals." However, adherence to the basic fundamentals of Scripture as divine prerogatives for Christian beliefs must be honestly viewed in light of our ability to understand and interpret those absolutes. Extreme Fundamentalists have tended to take the position that they are always correct in how they interpret basic Christian doctrine. In their most extreme form, some Hyper-Fundamentalists hold that only the King James Version of the Bible is "inspired." They reject not only other Bible translations, but the entire concept of translating the Bible as well. The opposite extreme is that taken by the worldly Evangelicals, who are so open-minded that they are willing to renegotiate almost any area of evangelical belief. As a result, they tend to be swayed by every new wind of doctrine blowing across the Atlantic from Europe.

The issue of taking a stand in relation to one's belief is vital to the fundamentalist mentality. Fundamentalist criticisms of compromise by the New Evangelicals have blossomed. Fundamentalists have been shocked over and again by the willingness of the evangelical left to accept almost any kind of theologian as making a legitimate contribution to the cause of Christianity. While the worldly Evangelicals tend to praise the contributions of Barth, Brunner, Pannenberg, and Achtemeier, they have had almost nothing but words of ridicule and contempt for the fundamentalist wing of Evangelicalism. Content to puff on their theological pipes, they seem to be embarrassed to admit any association at all with their Bible-toting cousins from the right. In contrast to this, Fundamentalism has been driven by overreaction to worldly Evangelicalism into an extreme militancy. In a sincere attempt to maintain strict Fundamentalism, this has led to overt labeling, categorization, and castigation of almost everybody. George Dollar has incorporated militancy into the very definition of Fundamentalism. The problem is that while Fundamentalists are known as militant defenders of the faith, at the same time Hyper-Fundamentalists have become militant critics of most other Fundamentalists as well. Their criticisms have been leveled against such people as Jerry Falwell, Jack Wyrtzen, Jack Van Impe, Lee Roberson, Jack Hyles, and John R. Rice (normally looked upon as extreme conservatives by most Evangelicals).

The atmosphere of New Evangelicalism is generally that of conformity to society. This conformity takes place in the theological, philosophical, and practical areas of life. A careful reading of Quebedeaux's writings makes it clear that this mentality leads from Evangelicalism to young Evangelicalism to worldly Evangelicalism and probably right back to Liberalism itself.

Another area of strong contrast between the extreme Evangelicals and the extreme Fundamentalists is that of the social implications of the Gospel and the involvement of Christians in society. Left-wing Evangelicals tend to be not only theologically liberal but somewhat politically liberal as well.[50] While rightly calling the Evangelical Movement to much needed social involvement, they generally tend to define that involvement in terms of a more liberal political ethic. Many of the writers of this movement are now middle-aged professors who came out of the student revolutionary movement of the 1960s. Instead of recognizing that America is now in a back-to-basics move, these out-of-step-with-the-times professors are still advocating a Christian return to the social revolution that failed with the defeat of McGovern in 1972. Hence the political mood on the average Christian liberal arts campus is often quite different from that of the Bible colleges and the fundamentalist schools. Again, by contrast, Hyper-Fundamentalists (who hold to strong conservative, right-wing political convictions) also tend to be very weak in their social and political involvement in society. They have tended to be content with delivering sermonizing blasts at the political left while remaining within the fortress of their own churches. Some of these more extreme groups have actually criticized the conservative Christian right for its involvement in the recent political campaign of Ronald Reagan. They have looked upon such men as Jerry Falwell as "dangerous" to the cause of Fundamentalism in the sense that they do not feel that they have total control over him. At the same time, it should be observed that these same groups gave strong support in the past to the Christian political activities of Carl McIntire and Billy James Hargis.

The approach of left-wing Evangelicalism to theological and social issues has generally been one of infiltration and dialogue as opposed to the fundamentalist emphasis on confrontation and proclamation. The Fundamentalist proclaims the truth in a strong confrontation with society. He is without a doubt a nonconformist when it comes to contemporary fads and trends. Unfortunately, at times he tends to identify all new fads as dangerous and immoral (hence, confusing the issue of sideburns with that of bikinis). By contrast, the evangelical left has proposed a dialogue with Catholics, Jews, and Marxists, among others.[51] In the area of missiology, they have called for moratoriums on evangelism in order to study the contextualization of Christianity within existing cultures, even going so far as to advocate the parallel existence of Christian belief with the religious practices of pagan tribalism. They have courted the PLO, Castro, and others. It is amusing, though, to observe that when commenting on one another the extreme Evangelicals can be just as belligerent in their references to Fundamentalists as the Hyper-Fundamentalists are to the Evangelicals.

Finally, we would observe that the evangelical left is a movement that is basically led by religious and theological professors who work for para-church organizations, as opposed to the fundamental right, which is led by pastors who are strongly pro-church in their commitment. As a result, the Fundamentalists have been more effective in leading large numbers of ordinary people under their banner than are the Evangelicals, who are appealing to an intellectual elite within conservative Christianity. This became obvious in the political campaign of 1980, in which the evangelical left tended to favor the campaign of John Anderson, while the evangelical right was overwhelmingly in favor of Ronald Reagan.

While Fundamentalism has been known for its "wars and rumors of wars" and its endless splits, it should also be observed that the evangelical ship is also breaking up at sea. Weak commitments and positions held by Evangelicals have tended to foster the rise of the new, young, and worldly Evangelicals, who have gone far beyond what their evangelical forefathers ever intended. As Evangelicalism divided into further subgroups from new to young to worldly, it moved so radically far to the left that it has become almost indistinguishable from contemporary Liberalism.

One of the major criticisms of the New Left is that Fundamentalists tend to give simplistic answers to the complicated issues of society. It is just as obvious, however, that left-wing Evangelicals give too complicated answers to the simple questions that society is really asking. Most honest pastors and Christian laity within the conservative framework are tired of the pseudo-intellectualism of ivory-tower Evangelicalism. The common mentality of the evangelical left is to give such equivocated answers to any questions that when its members are done speaking they've really given no answer at all! Ask an Evangelical whether or not he believes there are flames in hell, and after a thirty-minute philosophical recitation on the theological implications of eternal retribution in light of the implicit goodness of God, you will still not know what he really believes. Ask a Fundamentalist whether he believes there are really flames in hell and he will simply say, "Yes, and hot ones too!" This is why left-wing Evangelicalism has failed to make any substantial use of the media. It cannot express its theology in the concrete terminology of television English. The entire movement is confined to literary approaches, and whenever it has attempted to make use of radio and television it has failed miserably. At the same time, the radical right of Hyper-Fundamentalism has also failed to substantially capture the media. Hyper-Fundamentalism suffers on television because of the ability of the viewer to change channels. Its attempted invasion of the American home is thwarted by an ultra-negativistic approach. Accustomed to a captive audience within the local church, the Hyper-Fundamentalist cannot survive in the open marketplace of modern-day American communication media.

Strong and Weak Groups

The resurgence of Fundamentalism in the 1980s was a shocking event to those who assumed it was a dying, divided movement. This is evident when one considers its extensive fragmentation as a result of its practice of separatism. Conversely, the tolerance and outward cohesiveness of Evangelicalism generated the prospect that it would be the explosive religious movement of the 1980s. Why did Fundamentalism resurge?

Dean M. Kelley, in his book *Why Conservative Churches are Growing*, identifies important reasons for the growth of conservative churches and the decline of more liberal ones. In dealing with these reasons, he discusses the characteristics of "strong" (growing) and "weak" (declining) groups. These characteristics provide interesting insight into the growth of the Fundamentalist Movement. Setting aside theological criteria, the Fundamentalist Movement resembles Kelley's "strong," or growing, groups, while the Evangelical Movement resembles the "weak," or declining, groups.[52]

Characteristics of a "Strong" Group

1. Commitment
   - Willingness to sacrifice status, possessions, safety, life itself, for the cause or the company of the faithful.
   - A total response to a total demand.
   - Group solidarity.
   - Total identification of individual's goals with the group's.

The Fundamentalist Movement generates a high level of commitment from its participants. It demands sacrifice on the part of its members. Time, money, effort, planning, and organization have all been required. The secret of its unity has been a synthesis of individual goals into the goals of the total movement. Following the 1980 election, several liberal senators indicated that it would take years for the liberal political movement to catch up with the organization and structure of the right-wing conservative movement.

2. Discipline

- Willingness to obey the commands of (charismatic) leadership without question.
- Willingness to suffer sanctions for infraction rather than leave the group.

The Fundamentalist Movement has always been led by strong leaders. From the days of Norris, Riley, and Machen it has been directed and influenced by strong individual leadership. It is not, however, cultic in its relationship to leadership. There is definitely a willingness to follow that leadership, but not an absolute blind loyalty to the leaders.

3. Missionary Zeal

- Eagerness to tell the "good news" of one's experience of salvation to others.
- Refusal to be silenced (Acts 5:28–29).
- Internal communication stylized and highly symbolic: a cryptic language.
- Winsomeness.

The Fundamentalist Movement has always been committed to the Great Commission. While it may have been fighting Liberalism and the New Evangelicalism, it was concurrently involved in church planting and missionary outreach. The preaching of the Gospel, the baptizing of converts, and their personal growth have been foundational to the Fundamentalist Movement. One interesting characteristic of Fundamentalists is that the more they are attacked, the more strongly they react and the more they refuse to be silenced. It is indeed true that they have positive influence over people because of their aggressive attitude toward Evangelism.

4. Absolutism

- Belief that "we have the truth and all others are in error."
- Close system of meaning and value that explains everything.

- Uncritical and unreflective attachment to a single set of values.

Fundamentalists have a strong commitment to absolutism. The entire movement was born out of absolutism. The original liberal-fundamentalist war was a war of absolutes; it centered around the acceptance or rejection of God's Word as absolute, inspired, and inerrant. This commitment to absolute truth breeds great evangelistic zeal for Fundamentalism. Consequently, Fundamentalists tend to observe things with a black-or-white, right-or-wrong perspective.

5. Conformity

- Intolerance of deviance or dissent.
- Shunning of outcasts . . . shared stigmata of belonging. . . .
- Separatism.

Of the above characteristics related to conformity, separatism definitely identifies the Fundamentalist Movement. Fundamentalism rejects an attitude of conformity to culture and society. It has always stood in open confrontation to secularism. This characteristic of separatism and nonconformity breeds the problem of splitting and dissent.

6. Fanaticism

Kelley identifies two extremes related to fanaticism. One is "All talk, no listen," and the other extreme is "Keep yourselves unspotted from the world." Both of these characteristics are somewhat inherent in Fundamentalism. Fundamentalists are very quick and open to talk and much less apt to reflect and listen. Fundamentalism is an action-oriented movement, with little commitment to philosophy and reflection. Fundamentalism has also had a strong commitment to remaining unspotted from the world. This was clearly demonstrated in the historical development of its concept of separatism.

The above six characteristics, according to Kelley, are those of strong religious groups that make major impacts upon their society.

Many of these characteristics when carried to the extreme are dangerous. The challenge of Fundamentalism is to keep them within the context of love, and to remain balanced as its members seek to preach the Gospel to every creature.

Characteristics of a "Weak" Group

Although the Evangelical Movement represents a wide spectrum of people and organizations, it has failed to make a concerted impact as a movement. Carl F. H. Henry, the leading apologist of the Evangelical Movement, states: "Evangelical Christianity in our generation has come out of the closet. It has yet to discover what it means to come confrontationally and creatively into the culture."[53] Kelley's characteristics of "weak" groups reveal some substantive reasons for the inability of Evangelicalism to affect society strongly.

1. Relativism

   • Belief that no one has a monopoly on truth, that all insights are partial.
   • Attachment to many values and to various modes of fulfillment (not just the religious).
   • A critical and circumspect look.

It has already been established that the Evangelical Movement, in particular Quebedeaux's Young and Worldly Evangelicals, has long advocated a more tolerant approach to truth. It has proposed alternate concepts related to inerrancy. It has no clearly defined set of personal values. Its approach to Christianity is to let all Christians "do that which is right in their own eyes."

2. Diversity

   • Appreciation of individual differences (everyone should do his own thing?).
   • No heresy trials; no excommunications; no humiliating group confessions of error.
   • Leadership institutionalized, not charismatic.

One of the most prevalent weaknesses of the Evangelical Movement is that there is no strong individual leadership. Although there have been some influential individuals, such as Billy Graham and Carl F. H. Henry, the Evangelical Movement has been composed of a wide diversity of organizations, not individuals. Individual leadership that directs the entire movement is inherently absent from the Evangelical Movement. In their quest to be acceptable to Liberals and the secular society, Evangelicals allowed all those in the movement to "do their own thing." Consequently it has become almost impossible to describe or define the movement accurately.

3. Dialogue

- An exchange of differing insights, an exploration of divergent views.
- Appreciation of outsiders rather than judgment.

One of the major appeals of the Evangelical Movement is that of dialogue. Quebedeaux even advocated dialogue with the Liberals, socialists, and Marxists. The Evangelical Movement has called for a better understanding and tolerance of those who do not accept its ideas. The danger of tolerance is that ultimately the movement will lose its own identity and will begin to drift toward the position of the people with whom it carries on a dialogue.

4. Lukewarmness

- "If you have some truth and I have some truth, why should either of us die for his portion?"
- Reluctance to sacrifice all for any single set of values or area of fulfillment.
- Indecisiveness even when important values are at stake.

Because Evangelicals are committed to dialogue, relativism, and diversity, it is almost impossible for them to make a clear-cut, strong statement of their position. In dealing with social and theological issues, they have a tendency to vacilate. They have the distinct capability of answering the most simple of questions with the

most difficult of answers while not really answering the question at
all.

5. Individualism

- Unwillingness to give unquestioning obedience to anyone.
- Individuality prized above conformity.
- Discipline? For what?
- Leave group rather than be inconvenienced by its demands.

The Evangelical Movement can be characterized by this principle of individualism. However, this leads to a greatly weakened
movement. It produces hundreds of individuals going in different
directions and none moving in the same direction. For this reason,
Evangelicalism has failed to make an impact on society. The
members within the movement have never been committed to a
common goal.

6. Reserve

- Relucatance to expose one's personal beliefs or impose them
  on others.
- Consequent decay of the missionary enterprise.
- No effective sharing of conviction or spiritual insight within
  the group.

The Evangelical Movement has been so philosophically
minded that it has minimized its practical good. It has been consumed with dialogue, diversity, relativity, and the worth of the individual, but it has forgotten that the world is going to hell. The
Fundamentalist, who has little appreciation for the philosophical, is
totally consumed by the fact that the world needs a Savior. Fundamentalism interprets theology on a practical level, whereas Evangelicalism debates theology on a philosophical level.

In light of these "strong" and "weak" group characteristics,
Kelley concludes: "A group with evidence of social strength will
proportionately show traits of strictness; a group with traits of leniency will proportionately show evidences of social weakness rather
than strength. This idea is repugnant to some people, who insist

that 'lenient' organizations can also be 'strong.' Perhaps they can. No one would be happier than the author to see the hypothesis disproved, but it will take more than insistence to disprove it. . . . For twenty years I have been looking for one clear case that would disprove this theory, but I have not as yet found one."[54] It is unlikely that the Evangelical Movement, with the leniency of a "weak" group, can emerge as a movement with major social strength!

FUNDAMENTALISM: ITS WEAKNESSES

It has been well said that one's strength often becomes one's weakness. This is true of Fundamentalism just as it is of other movements. The qualities that make Fundamentalism the dynamic and powerful religious movement that it is today may also be blown up out of proportion and thereby become its most inherent dangers as well. Ten characteristic weaknesses of Fundamentalism are evident to the unbiased observer:

1. *Little capacity for self-criticism.* Because of its strong commitment to biblical truth, Fundamentalism tends to level scathing criticisms at Liberalism and the ecumenical movement and, in general, all ecclesiastical groups and organizations that are not a part of its own movement. By contrast, however, Fundamentalism is extremely sensitive to any self-criticism, causing a tendency to become overly defensive and ingrown. Constructive self-criticism is vital in order to maintain the vitality and direction of the movement. Fundamentalism must avoid the extreme tendency to blast, label, and excommunicate anyone and everyone who raises even the slightest objection to its beliefs and methods.[55]

2. *Overemphasis on external spirituality.* One of the great weaknesses within Fundamentalism is the tendency to overemphasize externals when dealing with spiritual issues, to the neglect of equally significant internal matters. Evangelicals are often quick to point out that spirituality is what you are, not just what you do. A proper understanding of spiritual maturity, however, cannot divorce what you do from what

you are. What you do is a reflection of what you are, and Fundamentalists rightly understand that. But in so emphasizing the significance of actions as a reflection of one's belief there is a tendency within Fundamentalism to reduce its emphasis on spirituality to only what you do and neglect the importance of what you are. Certainly there are times when people pass all of the external tests related to smoking, drinking, appearance, habits, and so on, and still remain bitter, hostile, unloving, and lustful. Fundamentalism as a movement certainly cannot argue that its strong emphasis on belief and external behavior has left it relatively free from morality crises. On the other hand, wholesale capitulation to accepting spirituality as merely an internal attitude of the mind and heart can be very destructive. One can make ethical matters so ethereal that they have no practical expression at all. Today, more than ever before, there are strong correctives at work within Fundamentalism to keep it properly balanced in this regard.[56]

3. *Resistance to change.* Since the basic mentality of Fundamentalism involves a nonconformity to secular culture, it tends to produce a resistance to change of any kind. This often results in an overreaction to fads. For example, many Fundamentalists preached against sideburns, wire-rimmed glasses, and flare-bottomed pants during the early seventies because of a supposed association with the hippies. In time, flare-bottomed pants became so stylish that the clothing companies were producing only that kind of pants. Some churches went to such an extreme that they began to provide seamstresses to ensure that all flare-bottomed pants be redesigned into straight-leg pants so as not to compromise with worldliness. However, in time, several fundamentalist leaders began to wear flare-bottomed pants, and then flare-bottomed pants were no longer an issue for the vast majority of Fundamentalists.

4. *Elevation of minor issues.* Because of our resistance to the corrupting influence of society, we tend to elevate minor issues into a place of focus and attention that often neglects major issues. In this regard, there is a strong pharisaical tendency among Fundamentalists that must be faced honestly to ensure that the "weightier matters" are not neglected. Some have

battled violently over the issue of women's wearing slacks, the inspiration of the King James Version only, and, in Holiness-fundamentalist circles, over whether "lifting hands" to God means that we are to lift both hands at the same time or whether everyone is to lift one hand collectively. While these issues have a place of honest concern to many sincere and well-meaning people, they must be recognized as side issues and not the central issues of Christianity. One will search in vain through the original editions of *The Fundamentals* to find such kind of bickering. It simply is not there. Nobody was arguing in those days about whether one should retain a moustache or beard in order to keep the dignity of the nineteenth century alive, or whether it was acceptable to be clean-shaven and thereby appear to be "modern." Every issue that arises within the movement must be evaluated on the basis of what the Bible alone teaches and not who yells the loudest.[57]

5. *The temptation to add to the Gospel.* While no true Fundamentalist wants to add anything to the Gospel (the death, burial, and resurrection of Jesus Christ), there is nevertheless a strong temptation to do just that. Some have the tendency to express themselves in such a manner as to imply that only their particular understanding of Christianity really represents the Gospel. Preaching on Bible prophecy, the dispensations, the evils of evolution, the ecumenical movement, and rising heresies certainly have their place, but they are not the Gospel. Hence it is possible to attend a fundamentalist church and hear a great deal of preaching about and against all sorts of things and almost never hear the Gospel. The central focus of all biblical preaching should be the Person and work of Christ. He is the topic, His resurrection our Good News, and calling people to faith in Him for their salvation is our task. Anything other than that may be legitimate in its place, but it must never supersede the centrality of proclaiming the message of salvation in Jesus Christ.

6. *Overdependence on dynamic leadership.* Within the Fundamentalist Movement there is very little concern for succession or perpetuity. Fundamentalism has been a movement of dynamic leaders committed to the task of changing their generation for the cause of Christ and providing unparalleled leader-

ship within Christianity. It is clear, however, from the study of
the history of Fundamentalism that once these individuals
have passed off the scene, their movements have usually died
with them. Very few have been able to leave behind well-es-
tablished organizations to carry on the task of their ministry.
If Fundamentalism is to effect a permanent change on
America in the generations ahead, it must begin now to build
the churches and schools that will effectively carry forth its
message to the next generation.

7. *Excessive worry over labels and associations.* In the desire to
be pure from the world, Fundamentalists have tended to
develop a kind of paranoid mentality toward the world they
are trying to reach. This has been true of the Evangelical
Movement as well. One finds that evangelical literature is
filled with statements about the importance of reaching racial
minorities, but an investigation of evangelical churches will
show that they rarely practice what they preach in this area.
In fact, it is safe to say that fundamentalist churches are actually reaching more of the minority population than the Evangelicals. For example, although the average evangelical
church has fewer than two hundred members, it is safe to say
that Dr. Jack Hyles's First Baptist Church of Hammond, Indiana, with its extensive Sunday school ministry to minority
children, is reaching thousands of young people in the minority communities. It would take at least one hundred evangelical churches even to compare with what his one church has
already accomplished in this regard.

The concern of Fundamentalists to have right relationships with all people has caused an exorbitant amount of
paranoia over fellowships, associations, and relationships.
Not only are Fundamentalists arguing about which groups
one ought to officially belong to, but now the argument has
degenerated to the level of whom one has had to speak in
one's church and for whom one has spoken, and in some cases
even with whom one has eaten dinner.[58] Perhaps more than
any other weakness, this is causing some Fundamentalists to
build such restrictive communities that they are in danger of
reverting to an Amish-like retreat from all contact with soci-

ety. Fear of being placed on someone's negative list has caused many Fundamentalists to capitulate to intimidation in order to remain "pure." Yet such capitulation is rarely satisfying to those whose tendency is to become more and more restrictive and exclusive. One list of "accepted" schools has reduced the number down to only five.[59]

The time has come for true Fundamentalists and sincere Evangelicals to rise above the excessive labeling and listing of people, groups, and schools. If there is a lesson to be learned from the history of the early Fundamentalist Movement, it is that divergent groups of Bible-believing Christians who hold to the basic tenets of the faith can cooperate together in order to develop a broadly united front against the real enemies of true Christianity. Let us once again focus the theological guns at Liberalism, humanism, and secularism.

8. *Absolutism.* Because of the Fundamentalists' commitment to the truth, there is a tendency among them to overabsolutism, that is, to approaching every conceivable issue with a totally black-or-white mentality. Our tendency is to view something as either totally right or totally wrong. While this is definitely the case in many situations, becoming locked into that kind of mentality has caused overstatement and overcriticism in many unnecessary matters.

9. *Authoritarianism.* Believing oneself to be right can easily lead to an overly authoritarian approach in disciplinary matters. This is true with regard not only to church discipline but to family discipline as well. Dr. Truman Dollar, a leading Baptist Fundamentalist, warns against the tendency of the overly authoritarian parent to produce rebellious children.[60] One need not look very far to find ample witness to the fact that many good people leave fundamentalist churches for doctrinally weaker churches because they are simply tired of all the fighting. Fundamentalism must become known for what it is for, not just for what it is against. The time has come to raise the standard for a generation of gentlemanly Fundamentalists who love equally the truth of God's Word and the people in whose lives it must be applied.

10. *Exclusivism.* Exclusivism is a characteristic of all religious

cults. It is the tendency to believe that they alone are saved. Unless you belong to their group, you are looked upon as suspect. This mentality breeds the tendency to judge Christians, not by what they *believe,* but by the group to which they *belong.* While belonging to a Bible-believing, Bible-preaching church is certainly a vital expression of one's commitment to Scripture, it must not be reasoned conversely that all people who belong to questionable churches or religious organizations are therefore necessarily and automatically lost. Whether Fundamentalists like it or not, a person may belong to a church that proclaims a liberal gospel and still be a genuine disciple of Jesus Christ. We all agree that they ought to know better and should be urged to "come out from among them," but Fundamentalism must never be guilty of pronouncing them unsaved because they do not join our group. True Fundamentalism recognizes that one's personal salvation has to do with one's belief in Jesus Christ as Savior. A person does not have to join a fundamentalist church in order to become a true believer in Christ.

Fundamentalists must also recognize that a person can pass all of their outward tests for spirituality and still be lost. A politician may have all of the outward requirements for conservative consistency set by the minimal moral standards as defined by conservative political action groups, and still be very amoral in his personal life. He needs Christ just as much as the person who is extremely liberal in his political stand. We must be reminded that even if we are successful in getting society to change its laws in favor of a more moral approach to life, that alone will not make America a moral or Christian nation. The preaching of the Gospel through aggressive evangelism has always been and must always be our major priority.

Fundamentalists are not interested in controlling America; they are interested in seeing souls saved and lives changed for the glory of God. They believe that the degree to which this is accomplished will naturally influence the trend of society in America. As Christians, we should remember that we are to be not only the Light of the world but also the Salt of the earth. Christian influence in society has always been the moral stability that has held this nation together. In calling this nation back to moral sanity, we want to see freedom preserved so that the work of the Gospel may go on unhindered in the generations ahead.[61]

FUTURE-WORD:

AN AGENDA FOR THE EIGHTIES

by Jerry Falwell

These are the greatest days of the twentieth century. We have the opportunity to formulate a new beginning for America in this decade. For the first time in my lifetime we have the opportunity to see spiritual revival and political renewal in the United States. We now have a platform to express the concerns of the majority of moral Americans who still love those things for which this country stands. We have the opportunity to rebuild America to the greatness it once had as a leader among leaders in the world.

The 1980s are certainly a decade of destiny for America. The rising tide of secularism threatens to obliterate the Judeo-Christian influence on American society. In the realm of religion, liberal clergy have seduced the average American away from the Bible and the kind of simple faith on which this country was built. We need to call America back to God, back to the Bible, and back to moral sanity.

Positive Christianity recognizes that reformation of the institutional structure of the Church is futile without the spiritual revitalization of people's lives. It is the people whose lives have been dynamically changed by their personal relationship to Christ who are the real strength of the Church. It is no "mere pietism" that will dynamically energize the evangelical church into social action. In our attempt to rally a diversity of morally conservative Americans together in Moral Majority, we were convinced that millions of people were fed up with the fruits of liberalism, both in politics and in religion. I am well aware that it is unpopular in some circles to equate the two. But I say that they must be viewed as cousins of the same family because both rest upon the same foundational presupposition of the inherent goodness of mankind. The ultimate product of theological Liberalism is a vague kind of religious humanism that is devoid of any true Gospel content.

In 1969 Dr. Harold O. J. Brown observed that there was still a "moral majority" left in America when he said: "The United States may have a great deal of Christianity deep down. There is evidence of this. There is much to indicate that something basic in America is still healthy, both in a spiritual and in a moral sense. But wherever it is and whatever it is doing, it is not setting the tone, it is not giving direction to mid-twentieth-century America. It is not immune to disease. There is plenty of reason to think that America has a large reservoir of Christian faith, sound morality, and of idealism. But there is also a great deal of reason to fear that this reservoir is in danger of being polluted."[1]

Dr. Brown further observed that it was the influence of the liberal impulse in American theology that had produced a climate that spawned celebrated "theologians" who openly taught atheism and left the average person in search of God as a "prisoner of the total culture."[2] During the sixties and seventies, people felt confused and began to turn away from the liberalized institutional church that was not meeting their real spiritual needs. As attendance drastically declined in the main-line denominations, it dramatically increased in conservative denominations. Liberalism is obviously losing its influence on America. The time has come for the Fundamentalists and Evangelicals to return our nation to its spiritual and moral roots.

MORAL ISSUES

Imperative of Morality

As a pastor, I kept waiting for someone to come to the forefront of the American religious scene to lead the way out of the wilderness. Like thousands of other preachers, I kept waiting, but no real leader appeared. Finally I realized that we had to act ourselves.

Something had to be done now. The government was encroaching upon the sovereignty of both the Church and the family. The Supreme Court had legalized abortion on demand. The Equal Rights Amendment, with its vague language, threatened to do further damage to the traditional family, as did the rising sentiment toward so-called homosexual rights. Most Americans were shocked, but kept hoping someone would do something about all this moral chaos.

ORGANIZING THE MORAL MAJORITY

Facing the desperate need in the impending crisis of the hour, several concerned pastors began to urge me to put together a political organization that could provide a vehicle to address these crucial issues. Men like James Kennedy (Fort Lauderdale, Florida), Charles Stanley (Atlanta, Georgia), Tim La Haye (San Diego, California), and Greg Dixon (Indianapolis, Indiana) began to share with me a common concern. They urged that we formulate a nonpartisan political organization to promote morality in public life and to combat legislation that favored the legalization of immorality. Together we formulated the Moral Majority, Inc. Today Moral Majority, Inc., is made up of millions of Americans, including 72,000 ministers, priests, and rabbis, who are deeply concerned about the moral decline of our nation, the traditional family, and the moral values on which our nation was built. We are Catholics, Jews, Protestants, Mormons, Fundamentalists—blacks and whites—farmers, housewives, businessmen, and businesswomen. We are Americans from all walks of life united by one central concern: to serve as a special-interest group providing a voice for a return to moral sanity in these United States of America. Moral Majority is a political organization and is not based on theological considerations. We are Americans who share similar moral convictions. We are opposed to abortion, pornography, the drug epidemic, the breakdown of the traditional family, the establishment of homosexuality as an accepted alternate life-style, and other moral cancers that are causing our society to rot from within. Moral Majority strongly supports a pluralistic America. While we believe that this nation was founded upon the Judeo-Christian ethic by men and women who were strongly influenced by biblical moral principles, we are committed to the separation of Church and State.

Here is how Moral Majority stands on today's vital issues:

1. *We believe in the separation of Church and State.* Moral Majority, Inc., is a political organization providing a platform for religious and nonreligious Americans who share moral values to address their concerns in these areas. Members of Moral Majority, Inc., have no common theological premise. We are Americans who are proud to be conservative in our approach to moral, social, and political concerns.

2. *We are pro-life.* We believe that life begins at fertilization. We strongly oppose the massive "biological holocaust" that is resulting in the abortion of one and a half million babies each year in America. We believe that unborn babies have the right to life as much as babies that have been born. We are providing a voice and a defense for the human and civil rights of millions of unborn babies.

3. *We are pro–traditional family.* We believe that the only acceptable family form begins with a legal marriage of a man and woman. We feel that homosexual marriages and common-law marriages should not be accepted as traditional families. We oppose legislation that favors these kinds of "diverse family form," thereby penalizing the traditional family. We do not oppose civil rights for homosexuals. We do oppose "special rights" for homosexuals who have chosen a perverted life-style rather than a traditional life-style.

4. *We oppose the illegal drug traffic in America.* The youth in America are presently in the midst of a drug epidemic. Through education, legislation, and other means we want to do our part to save our young people from death on the installment plan through illegal drug addiction.

5. *We oppose pornography.* While we do not advocate censorship, we do believe that education and legislation can help stem the tide of pornography and obscenity that is poisoning the American spirit today. Economic boycotts are a proper way in America's free-enterprise system to help persuade the media to move back to a sensible and reasonable moral stand. We most certainly believe in the First Amendment for every-

one. We are not willing to sit back, however, while many television programs create cesspools of obscenity and vulgarity in
our nation's living rooms.

6. *We support the state of Israel and Jewish people everywhere.*
It is impossible to separate the state of Israel from the Jewish
family internationally. Many Moral Majority members, because of their theological convictions, are committed to the
Jewish people. Others stand upon the human and civil rights
of all persons as a premise for support of the state of Israel.
Support of Israel is one of the essential commitments of Moral
Majority. No anti-Semitic influence is allowed in Moral Majority, Inc.

7. *We believe that a strong national defense is the best deterrent
to war.* We believe that liberty is the basic moral issue of all
moral issues. The only way America can remain free is to
remain strong. Therefore we support the efforts of our present
administration to regain our position of military preparedness
—with a sincere hope that we will never need to use any of
our weapons against any people anywhere.

8. *We support equal rights for women.* We agree with President
Reagan's commitment to help every governor and every state
legislature to move quickly to ensure that during the 1980s
every American woman will earn as much money and enjoy
the same opportunities for advancement as her male counterpart in the same vocation.

9. *We believe ERA is the wrong vehicle to obtain equal rights
for women.* We feel that the ambiguous and simplistic language of the Amendment could lead to court interpretations
that might put women in combat, sanction homosexual marriages, and financially penalize widows and deserted wives.

10. *We encourage our Moral Majority state organizations to be
autonomous and indigenous.* Moral Majority state organizations may, from time to time, hold positions that are not
held by the Moral Majority, Inc., national organization.

FACING THE OPPOSITION

We have been labeled by our critics as arrogant, irresponsible, and
simplistic. They accuse us of violating the separation of Church

and state. However, the National Council of Churches (NCC) has been heavily involved in politics for years, and virtually no one has complained. Since many moral problems, such as abortion, require solutions that are both legal and political, it is necessary for religious leaders to speak on these matters in order to be heard.

WHAT MORAL MAJORITY IS NOT

1. *We are not a political party.* We are committed to work within the multiple-party system in this nation. We are not a political party and do not intend to become one.

2. *We do not endorse political candidates.* Moral Majority informs American citizens regarding the vital moral issues facing our nation. We have no "hit lists." While we fully support the constitutional rights of any special-interest group to target candidates with whom they disagree, Moral Majority, Inc., has chosen not to take this course. We are committed to principles and issues, not candidates and parties.

3. *We are not attempting to elect "born-again" candidates.* We are committed to pluralism. The membership of Moral Majority, Inc., is so totally pluralistic that the acceptability of any candidate could never be based upon one's religious affiliation. Our support of candidates is based upon two criteria: (a) the commitment of the candidate to the principles that we espouse; (b) the competency of the candidate to fill that office.

4. *Moral Majority, Inc., is not a religious organization attempting to control the government.* Moral Majority is a special-interest group of millions of Americans who share the same moral values. We simply desire to influence government—not control government. This, of course, is the right of every American, and Moral Majority, Inc., would vigorously oppose any Ayatollah type of person's rising to power in this country.

5. *We are not a censorship organization.* We believe in freedom of speech, freedom of the press, and freedom of religion. Therefore while we do not agree that the Equal Rights Amendment would ultimately benefit the cause of women in America, we do agree with the right of its supporters to boycott those states that have not ratified the amendment. Like-

wise, we feel that all Americans have the right to refuse to purchase products from manufacturers whose advertising dollars support publications and television programming that violate their own moral code.

6. *Moral Majority, Inc., is not an organization committed to depriving homosexuals of their civil rights as Americans.* While we believe that homosexuality is a moral perversion, we are committed to guaranteeing the civil rights of homosexuals. We do oppose the efforts of homosexuals to obtain special privileges as a bona fide minority. And we oppose any efforts by homosexuals to flaunt their perversion as an acceptable life-style. We view heterosexual promiscuity with the same distaste which we express toward homosexuality.

7. *We do not believe that individuals or organizations that disagree with Moral Majority, Inc., belong to an immoral minority.* However, we do feel that our position represents a consensus of the majority of Americans. This belief in no way reflects on the morality of those who disagree with us or who are not involved in our organizational structures. We are committed to the total freedom of all Americans regardless of race, creed, or color.

OUT OF THE PEW AND INTO THE PRECINCT

Many Christians are raising the question of whether or not they should be involved in politics at all. Some raise the question of the separation of Church and State; others feel that politics is the devil's arena and Christians should stay out; and others say politics requires compromising and Christians should not compromise. Many liberal church people are also claiming that Evangelicals are violating the separation of Church and State. Recently Richard Dingman said: "As one who has held local public office for 10 years and worked in congress for 11 years, it is my opinion that it is not only proper for Christians to become involved, but it is absolutely biblical and absolutely necessary."[3]

The recent emergence of the Fundamentalists and Evangelicals into politics in no way violates the historical principles of this nation. The incorporation of Christian principles into both the structure and the basic documents of our nation is a matter of historical fact. The doctrine of the separation of Church and State simply means that the state shall not control religion and religion shall not control the state. It does not mean that the two may never work together.

HERE IS HOW MORAL MAJORITY, INC., IS CONTRIBUTING TO BRINGING AMERICA BACK TO MORAL SANITY

1. *By educating millions of Americans concerning the vital moral issues of our day.* This is accomplished through such avenues as our newspaper, called the *Moral Majority Report,* a radio commentary by the same name, seminars, and other training programs conducted daily throughout the nation.

2. *By mobilizing millions of previously "inactive" Americans.* We have registered millions of voters and reactivated more millions of frustrated citizens into a special-interest group who are effectively making themselves heard in the halls of Congress, in the White House, and in every state legislature.

3. *By lobbying intensively in Congress to defeat any legislation that would further erode our constitutionally guaranteed freedom* and by introducing and/or supporting legislation that promotes traditional family and moral values, followed by the passage of a Human Life Amendment, which is a top priority of the Moral Majority agenda. We support the return of voluntary prayer to public schools while opposing mandated or written prayers. We are concerned to promote acceptance and adoption of legislation that keeps America morally balanced.

4. *By informing all Americans about the voting records of their representatives so that every American, with full information available, can vote intelligently following his or her own convictions.* We are nonpartisan. We are not committed to politicians or political parties; we are committed to principles and issues that we believe are essential to America's survival at this crucial hour. It is our desire to represent these concerns to the American public and allow it to make its own decisions on these matters.

5. *By organizing and training millions of Americans who can become moral activists.* This heretofore silent majority in America can then help develop a responsive government

which is truly "of the people, by the people, for the people" instead of "in spite of the people," which we have had for too many years now.

6. *By encouraging and promoting non-public schools in their attempt to excel in academics while simultaneously teaching traditional family and moral values.* There are thousands of non-public schools in America that accept no tax moneys. Some of these schools are Catholic, Fundamentalist, Jewish, Adventist, or of other faiths. Some are not religious. But Moral Majority, Inc., supports the right of these schools to teach young people not only how to make a living, but how to live.

Moral Majority, Inc., does not advocate the abolition of public schools. Public schools will always be needed in our pluralistic society. We are committed to helping public schools regain excellence. That is why we support the return of voluntary prayer to public schools and strongly oppose the teaching of the "religion" of secular humanism in the public classroom.

The First Amendment says: "Congress shall make no law respecting an establishment of religion, or prohibiting the free exercise therof." This does not rule out church influence in government. Presbyterian theologian John Gerstner has said: "Establishment of religion is not the same thing as no influence of religion. I think Moral Majority is right in stating that the church should seek to have influence in political matters."[4]

California pastor Dr. Tim La Haye, believes that the pulpit must be active in resisting encroaching federal bureaucracy that threatens both the Church and the traditional family. He has stated: "God founded the government to protect the home against external enemies. The prophet of God is derelict if he does not, in God's name, rebuke goverment when it fails to protect the family."[5]

Catholic theologian and journalist Father Robert Burns, C.S.P., stated in the national Catholic weekly *The Wanderer:* "If our great nation collapses, it will not be because of the efforts of some foreign power, Soviet or otherwise, but rather for the same reason that ancient Rome collapsed because it was morally rotten to the core." He further comments: "The members of Moral Majority believe in fighting for the basic moral values on which this nation was built and upon which its strength rests. They are determined to prevent materialists, secular-humanists, and non-believers from destroying these values by replacing them with a valueless, amoral society."[6]

Christians are now realizing that governmental actions directly affect their lives. They are questioning the government's right to carry out such programs. They are beginning to realize that the only way to change the actions of government is to change those elected to govern. We are now beginning to do just that. We must continue to exert a strong moral influence upon America if our children and grandchildren are to enjoy the same freedoms that we have known.

Sanctity of Human Life

Life is a miracle. Only God Almighty can create life, and he said, "Thou shalt not kill." Nothing can change the fact that abortion is the murder of human life.

As I warned in my book *Listen, America!*, an article in the January 9, 1980, issue of the Washington *Post* stated the grave fact that in 1978 nearly 30 percent of all pregnancies were terminated by legal abortions. A family-planning study estimated that there were 1,374,000 legal abortions during that year. About one third of these were obtained by teenagers, and about three quarters were for unmarried women. In 1979 more than 1.5 million babies were aborted in America. Experts now estimate that between 8 million and 10 million babies have been murdered since January 22, 1973, when the Supreme Court, in a decision known as *Roe* v. *Wade*, granted women an absolute right to abortion on demand during the first two trimesters of pregnancy—that is, the first six months of pregnancy. No other major civilized nation in history has ever been willing to permit late abortion except for the gravest of medical reasons.

Human life is precious to God. Christ died upon the cross for every man and woman who has ever lived and who ever will live. In the past, America was known for its honoring and protecting the right of a person to live. No one disagrees that the state exists to protect the lives of its citizens. But we are in danger of losing our respect for the sanctity of human life. America has allowed more persons to be killed through abortion than have been eliminated in all our major wars. Only a perverted society would make laws protecting eagles' eggs and yet have no protection for precious unborn human life.

Equally ironic, there is a great debate going on today regarding capital punishment. In America we kill babies and protect criminals, even though the death penalty is definitely a deterrent to crime. The time has now come that we must speak up in defense of the sanctity and dignity of human life.

In reality, life began with God and, since Adam, has simply passed from one life cell to another. From the moment of fertilization any further formulation of the individual is merely a matter of time, growth, and maturation. This is a growth process that continues throughout our entire lives. At three weeks, just twenty-one days after conception, a tiny human being already has eyes, a spinal cord, a nervous system, lungs, and intestines. The heart, which has been beating since the eighteenth day, is pumping a blood supply totally separate from that of the mother. All this occurs before the mother may even be aware of the new life within her body. By the end of the seventh week we see a well-proportioned small-scale baby with fingers, knees, ankles, and toes. Brain waves have been recorded as early as forty-three days. By eleven weeks all organ systems are present and functioning in this new embryonic life.

Dr. Thomas L. Johnson, professor of biology and embryology at the University of Virginia, observes that "an individual organism (the zygote) cannot be a part of the mother . . . it has an entirely different set of chromosomes . . . it has a separate and unique life."[7] In reply to the statement that life begins as the infant leaves the mother's womb, Dr. Johnson says that the moment of birth is not a moment of magic when a potential being is transformed into an actual being. The unborn child is merely moving from a required aquatic environment to a required gaseous environment so that it can develop into its next stage of life.

Recently Doug Badger, the legislative director of the Protestant pro-life organization the Christian Action Council, stated: "The conviction that each human life is sacred has its roots in the scriptures. There God is revealed as the living God who bestows life. In contrast to the Gentile nations who manufacture gods in their image, Yahweh fashions human beings in God's image (Genesis 1:26, 28). Each person thus is vested with an inviolable dignity on the basis of his or her creation. From this flows the Torah's sixth commandment (Exodus 20:13) which functions not only as a prohibition of murder, but as a positive injunction to respect human life. Thus when Jesus assumes the role of Moses and expounds the law in the Sermon on the Mount (Matthew 5:17–20) he reveals that the commandment in fact requires that we love our neighbors, not merely that we do them no physical harm (Matthew 5:21–26)."[8]

One of the major arguments of the pro-abortionists is that the unborn child is a fetus, not a person. It should be noted that "fetus" is Latin for "unborn child." Unfortunately, the tendency today is to change traditional terminology and substitute words like "conceptus" for "child." No one wants to use the term "murder" for abortion, so we simply call it "termination of pregnancy." This technique is usually employed to defend the indefensible. It is much easier to refer to the elimination of "P.O.C.s" (products of conception) than to the slicing, poisoning, and flushing away of a million little boys and girls. In her clever parody on this issue, Juli Loesch points out: "Here's what Planned Parenthood said in 1963: 'an abortion kills the life of a baby after it has begun' (*Plan your children for health and happiness*. Planned Parenthood/World Population, 1963). Here's what Planned Parenthood says today: 'The fetal tissue . . . the uterine contents . . . the products of conception . . .' What changed? The baby? Or Planned Parenthood?"[9]

Theologian Francis A. Schaeffer and Dr. C. Everett Koop, Surgeon General of the United States, recently released a movie and book entitled *Whatever Happened to the Human Race?* These men raised this vital issue: "Once the uniqueness of people as created by God is removed and mankind is viewed as only one of the gene patterns which came forth on earth by chance—there is no reason not to treat people as things to be experimental on and to make over the whole of humanity according to the decisions of a relatively few individuals. If people are not unique, as made in the image of God, the barrier is gone. Since life is being destroyed before birth, why not tamper with it on the other end?" They further ask: "Will a society which has assumed the right to kill infants in the womb—because they are unwanted, imperfect, or merely in-convenient—have difficulty in assuming the right to kill other human beings, especially older adults who are judged unwanted, deemed imperfect physically or mentally, or considered a possible social nuisance?"[10]

Dr. Mildred F. Jefferson is a surgeon on the staff of the Boston University Medical Center. She is a remarkable woman who serves in key roles on many medical boards and committees. She is a diplomate of the American Board of Surgery and has received numerous honors and awards for her work. As a guest on the February 10, 1980, "Old-Time Gospel Hour" television broadcast, she made these comments regarding abortion: "Many people try to hide behind the confusion of not knowing what happens before a baby is born. But we do not have to be confused. We in medicine and science have a different name for every stage of the development of the baby, but it does not matter at all whether you know those names or not. When a young woman has not had much opportunity to go to school and she becomes pregnant no one has to tell her that she is going to have a baby." She went on to say: "I became a doctor in the tradition that is represented in the Bible of looking upon medicine as a high calling. I will not stand aside and have this great profession of mine, of the doctor, give up the designation of healer to become that of the social executioner. The Supreme Court justices only had to hand down an order. Social workers only have to make arrangements, but it has been given to my profession to destroy the life of the innocent and the helpless."

The surgeon further stated: "Today it is the unborn child; tomorrow it is likely to be the elderly or those who are incurably ill. Who knows but that a little later it may be anyone who has political or moral views that do not fit into the distorted new order. To that question, 'Am I my brother's keeper?' I answer 'Yes.' It is everyone's responsibility to safeguard and preserve life. A child is a member of the human family and deserves care and concern.

"We are in a great war for the hearts and minds of our people, for the moral future of our country, and for the integrity of a nation. It is a war that we must win. When we win, that victory will not be for ourselves but for God, for America, and for all mankind."[11]

Humanism in the Public Schools

In his recent book *The Battle for the Mind*, Dr. Tim La Haye defines humanism as "man's attempt to solve his problems independently of God."[12] Humanism has its origin in man's attempt to place human wisdom above divine revelation. La Haye traces its formulation back to the Greek thinkers' belief that "man is the measure of all things." He then identifies the five basic tenets of humanism as (1) atheism; (2) evolution; (3) amorality; (4) autonomy of man; (5) one-world socialism.

In a recent interview in *Moral Majority Report*, Mel Gabler of Longview, Texas, who, with his wife, Norma, heads a group called Educational Research Analysis, stated: "Most parents don't realize the viewpoint in their children's textbooks . . . the vast majority of the textbooks in use today are written from a humanistic viewpoint. It's totally woven into the textbooks at all levels. And sometimes, it's not even so evident in the pupil's book—you have to look at the teacher's book to see the additional material they are asked to present, and the questions and exercises they are to give the students."[13]

Gabler also denounced the move away from teaching academic skills in the public schools. He has warned that even Christian schools often fail to fully examine the content and world view of the textbooks they adopt. He cited several areas in which he claims humanism manifests itself in the textbooks: situation ethics, self-centeredness, evolution, the neglect or negation of Christianity, sexual freedom, death education, and internationalism. In the area of morals, he notes that humanist textbooks belittle the concept of sexual virginity and sexual abstinence and teach the legitimacy of abortion, premarital sex, homosexuality, lesbianism, and incest.

Today, however, more and more parents are beginning to read their children's textbooks and to take more of an interest in what their children are being taught. The Gablers are living proof that ordinary parents, without a specialized education or a background of public involvement, can be a potent force in public education.

Sex Education in the Public Schools

In a head-on debate on NBC's "Today" show with Dr. Sol Gordon, Syracuse University professor and leading sex educator, I stated that I believe in teaching sex education in public schools as a biological science. My objection to the current public school sex education program as it is now being taught is that it is "academic pornography." The materials used include wholesale endorsements of masturbation, premarital sex, extramarital sex, and homosexuality. They even include allusions to the acceptability of sex with animals!

It is no secret that the increase of an emphasis on sex education has paralleled the rise in teenage pregnancies, which is at epidemic proportions in the United States, with nearly one million teenage girls becoming pregnant out of wedlock every year! In a carefully documented study, Claire Chambers traces the "SIECUS Circle" to the larger humanist interest in population control, genetic engineering, legalized abortion, pornography, and homosexuality.[14] The Sex Information and Education Council of the United States (SIECUS) has conducted sex education training seminars and produced a series of ten study guides for use in public schools. Based totally on the philosophy of situation ethics, one study guide claims: "The newer relativistic position on sexual morality is a rational one, backed up by research . . . this is the approach that seems to offer the most hope for consensus under modern conditions."[15]

In a new wave of acceptance of immorality, Professor Benjamin DeMott wrote in a recent issue of *Psychology Today* that the idea of incest (sex between nonmarried family members) being immoral is now being challenged in reports presented to the American Psychiatric Association claiming that "some incest experiences appear to be positive and even beneficial."[16] The attempted "normalization" of incest on the American public is being further fostered by a rash of new books and movies.

In the newsletter *Impact 80,* published by the Institute for Family Research and Education, of which Sol Gordon is the director, Moral Majority is labeled as "perennially dubious and chilling."

The newsletter includes a full-page advertisement urging people to join the "United to Save America" group in order to protect the nation from "the so-called Moral Majority and the Bible Bigots." The same issue urges support of Planned Parenthood, the National Abortion Rights Action League, the Religious Coalition for Abortion Rights, and the National Organization of Women.

We must work to make sex education what it claims to be and not allow this avalanche of pornography to go on masquerading as a form of education. It is nothing more than pornographic brainwashing.

Pornography

The pornographers have labeled Moral Majority the "Extreme Right" because we speak out against Extreme Wrong! Pornography is a $4-billion-a-year business. Much of this money is used to influence legislators, judges, and juries, as well as the American people. I have often wondered how the majority of the people in this country feel about pornographers and pornography. My recent escapade with *Penthouse* magazine has brought a response of millions of letters from concerned Americans who have come to our defense. It is, as I have stressed, past time that a strong stand is taken against pornography. Why is it that when national polls show that nearly 80 percent of Americans oppose pornography, no major strides are being taken to rid our country of this menace?

Pornography is not something that is nice to discuss. I was sickened when I read in the book entitled *How to Stop the Porno Plague* by Neil Gallagher his description of the Bicentennial (July 1976) issue of *Hustler* including "a full-page color cartoon, 'Chester the Molester,' showing a man seducing a doll-clutching, pig-tailed girl; a centerfold showing caricatures of Jerry Ford, Henry Kissinger, and Nelson Rockefeller involved in sexual acts with an animated Statue of Liberty; and caricatures of George Washington, Paul Revere, and Ben Franklin involved in a variety of sex acts with prostitutes."[17]

Child pornography is escalating at a frightening rate in the United States of America. I read of one social club that has a slogan on its letterhead that reads: "Sex before eight or it's too late."

There are even such things as child seducers' manuals. There are such things as playing cards that picture naked children in sexual acts with adults. Children are a heritage of the Lord, and to review the violent, filthy acts committed against them by evil men is enough to prove that there is indeed a devil! Child pornography is certainly one of the vilest forms of child abuse and must be stopped.

A Christian author and professor of pediatrics at the University of Southern California, Dr. James Dobson, has also lamented what he calls "chicken porn" (which depicts sex between young girls and adult men). He cited one study of eighty other civilizations that degenerated to the level of sexual child abuse, all of which collapsed.[18]

The pornographic explosion distorts the biblical view of women, perverts American youth, and corrupts the moral fiber of society. Moral Americans must hold up a standard. Proliferation of pornography into our society is striking evidence of our decadence. The moral fiber of our nation is so deteriorated that we cannot possibly survive unless there is a complete and drastic turnabout soon. A permissive society that tolerates pornography has the same hedonistic attitude that destroyed ancient civilizations. Pornographers are idolaters who idolize money and will do anything for materialistic gain. They are men who have reprobate minds and who need divine deliverance.

Dr. Harold Voth, professor of psychiatry at the University of Kansas, spoke at a recent American Family Forum in Washington, D.C., stating that pornography results in "serious psychological disturbances" for millions of Americans. William Stanmeyer, professor at the Indiana University School of Law, stated to the same audience that criminal studies are now clearly contradicting ACLU claims that there is no link between pornography and crime.[19]

Christian physician Dr. Gary Hall (a former Olympic gold medalist) recently stated: "Children and adolescents are very susceptible to pornography, when moral principles are not deeply established, and when peer pressure is as important as parental approval. If it is the 'in thing' to accept pornography, to go to 'adult' movies or to watch 'mature' TV shows, then that is what adolescents will do."[20]

The most organized effort against the plague of pornography

has been the work of Charles Keating's Citizens for Decency through Law (CDL) organization. Founded in 1957, CDL has recently taken aggressive action against so-called adult bookstores and movie theaters in Cincinnati, with the result of closing down every one of them in that area. Keating states that there are nearly three hundred smut magazines in the United States alone. He warns: "I frequently speak before Christian groups on the Christian's duty to fight pornography. I am happy to say that the mistaken notion that the Lord has no work for moral Americans to do in the public policy arena is fast dissipating. Still, some Christians are unfamiliar with politics, the law, and the whole field of policy-formation."[21]

In light of the concern of decent Americans who are shocked at the impact of pornography in our society, it is distressing to read the comments of left-wing Evangelical Richard Quebedeaux when he states: "Pornography is not condoned, yet it does not warrant undue concern; there are worse evils to fight than pornography."[22] What could be worse in Quebedeaux's scheme, since he "rejects legalism in sexual matters," regards oral sex as mere "petting," and views abortion as a "tragic choice"?[23] I recall what the poet Dante wrote centuries ago: "The hottest places in hell are reserved for those who, in time of great moral crises, maintained their neutrality."

Homosexuality

Less than a decade ago, the word "homosexual" was a word that was disdained by most Americans and represented the nadir of human indecency. It was utilized as a word of contempt. All of this has changed. What was once considered a deviant life-style is now considered by many Americans as an alternative life-style. There is even legislation pending that would legitimize homosexuals as "normal." Today thousands of men and women in America flaunt their sin openly. The entire homosexual movement is an indictment against America and is contributing to its ultimate downfall.

History confirms that when homosexuality reaches epidemic levels in society, that society is in serious crisis and on the verge of collapse. God considers the sin of homosexuality as abominable. He destroyed the cities of Sodom and Gomorrah because of their involvement in this sin. The Old Testament law is clear concerning this issue: "Thou shalt not lie with mankind, as with womankind: it is abomination" (Lev. 18:22). God still abhors the sin of homosexuality. In the New Testament, there are numerous references to it. In Romans 1:26-28, we read: "For this cause God gave them up unto vile affections: for even their women did change the natural use into that which is against nature: And likewise also the men, leaving the natural use of the woman, burned in their lust one toward another; men with men working that which is unseemly, and receiving in themselves that recompence of their error which was meet. And even as they did not like to retain God in their knowledge, God gave them over to a reprobate mind, to do those things which are not convenient." These people willingly rejected God's revealed truth. Consequently, God "gave them up to uncleanness through the lusts of their own hearts, to dishonour their own bodies between themselves" (Rom. 1:24).

A bill has been introduced in Congress which, if passed, would establish homosexuals in America as a bona fide minority like women, blacks, or Hispanics. This "Gay Rights" bill, H.R. 2074, would require every employer to employ a minority of homosexuals commensurate with the population in that area. Pastors, private school administrators, and employers would be adversely affected by this new bill. There are currently fifty-one cosponsors of this bill in the House of Representatives. This is a clear indication of the moral decay of our society. Americans began by accepting homosexuality as an alternate life-style, recognizing it as legitimate, and now they are attempting to legalize it.

The October 12, 1979, Washington *Post* contained an article: "50,000 Marchers Turn Out for Gay Rights Demonstration." It reported that "the turnout of an estimated 50,000 marchers here Sunday shows that gay rights are a 'matter of national concern,' says a congressman who wants to extend this Civil Rights Act to protect homosexuals. 'I think most Americans are ready for it,' Republican Ted Weiss, New York, said. . . . Weiss' bill has spurred Rep. Larry McDonald, (D-Ga.,) to introduce a resolution . . . opposing any special legal status for homosexuals."[24]

In light of our opposition to the sin of homosexuality, we must always make it clear that we love people and are genuinely interested in their personal needs. I believe that homosexuals require love and help. We must not allow homosexuality to be presented to our nation as an alternate or acceptable life-style. It will only serve as a corrupting influence upon our next generation and will bring down the wrath of God upon America. I love homosexuals as people for whom Christ died, but I must hate their sin. Jesus Christ offers forgiveness and deliverance from that sin and from all other sins.

SOCIAL ISSUES

Dignity of the Family

There are only three institutions ordained by God in the Bible: the government, the Church, and the family. The family is the God-ordained institution of the marriage of one man and one woman together for a lifetime with their biological or adopted children. The family is the fundamental building block and basic unit of our society, and its continued health is a prerequisite for a healthy and prosperous nation. No nation has ever been stronger than the families within it. America's families are its strength, and they symbolize the miracle of America.

In the "war against the family" today, the most dangerous issue, as I have said before, is the "cult of the playboy." This attitude has permeated our society in the last twenty years. The playboy philosophy tells a man that he does not have to be committed to his wife and his children, but that he should be some kind of "cool free-swinger." Sexual promiscuity has become the life-style of America. The cult of the playboy is more than just a revolution of dirty magazines. It represents a life-style that ultimately corrupts the family. Men are satisfying their lustful desires at the expense of the family.

One million couples will divorce during the coming year! Sociologists now estimate that by the twenty-first century the divorce rate in America will climb to 50 percent. Contrast this with the fact that the marriage rate is declining! The American family faces its most crucial days in the decade ahead. The "war against the family" has already begun. One million American teenagers will become pregnant in 1981, and 600,000 will abort their babies. In many of our major cities, abortion rates outnumber birth rates. Promiscuous sex is advertised on almost every street corner of our major urban centers with lewd pornography tantalizing with "ultimate" sex thrills. The morality crisis has already gone too far in America. It is leaving countless broken families in its path. We cannot wait any longer to speak out against the avalanche of corruption that is threatening the moral stability of our nation.

The strength and stability of families determine the vitality and moral life of society. The most important function performed by the family is the rearing and character formation of children, a function it was uniquely created to perform and for which no remotely adequate substitute has been found. The family is the best and most efficient "department of health, education, and welfare." In response to the attack against the family, Congressman John Ashbrook (R-Ohio) has proposed the National Pro-Family Coalition, which recognizes that the family is the most important unit in society. We also support Senator Paul Laxalt's Family Protection Act, which encourages family, community, and local initiative to aid the family in place of complicated and unnecessary proliferation of bureaucratic government intervention. Senator Jesse Helms summarizes the importance of the family: "We must restore and preserve the family as the focus of our personal and social well-being and the strongest defense we have against the totalitarian state."[25]

Racial Injustice

In spite of the great advances made in the Civil Rights Movement of the 1960s and '70s, we must see to it that the socially and economically underprivileged minorities in our nation have every opportunity of advancement. We must insist that equal education and employment opportunities are available to all Americans regardless of sex, race, religion, or creed. Fundamentalists have been woefully negligent in addressing this issue. We can no longer be silent on this matter, which is so crucial to millions of our fellow Americans.

We may not have all the answers, but we must make it clear that we really do care.

We must encourage government to allow the free-enterprise system to develop in a healthy manner so that it will create its own job opportunities. We must help free minority groups from the virtual "prison" of the welfare system, which threatens to strangle their life and hope from generation to generation. Black economist Dr. Walter Williams of George Mason University, Virginia, has pointed out that increased government spending to create jobs only hinders the economy by increasing tax burdens that discourage both blacks and whites from moving ahead.

We need government policies that are pro-business, pro-consumer, and pro-worker. We must help our racial minorities to genuinely feel that they are fully accepted, first-class citizens in our society. Christianity destroyed the ethnic and social structure of slavery in the Roman Empire. The New Testament clearly states that in Christ there is neither "Greek nor Jew . . . Barbarian, Scythian, bond nor free: but Christ is all, and in all" (Col. 3:11). The power of the Gospel is that it knows no racial bounds. All prejudice is swept aside by Jesus Christ, who died that all people might be saved.

Dr. Andrew Billingsley, president of Morgan State College, Maryland, wrote an excellent article on "Black Families in White America" in a recent issue of *Black Family* magazine. He traced the changing phases of the black family in America from the days of slavery to the Civil Rights Movement. He wrote: "Many of the contributions black people have made to American culture grow out of the agonizing determination of our people not to let slavery dehumanize them. The tenacious fidelity to the very idea of the family along with religion and learning was central to that remarkable achievement." He went on to urge a pro-family policy on the part of the federal government as we move into the decade of the eighties, reminding us that "if we lose the vitality of our family life, we lose the major source of our strength as a people."[26] This is true of all American families, whatever their racial or ethnic heritage. The old Sunday school song is still true.

> *Jesus loves the little children;*
> *All the children of the world.*

Red and yellow, black and white;
They are precious in His sight.
Jesus loves the little children of the world.

World Hunger

Millions of human beings are starving to death all over the world. I have personally visited the drought-stricken regions of Haiti and Africa. I have walked hand in hand with Cambodian children in their refugee camps in Thailand. I am convinced that we Christians who have so much must be our "brother's keeper" in the poverty-stricken regions of the world. A "God bless you" is not enough. We must earn the right to be heard.

While liberal theologians have been talking and theorizing about world hunger, we have been raising millions of dollars to feed starving people. We have sent hundreds of thousands of dollars to the impoverished people of Haiti, Guatemala, Cambodia, Thailand, and the Vietnamese "boat people." While others have talked, we have acted. We have been involved in food programs, building programs, agricultural programs, and long-term programs that deal with the roots of hunger and not simply the current symptoms.

The Gospel is never devoid of social implications. Genuine Christian revival will always change society. We must, however, remind ourselves that feeding the masses without giving them the Gospel will not change them. Great debates are raging among missiologists about the interrelationship of evangelism and social concern. But there is no time for debate. We must do both and we must do it now.

ETHICAL ISSUES

As we approach the end of the twentieth century, the Church faces ever-escalating technological advances that pose the most serious ethical questions Christianity has ever faced. Today's choices pose dilemmas previously unfathomable. A recent congress on human values raised the question "Is a person more responsible for that which he does intentionally than for that which he allows to happen through passive acceptance?" We must not ignore these serious ethical issues and through passive inactivity abrogate our responsibility to scientists in a laboratory. We must struggle with these issues and thus define the ethical parameters within which science must live.

Artificial Insemination

In 1962 J. Robert Moskin wrote in *Look* magazine: "In the next 25 years, it is likely that man will create life in a test tube. He will transform dead chemicals into living material that can grow and reproduce itself. He will perform an act of God."[27] The reproduction of human life apart from sexual intercourse is now an option to millions of Americans. Artificial insemination has already been used to bring 300,000 children to birth in the United States alone. Ninety percent of those were conceived by donor semen (AID's) while virtually no one raised any moral objection.

On July 18, 1978, Louise Brown was born in England, having been conceived in a glass dish by means of in vitro fertilization. Experiments with this process have gone on since the 1940s, but were denied federal funding in the United States because thousands of fertilized embryos were aborted in the process.

This approach to baby-making has been hailed by women with blocked fallopian tubes as their only hope to bear children. However, this great technological breakthrough has caused a series of unresolved problems and unanswered questions. In his article in *Moral Majority Report*, Dr. Woodrow Kroll raises these crucial questions: What rights do the nonselected embryos have? Is it right to do scientific experimentation on a human life that leads to abortion? Whose consent is needed to abort—parents' or researchers'? Who really owns these children? What of the semen donor who gives away his seed, contrary to biblical teaching? What of the surrogate (substitute) mother who "rents" her egg and womb for conception of the child of a man who is not her husband? What psychological effects will there be years from now on parents, children, donors, and doctors? These questions must be answered before science is given a license to continue its program of artificial insemination.[28]

Selective Breeding

Early in the spring of 1980, the Los Angeles *Times* reported that seventy-four-year-old Robert K. Graham, a wealthy California businessman, had established an exclusive sperm bank for Nobel Prize winners. It was called the Hermann J. Muller Repository for Germinal Choice, named after a late friend of Graham and a Nobel Prize winner in physiology. The idea was really quite simple: several years ago Graham began writing to Nobel laureates asking for sperm donations; thus far five are known to have complied.

The sperm is frozen and stored in his subterranean sperm bank built on a ten-acre estate in Escondido, California. Then Graham, a member of Mensa (a group of 33,000 people with very high IQ's), announced last summer in the Mensa *Bulletin* that he was looking for bright women, under thirty-five and preferably married to sterile men, who would volunteer to become impregnated with Nobel sperm. Dozens of women applied.

In his dramatic article in *Moral Majority Report* of May 26, 1980, Dr. Woodrow Michael Kroll states: "To think that by engineering the genetic makeup of a human being through selective conception and thus producing more 'desirable' or 'superior' people presumes that we have more intelligence than God in deciding what kind of human beings are desired and what kind are not." Rev. Richard McCormick, head of Georgetown University's Kennedy Institute for Ethics, which specializes in biomedical issues, sarcastically notes that Graham's procedure fosters a "stud farming mentality in human procreation" and "makes a consumer item out of the child."[29]

It is obvious that if Graham's sperm bank is allowed to continue, he will foster an attitude that technical intelligence is a quality to be preferred over moral sensitivity. When technology becomes god and engineered intelligence takes precedence over traditional moral and family values, we will know that "future shock" has become a present reality.

Genetic Engineering

On June 16, 1980, the U. S. Supreme Court ruled that life created in a laboratory may be patented just like any other product. A controversy centered around the General Electric microbiologist who "manufactured" a new oil-eating bacteria to be used to clean up oil spills. However, the precedent set by the decision put genetic engineering into the realm of commercial patents related to everything from cloning to prefabricated human forms.

This and other new scientific advances arise out of research into recombinant DNA. A laboratory technique discovered in 1973, recombinant DNA is a kind of biological sewing-machine technique that takes genes from one organism and splices them into the genes of another. Genes consist of strands of the chemical deoxyribonucleic acid (DNA), which dictates what the characteristics of a cell will be. By splicing genetic material together from unrelated organisms, microbiologists are actually "manufacturing" new life forms.

Jeremy Rifkin, co-author of the book *Who Should Play God?*, appeals to the Church: "Frankly, I am shocked at the lack of response up to now even within the Judeo-Christian community. . . . If the church does not have the wherewithal to come out in opposition to the genetic age, then it seems to me that it's time to admit, once and for all, that Christianity has become little more than a permanent apologist for the secular order."[30]

Euthanasia (Mercy Killing)

The nationally known pediatric surgeon and now Surgeon General designee, Dr. Everett Koop, has observed: "The decision of the Supreme Court in favor of abortion on demand literally hands over the decision on the survival of one person's life to another person. All of the economic, social, emotional, and compassionate arguments that are used in favor of abortion very suddenly become the arguments for euthanasia."[31]

Even in the cases of those massively defective, miserably infirm, or terminally ill, I find no biblical justification or encouragement for euthanasia. God supremely values every life. Christ died for every life. Healing and restoration are potential for every life. We must face death with confident faith in a commitment to the utter sanctity of life.

Euthanasia will certainly be one of the most hotly contested ethical issues of the eighties. In his book *Death Before Birth*, Dr. Harold O. J. Brown argues that the wave of abortions in the seventies will mature into a wave of euthanasia in the eighties.[32] He is undoubtedly correct. How will Christian America react? Will we passively acquiese as well-meaning, misguided, or morally devoid medicine allows expedience to overrule the sanctity of life? When the sanctity of life is sacrificed on the altar of expense or expedience, the result is euthanasia.

POLITICAL ISSUES

The structure of American society makes political issues out of moral and ethical issues. We are not and dare not be naïve Americanistic chauvinists. America is not the Kingdom of God. The United States is not a perfect nation, but it is without a doubt the greatest and most influential nation in the world. We have the people and the resources to evangelize the world in our generation. In Scripture we are told to pray for peace that we might be free to live godly lives and spread the Gospel of Christ in society (1 Tim. 2:1–4).

National Defense

If ever there was a time for a strong national defense, it is today. While communism has been spreading around the globe, the United States has been declining in its military power for the last fifteen years. We have been surrendering our rights and sovereignty by this program of military disarmament. The final step of this direction is the ultimate surrender of our freedoms and liberties.

America is in serious trouble today. It has lost its economic and military prominence among the nations of the world. Exercising influence and leadership from this weakened position is an exercise in futility. Our leaders are finally realizing what many have tried to state for years: that the Soviets are liars and cheaters, and that they are determined to conquer our free country and to infiltrate the American people with godless communism. The security of our country is at stake. The balance of world power is at stake. We must return to a strong program of national defense.

General Lewis Walt, assistant commandant of the Marine Corps from 1968 to 1971, said in his recent book *The Eleventh Hour:* "The United States has been brought, by its own civilian leaders, to a position of military inferiority to the Soviet Union. At this moment, you and your loved ones stand exposed to physical destruction. The option of whether you shall live or die rests primarily with the hardened men who occupy the Kremlin. . . . No generation of Americans has ever been so recklessly placed at the mercy of so pitiless and powerful an enemy."[33]

General Walt outlines his belief that in a short time the Soviet Union may force the United States into a decision of surrender, a handing over of the American people to "an oligarchy of tyrants whose viciousness and brutality have no match in the long, bloody history of man's cruelty. . . . Today the U.S. has no civil-defense program, no antiballistic missiles, and no appreciable defense against even a bomber attack. This stripping of our defense forces has been a deliberate policy move of our civilian defense officials."[34]

We must continue to insist that our new government officials provide a strong national defense for our people. Certainly I believe that God can sovereignly overrule the weapons of human warfare. But what Christian parent would refuse an inoculation for his children during a widespread epidemic? Who would jump out of an airplane without a parachute and pray for the angels to deliver him? Jesus told us not to "tempt" God by placing ourselves recklessly in a position of jeopardy and expecting God to bail us out (Matt. 4:6–7).

Communist Threat

The goal of international communism has never changed. In 1973, speaking to a meeting in Prague, Czechoslovakia, Leonid Brezhnev stated: "We are achieving with détente what our predecessors have been unable to achieve with the mailed fist. . . . Trust us, comrades, for by 1985, as a consequence of what we are now achieving with détente, we will have achieved most of our objectives in Western Europe. We will have consolidated our position. We will have improved our economy. And a decisive shift in the correlation of forces will be such that, come 1985, we will be able to exert our will wherever we need to."[35]

In 1977 *The Communist Daily World* recorded Y. Krasin quoting Breshnev as saying, "Détente does not in the slightest abolish or alter the laws of the class struggle. International détente and the class struggle are two sides, two organically interconnected aspects of the dialectics of social progress in the epic of transition from capitalism to socialism." Vietnam, Laos, Cambodia, Mozambique, Angola, South-West Africa, Zimbabwe, Ethiopia, and Afghanistan are constant reminders of the ultimate objective of communism.

The communist takeover of other nations has always followed a particular agenda. Churches are shut down, preachers are killed or imprisoned, and Bibles are taken away from the people. The communists are expert deceivers. There are little churches in Moscow that serve as window dressing to fool people to the real intentions of communists. There is in the Soviet Union today no religious freedom, no freedom of speech, no freedom of the press. In his speech to the AFL-CIO on July 9, 1975, Russian exile Alexander Solzhenitsyn stated: "The communist ideology is to destroy your society. That has been their aim for 125 years and has never changed; only the methods have changed. . . . The primary, the eternal concept is humanity. And communism is antihumanity."[36]

Our founding fathers shed their blood to give us freedom from tyranny and we who have so long enjoyed its benefits must now demand freedom from apathy. We must be willing to defend the free nations of the world which are threatened by communism: Taiwan, South Korea, South Africa, and our European allies.

State of Israel

We believe that God in Genesis 12:1-3, very clearly promised a blessing for those who bless Israel and a curse for those who curse Israel. I take that as literally as I take John 3:16 in the New Testament.

To stand against Israel is to stand against God. We believe that. I love the Jew because God loves the Jew. As a follower of God, I am under an obligation to love as he loves. My life is committed to a number of priorities, and one of them is to promote, protect, and stand alongside the Jewish people. History and Scripture prove that God deals with nations in relation to how they deal with Israel. My deep conviction is that America will not remain a free nation unless we defend the freedom of Israel. We must proclaim this from our church pulpits as ministers, as well as in our daily lives as private citizens with a Christian obligation to the Jewish people.

The land and people of Israel are important because, as members of the human family, they have the right to exist. Israel's battle is not one for superiority or a jockeying for position but rather one of survival. We believe that Genesis 15 sets the boundaries of Israel and supports its claim to the land. We do not condone unrighteous acts by Israelis, Arabs, or any other people. But we do believe that the Jews have the historical, theological, and legal right to the land called Israel.

Probably the most important reason for Israel's survival and for Christians' support is that Our Savior came from a Jewish family and the Lord Jesus Christ was a Jew. This demands of all of us a warm and a gracious spirit toward the Jewish people. We received our Bible—Old and New Testaments—from Jewish writers. The Oracles of God were transmitted to us by the Jewish people, and so we owe a great deal to Israel. Any who do not support Israel are inviting the judgment of God upon themselves. I think the Adolf Hitlers, all the various leaders of the nations who through the centuries have persecuted the Jew, stand as mute testimony to the fact that God keeps His word to punish those who punish the Jews.

I am not against Arabs or Palestinians. I believe in their right to exist in peace. But I do not believe in the efforts of the P.L.O. to exterminate the Jews and drive Israel into the sea. The majority of Americans are deeply and sincerely concerned about the well-being of Israel. Israel has a right to exist among the nations of the world. It has been persecuted long enough. We must defend it at all costs while maintaining an equal concern for the Arab nations.

RELIGIOUS ISSUES

As a minister of the Gospel, I am convinced that our greatest national issues are spiritual in nature. A national poll revealed that 84 percent of all Americans claim they believe the Bible, but only 11 percent read it regularly. We are a people of promises, intentions, and beliefs, but all too often we are not practical producers of righteousness. We have run into our church-fortresses to sing the praises of God, only to return to society as "secret agents" for Christ. It is time for Christians to come out of their ecclesiastical closets. It is time for us to stand up and be counted. We can have a better America, and we can have it now!

National Revival

We need a genuine revival to revitalize our churches. We need a revival of national repentance because of our self-indulgent sins. We need a revival of old-fashioned prayer. We need to get down on our faces before the God who holds this nation in the balance of His judgment. We need to act like the Christians we claim to be!

We cannot expect America to change until we have changed. We must reject pride in ourselves and our positions. Evangelical Christians have a tendency to pride themselves on their intelligent comprehension and defense of the faith. Fundamentalists tend to pride themselves on their strong, uncompromising stand for the faith. We must have both! We must stop polarizing each other by constant and unnecessary attacks on "straw men." All Evangelicals are not "Judas-goat compromisers ready to sell their souls for academic acceptability." By the same token, as Don Boys put it in his recent article in *The Sword of the Lord,* not all Fundamentalists feel that "a man must be a fundamentalist if he believes: hair on top of the ears is worldly; slacks are sinful; TV is forbidden; a bus ministry is absolutely essential; no mixed swimming; no Sunday School literature; and the King James Bible as the only reliable text."[37]

America needs the impact of a genuine spiritual revival led by Bible-believing pastors, whatever their ecclesiastical labels. Our people are more cooperative than we pastors are. My extensive travels have convinced me that the members of conservative churches are not as narrow as their pastors, and the members of more liberal churches are much more conservative than their leaders. In reality, the Bible-believing church members of America are very close to one another theologically. They believe the Bible is the Word of God; they believe in heaven, in hell, and in life after death. They believe that Jesus died for our sins, rose from the dead, and is coming again. They are the "bread and butter" Middle Americans who are holding this country together.

As pastors, we have an obligation to God and to His people to lead them according to the truths of Scripture. America is ripe for revival for the first time in this century. We cannot dissipate our efforts by chasing down "rabbit trails." As Fundamentalists, we must stand strong on biblical truth. But we must also stand together. The Apostle Paul urges us in Ephesians 4:3 that we should endeavor "to keep the unity of the Spirit in the bond of peace." We must do all we can to maintain a united testimony to the unsaved world without compromising on biblical principles.

All too often we conservatives make doctrines out of our traditions much as the Pharisees did in Jesus' day. We take our preferences and preach them as if they were the Gospel itself. In fact, sometimes we preach them to the neglect of preaching the Gospel. As B. R. Lakin has often said, "If you take away long hair, short skirts, cigarettes, and the Masons . . . some fellows wouldn't know what to preach on!" Let us be known for what we are for, not just for what we are against. You can be against everything and still accomplish nothing for God.

Church Planting

We not only need a sin-cleansing and a life-changing revival in our churches, but we need to establish ten thousand to twenty thousand new churches in North America by the end of this century. Our school alone has set a goal of training five thousand new pastors to plant five thousand new churches in the next twenty years.

Many existing churches are cold and dead. There is no real spiritual life in them. Many have turned a deaf ear to the Gospel in favor of social renewal without Christ. Their leadership is bound to an ecclesiastical structure that is as spiritually vibrant as an icicle. I am afraid this is the case with most of the churches affiliated with the National Council of Churches. It is certainly true of their national leadership. The NCC has supported every kind of left-wing social program imaginable. In most cases, its leaders do not really speak for their people. Many church members are deeply disturbed about the direction their churches are taking. Some denominations have gone so far as to legitimatize and officiate homosexual marriages and to ordain homosexual clergy.

Unfortunately, many of our conservative churches represent little more than dead orthodoxy. They believe the right things but their practical evangelism is nil. Some churches are spending as much as $100,000 per convert! They have programs, budgets, and conferences, but they have very limited vision. They have sacrificed the breadth of their ministry for depth, and in reality have neither. When a church is not aggressively winning people to Christ, it will become introspective and introverted until it is isolated from any real influence in the community. In time it will virtually die. I believe we can and must have solid Bible teaching and preaching churches coupled with positive and aggressive evangelism.

Church planting must be a major priority on our agenda for the eighties. We must establish thousands of new Bible-believing churches committed to practical evangelism and political activism. Our goal at Liberty Baptist College is to train pastors who can effectively explain the Scriptures, preach the word with power and conviction, and lead their congregations as sincere men of God. We must turn America around at the grass-roots, local-church level.

Spiritual living must be channeled into positive church growth in the decade ahead.

Christian Education

There are now well over eighteen thousand fundamental Christian and evangelical schools in America. Three new schools are being established every day! The Christian school movement is the movement of the future. We are training a veritable "army" of Christian leaders for the next generation. We must not destroy our testimony to and influence on the public schools. There are thousands of Christian teachers and millions of Christian students in our public schools. The secular school will always have a place in our society, but not to the exclusion of the Christian school.

Private Christian schools are relatively small in enrollment compared to the public schools, but they are beginning to emerge as a valid part of the American educational system. We must build as many new schools as we do new churches. We must therefore train thousands of Christian school teachers who are spiritually and academically equipped to teach our children. We must pass on the heritage of a free America to the next generation.

Our unique philosophy of education rests upon our belief that the Bible is the authentic and reliable guide and authority for all areas of life. Our view is based on the conviction that knowledge of Christ is essential to the physical, mental, and social aspects of our faith and practice. It emphasizes a proper relationship among the family, the church, and the school. Our goal should be to produce a new generation of thousands of young people who will make solid citizens for America's future. We need a spiritual army of young people who are pro-life, pro-moral, and pro-American. We need to train a generation of young people who can carry this nation into the twenty-first century with dynamic Christian leadership.

AN APPEAL TO FUNDAMENTALISTS

I have always made it clear that I am a Fundamentalist—big F! A Fundamentalist is one who believes the Bible to be verbally in-

spired by the Holy Spirit and therefore inerrant and absolutely infallible. True Fundamentalists believe in the deity of Jesus Christ.
They readily accept His virgin birth, sinless life, and vicarious
death. They believe in His literal resurrection, His ascension into
heaven, and His second coming. A Fundamentalist believes in
evangelism and discipleship through the local church as the proper
fulfillment of the Great Commission of our Lord.

I am also a separatist. We practice separatism from the world
and all of its entanglements. We refuse to conform to the standards
of a sinful society. We practice personal separation as well as ecclesiastical separation. Most of us are "independents" in our associations. We are at our best when we are free from hierarchical structures that would tie us down to denominational mediocrity. We are
our own people. We are not intimidated by academic degrees or
ecclesiastical positions. We do our own thinking, and we do not
care what liberals think about anything!

However, we are not without our weaknesses. We tend to be
negative and pessimistic. For too many years now, we have been
sitting back waiting for apostasy to take over at any moment, and
have nearly let the country go down the drain. We have been irresponsible as Christian citizens. We have almost totally avoided the
political process and the social life of our country. We have
neglected reaching the whole person for the cause of Christ. We
have blasted the Liberals and derided the Evangelicals for their
feeble attempts at the social application of the Gospel, while doing
almost nothing ourselves.

We love to extol the virtues of our fidelity to the faith. We
pride ourselves that we are not as others who have compromised.
Yet our lack of capacity for honest self-criticism has often left us
hiding behind our honorary degrees while attacking the value of
education. Our emphasis on belonging to the right group causes us
at times to overlook our own sins. We have just as many failures in
our ranks as do the Evangelicals—maybe more. We cannot be
blinded by our tendency to use our people to build our churches,
instead of using our churches to build our people.

In spite of our weaknesses, we have much to offer our Evangelical brethren that they need. We preach the Bible with authority
and conviction. Where they hesitate and equivocate, we loudly
thunder: "Thus saith the Lord!" Where they are overly theoretical

and impractically idealistic, we have become practical evangelists and experts at church growth. While the Evangelicals are always defining and redefining, we are out building great churches to the glory of God. We are experts at preaching the Gospel to the lost. We have the highest percentage of converts and the fastest-growing churches in America.

In a similar "Agenda for the 1980s" Evangelical spokesman Billy Graham appealed to pastors for three things that we Fundamentalists need:[88]

1. Integrity of Life
2. Compassion
3. Vision

If we are going to reach millions of Americans with the Gospel in our lifetime, we must live the message we proclaim. Personal integrity is a must in our own lives, in our families, in our churches, and in our communities. While we stand for the truth, we must also have genuine compassion for a lost world in need of our Savior. Our mission is to see, not how many people we can hate, but how many we can love for Christ's sake. Further, we must extend our vision to evangelize the world in our lifetime. We must stop being so negative and critical of everyone who is trying to reach people with the Gospel but does not wear our label. We must realize that it is going to take our full commitment to the task of evangelism, discipleship, and church-planting to do the job in our generation. The Lord has set before us an open door of opportunity, and we must use it to His glory.

An Appeal to Evangelicals

The Evangelical Movement has been a vital part of this country for two centuries. Evangelical pastors have provided mature and stable leadership for the churches of America. They have demonstrated the love of Christ to their congregations and have been expositors and defenders of the Christian faith. Where others have been extreme, they have remained balanced. They have attempted to apply the truth of the Gospel to the needs of society. In general, the Evangelical Movement has been faithful to the fundamental doctrines of the Christian faith.

In reality, there is little difference theologically between Fundamentalists and Evangelicals. We both hold to a strong belief in the inspiration and inerrancy of the Bible. We hold to the deity of Christ and to the necessity of personal salvation. Though Evangelicalism tends to be tolerant of varying viewpoints, the vast majority of evangelical pastors tell me that they are concerned about the drift of so-called Young Evangelicals to the left. They do not like the current trend within the movement, which is getting dangerously close to moderate Liberalism.

The lines are not clearly drawn today among Evangelicals. The movement is so broad that it at times takes in everything from Bible churches to Charismatic Catholics. Theologically it extends from Josh McDowell to Helmut Thielicke. Philosophically, it includes strong inerrancy defenders such as Norman Geisler and John W. Montgomery. It has provided the conservative movement in general with such able social critics as Harold O. J. Brown. But at the same time it unfortunately includes some who are ready to deny their fundamentalist heritage and exchange their theological birthright for a mess of socioacademic pottage!

We appeal to our evangelical brethren to stand with us for the truth of the Gospel in this hour when America needs us most. Stop looking down your theological and ecclesiastical noses at your fundamentalist brethren. As the English theologian James Barr has already pointed out, non-Evangelicals view Evangelicals and Fundamentalists alike anyhow. We have so much in common. Only the radicals among us (to the left and to the right) divide us. I say it is time we denied the "lunatic fringe" of our movements and worked for a great conservative crusade to turn America back to God. We do not need an organic unity. Such is not necessary in order to achieve a mutual appreciation and respect.

We appeal to you to reacknowledge your fundamentalist roots. Stop being intimidated by what others think. Stop worrying about academic credibility and social acceptability. If Evangelicals have one glaring weakness, it is that you are too concerned what the world thinks about you. You are hesitant to speak up on vital issues for fear of what the intellectual elite may think. Let them think what they wish. They have been wrong before, and they will be wrong again!

In his monumental book *Earnestly Contending for the Faith,* the late John R. Rice said:

> The greatest preachers, the greatest soul winners through the ages have earnestly contended for the faith. So did Luther and Calvin and Zwingli and Savonarola and Huss. The persecution, the slander and the blood of martyrs is their witness. Whitefield in England and America, T. DeWitt Talmage in Brooklyn, I. M. Haldeman and John Roach Straton in New York City, W. B. Riley in Minneapolis, Mark Matthews in Seattle, Bob Shuler in Los Angeles, Dr. R. G. Lee in Memphis, Criswell in Dallas, and many other faithful leaders in Christendom have earnestly contended for the faith as the Scripture commands a Christian to do.[39]

Evangelicals need to reaffirm the foundation. Come back to the fundamentals of the Christian faith and stand firm on that which is essential. Throw down the anchor of truth and stop drifting with every new wave of religious fad that comes along. Stop trying to accommodate the Gospel to the pitiful philosophies of unregenerate humankind. You have the truth, and the truth shall set you free.

You talk much of love, but often you have only words of bitter contempt for those of us who call ourselves Fundamentalists. Do not be embarrassed because we believe the same things you do. Acknowledge us. Accept us as Bible-believing brethren who love the same Christ you love. Let us work to reach the world for Christ.

We conservative Fundamentalists and Evangelicals can be used of God to bring about a great revival of true Christianity in America and the world in our lifetime.

NOTES

CHAPTER 1

1. British theologian James Barr has said that Fundamentalism will last at least another five hundred years, in *Fundamentalism* (Philadelphia: Westminster Press, 1977), to which, in a review of Barr, Southern Baptist historian E. Glenn Hinson remarked: "May God Forbid!" *Review and Expositor* 75:4 (Fall 1978), p. 635.

2. Martin E. Marty, "Fundamentalism Reborn," *Saturday Review* (May 1980), p. 38. Marty fails to distinguish properly between the fanatic "fundamentalism" of Iran with the Ayatollah and the growing Christian movement in America. He implies that all the militant religious movements of the world share a common denominator: fanaticism. He foresees the continued growth of these movements because "through such movements around the world they seek to ward off the devils, the shahs abroad, or the humanists at home." This may be clever editorializing, but it is certainly not respectable scholarship!

3. Ibid.

4. "A Tide of Born-Again Politics," *Newsweek* (Sept. 15, 1980), p. 36. Media articles have included: "The Electric Church," *The Wall Street Journal* (May 19, 1978); "Thunder on the Right: An Unholy War Breaks Out Over Politics," *People* (Oct. 13, 1980); "Where Is Jerry Falwell Going?" *Eternity* (July 1980); "Preachers in Politics," *U.S. News and World Report* (Sept. 15, 1980); "Politics from the Pulpit," *Time* (Oct. 13, 1980); "The Power of the Christian Right," *Family Weekly* (Oct. 26, 1980); and "Jerry Falwell's Marching Christians," *Saturday Evening Post* (Dec. 1980).

5. See the extensive study by James Barr, *Fundamentalism*, p. 2. His research is massive but confined almost totally to British Evangelicalism

(which American Fundamentalists do not accept as real Fundamentalism). His study is almost completely ignorant of the American fundamentalist movement and shows very little understanding of it. Barr does, however, correctly observe that there is ultimately very little difference theologically between Fundamentalists and Evangelicals, since their theology reduces down to biblical inerrancy in either case. Notice his clever and poignant critical analysis of B. Ramm, where he states: "Much good fun can be had from reading Ramm," p. 95.

6. Cf. E. J. Carnell, *The Case for Biblical Christianity* (Grand Rapids: Eerdmans, 1969), pp. 40–47. This posthumous collection of essays, edited by R. H. Nash, includes "Orthodoxy: Cultic vs. Classical," which originally appeared in the March 30, 1960, issue of *Christian Century*. In it the Fuller Theological Seminary president criticized Fundamentalism of a kind of mentality that "holds with obscurantism to the verbal inspiration and inerrancy of the Holy Scriptures." The same concept is expressed by B. Ramm in *A Handbook of Contemporary Theology* (Grand Rapids: Eerdmans, 1966). G. K. Clabaugh goes so far as to associate Fundamentalists with Nazis in *Thunder on the Right: The Protestant Fundamentalists* (Chicago: Nelson-Hall, 1974), p. xvii. He labels the radical right as "Fundarists" and likens them to Hitler! His study is almost completely limited to Carl McIntire and Billy James Hargis. The reader is referred to the Preface for the author's self-confessed hostility brought on by the reaction of an irate parent during his early teaching days.

7. See E. R. Sandeen, *The Roots of Fundamentalism: British and American Millenarianism 1800–1930* (Chicago: University of Chicago Press, 1970). While his careful scholarship and extensively annotated bibliographies are to be commended, Sandeen's reductionistic reasoning that Fundamentalism can be explained totally in light of nineteenth-century Millenarianism must be emphatically rejected. Although this certainly was an influence in the evangelical-fundamentalist ideology, the movement itself resulted from a much wider commitment to the infallibility of the Scriptures: cf. the chart on the various topical articles appearing in the original four-volume *Fundamentals* in M. L. Rudnick, *Fundamentalism and the Missouri Synod* (St. Louis: Concordia, 1966), pp. 40–41. Of the ninety-four total articles, only three were on the Second Coming. For a more careful study, see T. P. Weber, *Living in the Shadow of the Second Coming: American Premillennialism 1875–1925* (New York: Oxford University Press, 1979).

8. D. B. Stevick, *Beyond Fundamentalism* (Richmond, Va.: John Knox Press, 1964), p. 19. His assessments make extremely interesting reading through the anticipatory glee of his fictitious Spermologos over the (then) newly emerging neo-Fundamentalism. Quite reactionary, though, Stevick's character acts like an emancipated Amish boy who just traded in his buggy for a bicycle!

9. R. A. Torrey et al., *The Fundamentals: A Testimony to the Truth* (Los Angeles: B.I.O.L.A., 1917; reprinted Grand Rapids: Baker Book House, 1970), p. 5.

10. Rudnick, *Fundamentalism and the Missouri Synod*, pp. 40–41.

11. G. Marsden, "Fundamentalism as an American Phenomenon: A Comparison with English Evangelicalism," in *Church History* 46 (June 1977), p. 215. His excellent article (pp. 215–32) should be consulted *in toto*. He correctly observes that there was no exact British counterpart to the militancy of the American Fundamentalists, noting the tolerance of J. C. Ryle and James Orr, as well as of the British Keswick Movement in general.

12. Ibid., pp. 215–16. See also his "From Fundamentalism to Evangelicalism: An Historical Analysis," in D. F. Wells and J. D. Woodbridge, eds., *The Evangelicals* (Grand Rapids: Baker Book House, 1977), pp. 142–62, and his new book *Fundamentalism and American Culture* (New York: Oxford University Press, 1981). His careful scholarship and incisive evaluations are indispensable to a proper understanding of Fundamentalism in America.

13. See the extensive evaluation by C. Van Til, *The New Modernism: An Appraisal of the Theology of Barth and Brunner* (Philadelphia: Presbyterian and Reformed, 1946; rev. 1972). For original sources on the development from Liberalism to neo-orthodoxy, see W. R. Hutchison, ed., *American Protestant Thought* (New York: Harper & Row, 1968).

14. J. G. Machen, *Christianity and Liberalism* (New York: Macmillan, 1923). This book became the "Fundamentalist Manifesto" and represents the best scholarship of the day against Modernism. It has often been pointed out that the Modernists never adequately answered this book.

15. Ibid., p. 71. This statement appears in his defense of verbal inspiration in the light of historical verification.

16. This can readily be seen in the radical Liberals such as Harvey Cox, in his works *The Secular City* (New York: Macmillian, 1965); *The Feast of Fools* (Cambridge, Mass.: Harvard University Press, 1969); and *The Seduction of the Spirit* (New York: Simon & Schuster, 1973). In these he weaves theology (of sorts) with an autobiography of his secularized pilgrimage away from the tribal village of Malvern to the secular city, to the house of intellect, and on to the nudist baths at Esalen.

17. See J. Barr, Foreword to the American Edition, *Fundamentalism*, pp. vi, vii. Also Chap. 1, "What Is Fundamentalism?" (pp. 1–11).

18. On the variation of five to fourteen points of Fundamentalism, see S. G. Cole, *The History of Fundamentalism* (New York: Richard R. Smith, 1931), pp. 52–64; Sandeen, *The Roots of Fundamentalism*, pp. 273–77; and S. E. Ahlstrom, *A Religious History of the American People* (New Haven: Yale University Press, 1972), pp. 345–46.

19. This argument is also developed by Harold Lindsell, *The Battle for the Bible* (Grand Rapids: Zondervan, 1976), pp. 17–40. He raises strong objections to the drift away from inerrancy by left-wing Evangelicals, noting that "Fundamentalists and Evangelicals (both of whom have been traditionally committed to an infallible or inerrant Scripture) have been long noted for their propagation and defense of an infallible Bible" (p. 20). Apologetic expositions of biblical inerrancy are numerous: S. Custer, *Does Inspiration Demand Inerrancy?* (Philadelphia: Presbyterian and Reformed, n.d.); N. Geisler, ed., *Inerrancy* (Grand Rapids: Zondervan, 1979); J. Gerstner, *A Bible Inerrancy Primer* (Philadelphia: Presbyterian and Reformed, 1965); C. Henry, ed., *Revelation and the Bible* (Grand Rapids: Baker Book House, 1958), and *God, Revelation and Authority*, 4 vols. (Waco: Word Books, 1976); J. W. Montgomery, ed., *God's Inerrant Word* (Minneapolis: Bethany Fellowship, 1974); J. I. Packer, *Fundamentalism and the Word of God* (Grand Rapids: Eerdmans, 1958); C. Pinnock, *Biblical Revelation* (Chicago: Moody Press, 1971), and *A Defense of Biblical Infallibility* (Philadelphia: Presbyterian and Reformed, 1975); J. R. Rice, *The Bible: Our God-breathed Book* (Murfreesboro, Tenn.: Sword of the Lord, 1969); J. Walvoord, ed., *Inspiration and Interpretation* (Grand Rapids: Eerdmans, 1957); E. J. Young, *Thy Word is Truth* (Grand Rapids: Eerdmans, 1963). For departures, see D. M. Beegle, *Scripture, Tradition, and Infallibility* (Grand Rapids: Eerdmans, 1973), and J. Rogers, ed., *Biblical Authority* (Waco: Word Books, 1977). The latter is an attempted response to Lindsell. G. T. Sheppard of Union Theological Seminary states, however: "Despite all of [David] Hubbard's argument to the contrary," there is in practice little distinction between his brand of "evangelical" and "neoorthodox": in "Biblical Hermeneutics: The Academic Language of Evangelical Identity," *Union Quarterly Review* 32 (Winter 1977), p. 91.

20. Young, *Thy Word Is Truth*, states: "If the Bible is not a trustworthy witness of its own character, we have no assurance that our Christian faith is founded upon Truth" (p. 30). On p. 191 he adds: "It is equally true that if we reject this foundational presupposition of Christianity, we shall arrive at results which are hostile to supernatural Christianity. If one begins with the presuppositions of unbelief, he will end with unbelief's conclusion."

21. R. P. Lightner, *Neoevangelicalism Today* (Schaumburg, Ill.: Regular Baptist Press, 1978), p. 183. His perceptive revision of his earlier work provides an excellent study of the origin of the Fundamentalist movement. Also see his *The Saviour and the Scriptures: A Case for Biblical Inerrancy* (Grand Rapids: Baker Book House, 1978).

22. See the excellent and definitive work of W. M. Smith, *The Supernaturalness of Christ* (Boston: W. A. Wilde, 1940). He defends the deity of Christ from His sinless and supernatural life.

23. Moorehead was also one of the editors of the original *Scofield Reference Bible*. His article appears in *The Fundamentals*, Vol. 2 (1917), pp. 61–79.

24. Warfield, "The Deity of Christ," in *The Fundamentals*, Vol. 2 (1917), pp. 239–46. See also his extensive *The Person and Work of Christ* (Philadelphia: Presbyterian and Reformed, reprinted rev. ed. 1950).

25. J. Orr, "The Virgin Birth of Christ," in *The Fundamentals*, Vol. 2 (1917), pp. 247–60; quotation from p. 259. On the theological significance of the virgin birth, see R. Gromacki, *The Virgin Birth: Doctrine of Deity* (Nashville: Thomas Nelson, 1974), and E. Hindson, *Isaiah's Immanuel* (Philadelphia: Presbyterian and Reformed, 1978); also the classic work by J. G. Machen, *The Virgin Birth* (New York: Harper & Row, 1930).

26. In light of the current emphasis on the doctrine of inspiration, very little has been written recently on the atonement. See James Denny, *The Death of Christ* (London: Hodder & Stoughton, 1909); Leon Morris, *The Apostolic Preaching of the Cross* (Grand Rapids: Eerdmans, 1960) and *The Cross in the New Testament* (Grand Rapids: Eerdmans, 1965). On the continued controversy, see F. Humphreys, *The Death of Christ* (Nashville: Broadman, 1978), and D. F. Wells, *The Search for Salvation* (Downers Grove, Ill.: Inter-Varsity Press, 1978).

27. Cf. Luke 24:36–43 and John 20:20–29. On the significance of the resurrection, see the popular work of J. McDowell, *Evidence That Demands a Verdict* (Arrowhead Springs, Calif.: Campus Crusade, 1972); and E. H. Day, *On the Evidence for the Resurrection* (London: S.P.C.K., 1906); F. Morrison, *Who Moved the Stone?* (London: Faber & Faber, 1967); W. J. Sparrow-Simpson, *The Resurrection and the Christian Faith* (Grand Rapids: Zondervan, 1968; reprint of 1911 ed.); M. C. Tenney, *The Reality of the Resurrection* (New York: Harper & Row, 1963).

28. On the issues related to the doctrine of the second coming, see the national best seller by Hal Lindsay, *The Late Great Planet Earth* (Grand Rapids: Zondervan, 1970), and H. Lindsell, *The Gathering Storm* (Wheaton, Ill.: Tyndale House, 1980); S. Travis, *The Jesus Hope* (Downers Grove, Ill.: Inter-Varsity Press, 1974); J. Walvoord, *The Blessed Hope and the Tribulation* (Grand Rapids: Zondervan, 1976).

29. G. Gallup, Jr., and D. Poling, *The Search for America's Faith* (Nashville: Abingdon, 1980), pp. 15–22. This book is a valuable assessment of the current religious climate in America. It shows without a doubt that there is a definite swing back toward strongly conservative religious beliefs.

30. Ibid., pp. 51 ff.

31. Larry Christenson and Tim La Haye alone have sold over 2 million books each! Their titles include: Christenson, *The Christian Family* (Minneapolis: Bethany Fellowship, 1970) and *The Christian Couple* (Minneapolis: Bethany Fellowship, 1977); La Haye, *How to Be Happy Though Married* (Wheaton, Ill.: Tyndale House, 1969); *Spirit-Controlled Family Living* (Old Tappan, N.J.: Revell, 1978); *The Act of Marriage* (Grand Rapids: Zondervan, 1976).

32. Gallup and Poling, *The Search for America's Faith*, pp. 134–38.

33. Ibid., pp. 10–11.

34. "The Christianity Today–Gallup Poll: An Overview," *Christianity Today* (Dec. 21, 1979), pp. 13 ff. This was followed by a year-long series of articles related to various facets of the poll.

35. P. Wagner, "Aiming at Church Growth in the Eighties," *Christianity Today* 24:20 (Nov. 21, 1980), p. 26. Wagner predicts that the 1980s will be a decade of renewed church growth. For further comparison of denominational church growth versus fundamentalist church growth, see E. Towns, *Is the Day of the Denomination Dead?* (Nashville: Thomas Nelson, 1973), and D. M. Kelley, *Why Conservative Churches are Growing* (New York: Harper & Row, 1972).

36. Baptist Bible Fellowship International Directory, Box 191, Springfield, Mo. 65801 (1980).

37. Wagner, "Aiming at Church Growth," p. 27.

38. E. Towns, *The Ten Largest Sunday Schools and What Makes Them Grow* (Grand Rapids: Baker Book House, 1969), pp. 11 ff. This book hit the fundamentalist church scene like a blockbuster. It was widely read, quoted, and heeded by pastors everywhere. It may honestly be said that this book urged on church growth among Fundamentalists, who increased by more than 1 million members in ten years.

39. Statistics prepared for Towns's forthcoming book *The Complete Book of Church Growth* (Wheaton, Ill.: Tyndale House, 1981).

40. E. Towns, *Is the Day of the Denomination Dead?*, p. 25. This highly controversial and debatable book is still asking the questions that the denominations do not want to answer.

41. Ben Armstrong, *The Electric Church* (Nashville: Thomas Nelson, 1979), pp. 7–18. This is a comprehensive study of the current state of religious broadcasting. Armstrong is executive director of National Religious Broadcasters and an expert on the concerns of religious broadcasting. See his extensive statistical tabulations on Christian broadcasting.

42. See statistics in T. Bisset, "Religious Broadcasting: Assessing the State of the Art," in *Christianity Today* (Dec. 12, 1980), pp. 28–31. He

lists 1979 TV income for the broadcasters as: Oral Roberts, $60 million; Pat Robertson, $58 million; Jim Bakker, $51 million; Jerry Falwell, $50 million; Billy Graham, $30 million; Rex Humbard, $25 million; Robert Schuller, $16 million.

43. "Electric Church," *The Wall Street Journal* (May 19, 1978). His clever expression immediately caught on and now is the popular term for religious broadcasting. His article deals mainly with the broadcasting ministry of Jerry Falwell.

44. Ben Armstrong, *Religious Broadcasting Sourcebook* (Morristown, N.J.: National Religious Broadcasters, 1978), p. N-2.

45. This statement quoted from the brochure, "Now, There's an Organization for Christian Student Personnel Professionals" (Don Boender, President, Calvin College, Grand Rapids, Mich. 49506). While all the member schools do not necessarily consider themselves Fundamentalists per se, they agree to the strong doctrinal statement of the organization.

46. See its manual for Christian schools, edited by Paul A. Kienel, *The Philosophy of Christian School Education* (Whittier, Calif.: A.C.S.I., 1978). In addition it has produced numerous books, tapes, and materials on Christian schools.

47. R. Godwin, Ph. D. (Florida State), is now executive vice-president of Moral Majority and was formerly associated with the nation's largest Christian school, Pensacola Christian Schools, in Pensacola, Florida. For a detailed chart on the number of Christian schools in 1954–55, see L. Gasper, *The Fundamentalist Movement* (The Hague and Paris: Moulton, 1963), p. 125.

48. On the rise of Liberalism in America from a liberal perspective, see G. G. Atkins, *Religion in Our Times* (New York: Round Table Press, 1932). For its impact on American culture, see W. R. Hutchinson, *The Modernist Impulse in American Protestantism* (Cambridge: Harvard University Press, 1976). For a critical survey, see K. Hamilton, *Revolt Against Heaven: An Inquiry into Anti-Supernaturalism* (Grand Rapids: Eerdmans, 1965).

49. C. C. Ryrie, *Neoorthodoxy: An Evangelical Evaluation of Barthianism* (Chicago: Moody Press, 1956), pp. 14–15. This book is valuable in providing a layman's look at neo-orthodoxy. For a much more detailed analysis and evaluation, see Cornelius Van Til, *The New Modernism*.

50. J. I. Packer, *"Fundamentalism" and the Word of God* (Grand Rapids: Eerdmans, 1958), pp. 25–26. A classic defense of scriptural authority. Although Packer rejects the term "fundamentalist" ("the word is prejudicial, ambiguous, explosive, and in every way unhelpful to discussion" [p. 40]), his scholarly work merits reading by every Fundamentalist.

51. Ryrie, *Neoorthodoxy*, p. 62.

52. Van Til, *The New Modernism*, p. 304.

53. On this movement of Theothanatology, see the works of G. Vahanian, *The Death of God* (New York: Braziller, 1961); H. Cox, *The Secular City* (New York: Macmillan, 1965); T. Altizer and W. Hamilton, *Radical Theology and the Death of God* (Indianapolis: Bobbs-Merrill, 1966). For an evaluation, see K. Hamilton, *God is Dead: The Anatomy of a Slogan* (Grand Rapids: Eerdmans, 1966); J. W. Montgomery, *The "Is God Dead?" Controversy* (Grand Rapids: Zondervan, 1966); C. Van Til, *The God is Dead Movement* (Philadelphia: Presbyterian and Reformed, 1969).

54. See R. Webber and D. Bloesch, eds., *The Orthodox Evangelicals* (Nashville: Thomas Nelson, 1978), and their evaluation of the "Chicago Call," pp. 190–210; and C. Rene Padilla, ed., *The New Face of Evangelicalism* (Downers Grove, Ill.: Inter-Varsity Press, 1976), for discussions of evangelical relationships to the World Council of Churches.

55. These attitudes are fully expressed and evaluated by H. J. Ockenga himself in "From Fundamentalism, through New Evangelicalism, to Evangelicalism," in K. Kantzer, ed., *Evangelical Roots* (New York: Thomas Nelson, 1978), pp. 35–48.

56. R. E. Webber, *Common Roots: A Call to Evangelical Maturity* (Grand Rapids: Zondervan, 1978), p. 23. He subdivides Evangelicals into fourteen various groups: Fundamentalist, Dispensational, Conservative, Nondenominational, Reformed, Anabaptist, Wesleyan, Holiness, Pentecostal, Charismatic, Black, Progressive, Radical, and Main-line (p. 32).

57. This drift is well documented by R. Quebedeaux, *The Young Evangelicals* (New York: Harper & Row, 1974) and *The Worldly Evangelicals* (New York: Harper & Row, 1978). He has performed a great (though unintentional) service for Fundamentalists by defining and identifying the current trends in the evangelical drift to the left.

58. C. F. H. Henry, "Evangelicals: Out of the Closet but Going Nowhere?" in *Christianity Today* (Jan. 4, 1980), p. 22. This perceptive article proved true during the 1980 election campaign as the Fundamentalists, not the Evangelicals, led the political involvement effort.

59. This "take-over" is being admitted by left-wing Evangelicals who view it with great concern. See the comments of J. Scanzoni, "Resurgent Fundamentalism: Marching Backward in the 80's?" in *Christian Century* (Sept. 10, 1980), pp. 847–49, where he criticizes H. O. J. Brown's call to Evangelicals to condemn abortion.

60. R. Webber, *Common Roots*, p. 29.

61. Quebedeaux, *The Worldly Evangelicals*, p. 13. Far from being "chic," as he puts it on p. 168, too many Evangelicals have become

chicken! While the Evangelicals explain, define, and theorize, the Fundamentalists have kept on building a massive movement through their strong evangelism and church-planting programs. They are not hampered by the albatross of respectability, as are the Evangelicals, who are too worried about what the world thinks of them to change that world for God.

CHAPTER 2

1. See the valuable and detailed study of M. Green, *Evangelism in the Early Church* (London: Hodder & Stoughton, 1970), especially pp. 194–235. He has provided the most detailed study available of the methods, motives, and strategies of evangelism in the apostolic and post-apostolic Church.

2. See the very helpful and balanced study of the Uppsala scholar G. Westin, V. A. Olson, trans., *The Free Church Movement Through the Ages* (Nashville: Broadman Press, 1958), p. 1. His study should be consulted throughout, along with the selections in J. L. Garrett, ed., *The Concept of the Believers' Church* (Scottdale, Pa.: Herald Press, 1969); and the excellent and very readable work of D. F. Durnbaugh, *The Believers' Church: The History and Character of Radical Protestantism* (New York: Macmillan, 1968).

3. This is discussed at length by M. A. Smith in *From Christ to Constantine* (London: Inter-Varsity Press, 1971), pp. 17–46. Also see W. Oetting, *The Church of the Catacombs* (St. Louis: Concordia, 1970).

4. These may be found in Oetting, *The Church of the Catacombs*, pp. 98–125, and also in E. Goodspeed, *Apostolic Fathers* (New York: Harper & Row, 1950), and H. Bettenson, ed., *Documents of the Christian Church* (New York: Oxford University Press, 1947).

5. Westin, *The Free Church Movement Through the Ages*, p. 12.

6. Ibid., p. 21.

7. Smith, *From Christ to Constantine*, pp. 134–39. He traces the conflict involving Cyprian at Carthage and Novatian at Rome.

8. Westin, *The Free Church Movement Through the Ages*, pp. 21 ff. Also Smith, *From Christ to Constantine*, p. 137, and J. Stevenson, *A New Eusebius* (London: SPCK, 1957), pp. 248–58.

9. See R. Bainton, *The Medieval Church* (New York: Van Nostrand, 1962), pp. 51–52. See also the edited selection therein of readings from primary sources, pp. 138–43.

10. See R. Bainton, *The Travail of Religious Liberty* (Philadelphia: Westminster Press, 1951), pp. 33–53; also, on the use of the Inquisition against the Albigensians, see H. C. Lea, *A History of the Inquisition in the Middle Ages* (New York: Macmillan, 1922).

11. See Durnbaugh, *The Believers' Church*, pp. 40–51; and H. Daniel-Rops, *Cathedral and Crusade: Studies of the Medieval Church, 1050–1350* (London: Dent, 1957), pp. 515 ff., and W. Nigg, *The Heretics* (New York: Alfred Knopf, 1962).

12. The famous Baptist pastor Charles Spurgeon went so far as to say: "We believe that the Baptists are the original Christians . . . we never came from the Church of Rome, for we were never in it, but we have an unbroken line up to the apostles themselves" in *New Park Street Pulpit*, Vol. 7 (1861), p. 225. Others view Baptist origins as coming from the English Puritans: W. S. Hudson, *The Great Tradition of the American Churches* (New York: Harper & Brothers, 1953), pp. 27–41; or from the continental Anabaptists: F. H. Littell, *The Anabaptist View of the Church* (Boston: Starr King Press, 1958).

13. See H. B. Workman, *John Wyclif* (Oxford: Clarendon Press, 1926), and J. Stacey, *John Wyclif and Reform* (Philadelphia: Westminster Press, 1964).

14. For contemporary accounts, see J. Mundy and K. Woody, eds., *The Council of Constance* (New York: Columbia University Press, 1961). On the Bohemian "Unity of Brethren," see Durnbaugh, *The Believers' Church*, pp. 51–63; and G. H. Williams, *The Radical Reformation* (Philadelphia: Westminster Press, 1962), pp. 204–17.

15. P. Brock, *The Political and Social Doctrines of the Unity of Czech Brethren* (The Hague: Moulton, 1957), pp. 72 ff. See also M. Spinka, "Peter Chelčický, the Spiritual Father of the *Unitas Fratrum*," in *Church History* 12 (1943), pp. 271–91.

16. See Bainton, *The Medieval Church*, pp. 81–88; O. Thatcher and E. McNeal, *A Source Book for Medieval History* (New York: Scribners, 1905), pp. 301–30.

17. See A. Hyma, *Renaissance to Reformation* (Grand Rapids: Eerdmans, 1951), and H. S. Lucas, *The Renaissance and Reformation* (New York: Harper & Brothers, 1962). These both clearly distinguish the varying characteristics of the northern and southern European aspects of the Renaissance.

18. On Luther and the beginnings of the Reformation, see R. Bainton, *The Reformation of the Sixteenth Century* (Boston: Beacon Press, 1952) and *Here I Stand: The Life of Martin Luther* (Nashville: Abingdon Press, 1950); A. G. Dickens, *Reformation and Society in Sixteenth Century Europe* (New York: Harcourt, Brace & World, 1966); and V. Green, *Luther and the Reformation* (New York: Putnam, 1964).

19. See Durnbaugh, *The Believers' Church*, pp. 66–82.

20. On Zwingli, see S. M. Jackson, *Huldreich Zwingli* (New York: Putnam's Sons, 1901); O. Farner, *Zwingli the Reformer* (London: Lutterworth Press, 1952); and J. Courvoisier, *Zwingli: A Reformed Theologian* (Richmond, Va.: John Knox Press, 1963).

21. See the detailed account in Williams, *The Radical Reformation*, pp. 81–97, 296–389.

22. J. Wenger, *Even Unto Death* (Richmond, Va.: John Knox Press, 1961), p. 51. On Mennonite history, see T. Van Braght, *The Martyrs' Mirror* (Scottdale, Pa.: Herald Press, 1951); and W. R. Estep, *The Anabaptist Story* (Nashville: Broadman Press, 1963).

23. R. G. Torbet, *A History of the Baptists* (Philadelphia: Judon Press, 1963), pp. 25–30. He provides a thorough standard history of the Baptist Movement since the Reformation.

24. Ibid., pp. 26–39. Cf. also E. Cairns, *Christianity Through the Centuries* (Grand Rapids: Zondervan, 1967), pp. 362–69.

25. J. Brown, *The Pilgrim Fathers of New England and their Puritan Successors* (London: Religious Tract Society, 1897). This classic traces the transition from the Pilgrim beginnings to the Puritan Congregationalists.

26. Torbet, *A History of the Baptists*, pp. 36–39.

27. Ibid., p. 489.

28. On the Baptist separatists, see M. R. Watts, *The Dissenters* (Oxford: Clarendon Press, 1978), pp. 41–49; D. Davie, *A Gathered Church: The Literature of the English Dissenting Interest, 1700–1930*, Chap. 1: "The Nonconformist Contribution to English Culture," pp. 1–18.

29. K. S. Latourette, *A History of the Expansion of Christianity* (New York: Harper Brothers, 1941), Vol. 4, pp. 68–69; also Stephen Neill, *A History of Christian Missions* (New York: Penguin Books, 1964), pp. 197–268.

30. For a thorough discussion of the ideals and concepts of Pietism and its views of Scripture, experience, regeneration, and sanctification, see D. W. Brown, *Understanding Pietism* (Grand Rapids: Eerdmans, 1978); on the Free Church Pietists, see Durnbaugh, *The Believers' Church*, pp. 118–45.

31. On the influence of Pietism on the Lutherans, Methodists, Mennonites, Moravians, Brethren, and Reformed Churches in Colonial America, see F. E. Stoeffler, ed., *Continental Pietism and Early American Christianity* (Grand Rapids: Eerdmans, 1976).

32. For the finest recent study of Wesley, see R. G. Tuttle, *John Wesley: His Life and Theology* (Grand Rapids: Zondervan, 1978). Tuttle's work is filled with careful scholarship based on primary sources. He especially traces the early development of Wesley's life and doctrine thoroughly. See also F. Baker, *John Wesley and the Church of England* (Nashville: Abingdon, 1970); L. Church, *The Early Methodist People* (London: Epworth Press, 1948); T. W. Herbert, *John Wesley as Editor and Author* (Princeton: Princeton University Press, 1940); A. Outler,

ed., *John Wesley* (New York: Oxford University Press, 1964); M. Schmidt, *John Wesley: A Theological Biography* (Nashville: Abingdon, 1962); and C. W. Williams, *Wesley's Theology Today* (Nashville: Abingdon, 1960).

33. On the Puritan influence on Wesley's background and personal life, see R. C. Monk, *John Wesley: His Puritan Heritage* (Nashville: Abingdon, 1966); J. Newton, *Methodism and the Puritans* (London: Williams' Trust, 1964); and G. S. Wakefield, *Puritan Devotion: Its Place in the Development of Christian Piety* (London: Epworth Press, 1957).

34. On the social impact of the Wesleyan Revival in England, see W. J. Warner, *The Wesleyan Movement in the Industrial Revolution* (New York: Longmans, Green, 1930); on its impact in America, see T. L. Smith, *Revivalism and Social Reform* (New York: Harper & Row, 1965).

35. Quoted by D. F. Durnbaugh, ed., in *European Origins of the Brethren* (Elgin, Ill.: Brethren Press, 1958), p. 121.

36. See J. Schlingluff's edition of Alexander Mack, *Rights and Ordinances* (Philadelphia: John Binns, 1810).

37. For a brief and informative history of Darby's life and ministry, see H. A. Ironside, *A Historical Sketch of the Brethren Movement* (Grand Rapids: Zondervan, 1942).

38. For a thorough bibliography on dispensationalism, see A. D. Ehlert, *Bibliographic History of Dispensationalism* (Grand Rapids: Eerdmans, 1965).

39. On the origin, growth, and development of the Quaker movement over the years, see D. Elton Trueblood, *The People Called Quakers* (New York: Harper & Row, 1966). He provides an interesting popular history of his own religious heritage.

40. Quoted by Durnbaugh, *The Believers' Church*, pp. 107–8, from H. Brinton, *Friends for 300 Years* (New York: Harper & Brothers, 1952), pp. 12–13.

41. Ibid., p. 19.

42. Quoted in F. B. Tolles, *Quakers and the Atlantic Culture* (New York: Macmillan, 1960), p 25.

43. For the history of the Disciples, see J. DeForest Murch, *Christians Only* (Cincinnati: Standard, 1962), and W. E. Garrison and A. T. DeGroot, *The Disciples of Christ: A History* (St. Louis: Christian Board of Publication, 1948).

44. See Garrison and DeGroot, *The Disciples of Christ*, p. 90.

45. Durnbaugh, *The Believers' Church*, p. 158.

46. See W. S. Hudson, *The Great Tribulation of the American Churches* (New York: Harper & Brothers, 1953), pp. 64–65. He refers to the fearful anticipation of Lyman Beecher, who bitterly opposed the voluntary system in favor of retaining Congregationalism as the state church of Connecticut, and later admitted that what he had so greatly feared turned out to be "the best thing that ever happened in the State of Connecticut."

47. On the significance of the voluntary system and its unique impact on the American Church as a free-enterprise endeavor, see M. B. Powell, *The Voluntary Church* (New York: Macmillan, 1967).

48. See this observation by Durnbaugh in *The Believers' Church*, p. 249.

49. Ibid., p. 259.

50. D. M. Kelley, *Why Conservative Churches Are Growing* (New York: Harper & Row, 1972). He traces the strengths of the conservative religious movement to commitment, discipline, and missionary zeal, all of which are missing from Liberalism, with its lenient "diminishing demands."

CHAPTER 3

1. E. E. Cairns, *Christianity Through the Centuries* (Grand Rapids: Zondervan, 1967), p. 392.

2. On the development of Puritanism during the reign of Queen Elizabeth, see L. J. Trinterud, ed., *Elizabethan Puritanism* (New York: Oxford University Press, 1971). See also M. M. Knappen, *Tudor Puritanism* (Chicago: University of Chicago Press, 1939).

3. See the careful and thorough study of W. Haller, *The Rise of Puritanism* (Philadelphia: University of Pennsylvania Press, 1972), p. 27.

4. B. Shelley, "Preaching in Early New England," in K. Kantzer, ed., *Evangelical Roots* (Nashville: Thomas Nelson, 1978), p. 22.

5. B. Shelley, *Evangelicalism in America* (Grand Rapids: Eerdmans, 1967), p. 30.

6. E. Emerson, *Puritanism in America 1620–1750* (Boston: Twayne Publishers, 1977), p. 64. Also on the development of Puritanism in New England, see F. J. Bremer, *The Puritan Experiment* (New York: St. Martin's Press, 1976), and Perry Miller, *Errand into the Wilderness* (New York: Harper & Row, 1956).

7. On the influence of Puritanism in politics, see A. Woodhouse, ed., *Puritanism and Liberty* (Chicago: University of Chicago Press, 1965), and J. T. McNeill, *A History and Character of Calvinism* (New York: Oxford University Press, 1954), Chap. 20.

8. For a thorough history of the development of the Baptist Church in colonial America, see T. Armitage, *A History of the Baptists* (New York: Bryan, Taylor, 1887); R. G. Torbet, *A History of the Baptists* (Valley Forge, Pa.: Judson Press, 1963); and R. C. Newman, *Baptists and the American Tradition* (Des Plaines, Ill.: Regular Baptist Press, 1976).

9. See W. G. McLoughlin, *New England Dissent 1630–1833,* 2 vols. (Cambridge: Harvard University Press, 1968), pp. 1 ff.: Introduction.

10. C. C. Goen, *Revivalism and Separatism in New England 1740–1800* (New Haven: Yale University Press, 1962), p 216. He notes that Backus was converted during the Great Awakening in Norwich,' Massachusetts, in 1741.

11. See the excellent history of American Evangelicalism by J. Woodbridge, M. Noll, and N. Hatch, *The Gospel in America: Themes in the Story of America's Evangelicals* (Grand Rapids: Zondervan, 1979), p. 26.

12. See E. S. Gaustad, *The Great Awakening* (New York: Harper & Row, 1957), pp. 2–3. He contrasts the Enlightenment with Pietism, stating: "Whereas the Enlightenment was anthropocentric, pietism was theocentric." See also McLoughlin, *New England Dissent 1630–1833,* Vol. 1, p. 331.

13. For a thorough history of this movement, see Joseph Tracy, *The Great Awakening* (Boston: Tappen & Dennet, 1841; repr. Edinburgh, Scotland: Banner of Truth, 1976). For excellent collections of original sources on the revival, see J. M. Bumsted, ed., *The Great Awakening: The Beginnings of Evangelical Pietism in America* (Waltham, Mass.: Ginn, 1970), and A. Heimert and P. Miller, eds., *The Great Awakening: Documents Illustrating the Crisis and Its Consequences* (Indianapolis: Bobbs-Merrill, 1967).

14. For contrasting studies of Edwards' life and the impact of the revival, see E. H. Davidson, *Jonathan Edwards: The Narrative of a Puritan Mind* (Cambridge: Harvard University Press, 1968), and H. P. Simpson, *Jonathan Edwards: Theologian of the Heart* (Grand Rapids: Eerdmans, 1974).

15. On Whitefield's life and ministry, see the excellent biography by J. Pollock, *George Whitefield and the Great Awakening* (Garden City, N.Y.: Doubleday, 1972), and the epic work by A. Dallimore, *George Whitefield: The Life and Times of the Great Evangelist of the Eighteenth-Century Revival,* 2 vols. (Edinburgh, Scotland: Banner of Truth, 1970, 1980).

16. Their "Testimony Against George Whitefield" appears in Heimert and Miller, eds., *The Great Awakening,* pp. 340–62, reproduced from the 1744 original.

17. Shelley, *Evangelicalism in America,* p. 42.

18. Woodbridge, Noll, and Hatch, *The Gospel in America*, p. 31. On the relationship of the Awakening to the Revolutionary War and religious liberty, see A. Heimer, *Religion and the American Mind: From the Great Awakening to the Revolution* (Cambridge: Harvard University Press, 1966), and B. Weisberger, *They Gathered at the River: The Story of the Great Revivalists and Their Impact upon Religion in America* (Boston: Little, Brown, 1958).

19. See the suggestive insights of H. R. Niebuhr, *The Social Sources of Denominationalism* (New York: Henry Holt, 1929); also J. M. Cuddihy, *No Offense: Civil Religion and Protestant Taste* (New York: Seabury Press, 1978). On p. 17 Cuddihy quotes Talcott Parson's observation that religious denominations in America are "logically associated with the constitutional separation of church and state."

20. Cf. Weisberger, *They Gathered at the River*, and J. Edwin Orr, *Second Evangelical Awakening* (Fort Washington, Pa.: Christian Literature Crusade, 1955) and *The Eager Feet: Evangelical Awakenings 1792–1830* (Chicago: Moody Press, 1974).

21. On the impact of Finney and Moody, see H. Wessel, ed., *The Autobiography of Charles G. Finney* (Minneapolis: Bethany Fellowship, 1977), and W. R. Moody, *The Life of Dwight L. Moody* (Murfreesboro, Tenn.: Sword of the Lord, reprint, n.d.). For a different perspective, see J. F Findlay, *Dwight L. Moody: American Evangelist 1837–1899* (Chicago: University of Chicago Press, 1969).

22. On the manner of Moody's preaching, see S. N. Gundry, *Love Them In—The Proclamation Theology of D. L. Moody* (Chicago: Moody Press, 1976).

23. Shelley, *Evangelicalism in America*, p. 46.

24. On the history of the early Methodist movement in America, see A. B. Hyde, *The Story of Methodism* (Greenfield, Mass., 1887). Also, on the social impact of Methodism in America, see T. L. Smith, *Revivalism and Social Reform* (New York: Harper & Row, 1965), and D. G. Matthews, *Slavery and Methodism: A Chapter in American Morality* (Princeton: Princeton University Press, 1965). See the statistics compiled by Robert Baird, "Religion in America, 1844," in W. G. McLoughlin, ed., *The American Evangelicals, 1800–1900* (New York: Harper & Row, 1968), pp. 30–40. He numbers the Methodists in 1844 at 1,195,025 communicants, compared to only 103,000 Episcopalians.

25. On Wesleyan-Arminian Perfectionism, see the doctrinal study of L. G. Cox, *John Wesley's Concept of Perfection* (Kansas City: Beacon Hill Press, 1964).

26. Weisberger, *They Gathered at the River*, pp. 113–26, discusses this conflict with the older evangelists at great length. See also J. F. Thornbury, *God Sent Revival: The Story of Asahel Nettleton* (Grand Rapids:

Evangelical Press, 1977). On the influence of Finney on modern evangelism, see the interesting study by W. G. McLoughlin, *Modern Revivalism: Charles G. Finney to Billy Graham* (New York: Ronald Press, 1959).

27. V. Synan, "Theological Boundaries: The Arminian Tradition," in D. Wells and J. Woodbridge, eds., *The Evangelicals* (Grand Rapids: Baker, 1977), pp. 44 ff.

28. See Smith, *Revivalism and Social Reform,* pp. 148–77.

29. See the historic survey of Weisberger, *They Gathered at the River,* pp. 31–36. He also (p. 48) refers to the unusual experience of Cartwright at his conversion, when he claimed he heard a voice from heaven say: "Peter, look at me." This was followed by a flash of divine light that knocked him to the ground. Weisberger observes: "Men who 'got religion' in such ways thought that preaching was a failure if it did not induce an indentical saving agony in their listeners."

30. Ibid., p. 40.

31. See details in K. Kendrick, *The Promise Fulfilled: A History of the American Pentecostal Movement* (Springfield, Mo.: Gospel Publishing House, 1961), pp. 51 ff.

32. This is the conclusion of Pentecostal historian Vinson Synan in *The Holiness-Pentecostal Movement in the United States* (Grand Rapids: Eerdmans, 1971), pp. 33–34.

33. Synan, "Theological Boundaries," in Wells and Woodbridge, eds., *The Evangelicals,* p. 48.

34. On the explosive growth and influence of the Pentecostal impulse in American religion, see W. J. Hollenweger, *The Pentecostals: The Charismatic Movement in the Churches* (Minneapolis: Augsburg, 1972); R. Quebedeaux, *The New Charismatics* (Garden City, N.Y.: Doubleday, 1976); K. McDonnell, *Charismatic Renewal and the Churches* (New York: Seabury Press, 1976); J. M. Ford, *The Pentecostal Experience: A New Direction for American Catholics* (New York: Paulist Press, 1970).

35. For a criticism of Pentecostal theology, see W. Chantry, *Signs of the Apostles* (Edinburgh: Banner of Truth, 1973); W. A. Criswell, *The Baptism, Filling and Gifts of the Holy Spirit* (Grand Rapids: Zondervan, 1973); J. Dillow, *Speaking in Tongues* (Grand Rapids: Zondervan, 1975); R. Gromacki, *The Modern Tongues Movement* (Philadelphia: Presbyterian and Reformed, 1967); J. F. MacArthur, *The Charismatics* (Grand Rapids: Zondervan, 1978); C. Smith, *Tongues in Biblical Perspective* (Winona Lake, Ind.: BMH Books, 1972).

36. See the highly documented and interesting study by T. P. Weber, *Living in the Shadow of the Second Coming: American Premillennialism 1875–1925* (New York: Oxford University Press, 1979), pp. 15 ff.

Throughout, the entire study is most intriguing and helpful in recapturing the mentality of premillennialism on the eve of the fundamentalist controversy.

37. See E. S. Gaustad, *The Rise of Adventism* (New York: Harper & Row, 1974). On the Adventist controversy over justification, see G. J. Paxton, *The Shaking of Adventism* (Grand Rapids: Baker Book House, 1977).

38. See the premillennial defense by Charles Feinberg, *Millennialism: The Two Major Views* (Chicago: Moody Press, 1980), and the amillennial apologetic of A. Hoekema, *The Bible and the Future* (Grand Rapids: Eerdmans, 1979).

39. See the discussion of the early history of the Plymouth Brethren in D. F. Durnbaugh, *The Believers' Church* (New York: Macmillan, 1968), pp. 161–72; H. A. Ironside, *A Historical Sketch of the Brethren Movement* (Grand Rapids: Zondervan, 1942); and N. Noel, *The History of the Brethren* (Denver: W. F. Knapp, 1936).

40. Though he certainly overemphasizes the influence of Millenarianism on the fundamentalist controversy, E. R. Sandeen nevertheless provides an excellent, though biased, study of the rise and development of dispensationalism in *The Roots of Fundamentalism: British and American Millenarianism 1800–1930* (Chicago: University of Chicago Press, 1970), pp. 59–80.

41. Quoted by Sandeen, Ibid., pp. 273 ff.

42. The official liberal organizational effort is usually dated from the controversy in 1914 involving McCormick Seminary professor J. Ross Stevens until the drafting of the Auburn Affirmation in 1922.

43. W. B. Riley, *The Evolution of the Kingdom* (New York: Charles C. Cook, 1913), p. 5. Though an ardent premillennialist, Riley also held to the Day-Age Theory of creation.

44. Original sources include: C. H. Mackintosh, *Papers on the Lord's Coming* (New York: n.d.); A. B. Simpson, *The Apostolic Church* (Nyack, N.Y.: n.d.); A. J. Gordon, *Ecce Venit* (New York: Revell, 1889).

45. On the history of Moody Bible Institute, see D. Martin, *God's Power in Action* (Chicago: Moody Press, 1979). In its nearly one hundred years of existence, Moody has produced thousands of pastors, teachers, and missionaries, who are serving the Lord in almost every country of the world.

46. It should also be noted that Baptist leader J. R. Graves wrote *The Word of Christ in the Covenant of Redemption: Developed in Seven Dispensations* (Memphis) in 1883.

47. Quoted by H. Drummond in *Dwight L. Moody: Impressions and Facts* (New York: McClure, Phillips, 1900), pp. 25 ff.

48. For a biblical defense and historic evaluation, see C. Ryrie, *Dispensationalism Today* (Chicago: Moody Press, 1965). Cf. C. Bass, *Backgrounds to Dispensationalism* (Grand Rapids: Eerdmans, 1960), and N. Kraus, *Dispensationalism in America* (Richmond: John Knox Press, 1958). On post-tribulational premillennialism, see R. H. Gundry, *The Church and the Tribulation* (Grand Rapids: Zondervan, 1973).

49. See B. B. Warfield, *The Inspiration and Authority of the Bible* (Philadelphia: Presbyterian and Reformed, 1948 reprint). Warfield's position is defended in *The Infallible Word: A Symposium* (Philadelphia: Presbyterian and Reformed, 1946), and by E. J. Young, *Thy Word Is Truth* (Grand Rapids: Eerdmans, 1957).

50. Shelley, *Evangelicalism in America*, p. 67. He evaluates Fundamentalism as reactionary Evangelicalism responding to the threat of liberalism (pp. 59–67).

CHAPTER 4

1. *American Protestant Thought: The Liberal Era*, ed. William R. Hutchison (New York: Harper & Row, 1968). One cannot fully understand the liberal mind without reading these selected writings of prominent liberal theologians and preachers.

2. DeWitte Holland, ed., *Preaching in American History* (Nashville: Abingdon Press, 1969), p. 263. This book is a treatment of the issues that occupied the preaching of American clergymen. Each report in the book follows a defined format. "1. Definition and vivification of the issue being treated; 2. Description of the factors giving rise to the issue; 3. Analysis of the conflict of ideas on the issue as presented in sermons; 4. Tracing and interpretation of developments from the interaction on the issue" (p. 13).

3. Norman F. Furniss, *The Fundamentalist Controversy, 1918–1931* (Hamden, Conn.: Yale University Press, 1954), pp. 12–13. An interesting feature of this book is Furniss' listing of the characteristics of Fundamentalists (pp. 35–45). He includes a comprehensive history of the northern Baptists, Southern Baptists, northern Presbyterians, southern Presbyterians, Methodists, Episcopalians, and Disciples of Christ.

4. John D. Woodbridge, Mark A. Noll, and Nathan O. Hatch, *The Gospel in America* (Grand Rapids: Zondervan, 1979), p. 59. The authors provide a history of America's evangelicals and utilize hymn titles for chapter headings.

5. Furniss, *The Fundamentalist Controversy, 1918–1931*, p. 50.

6. George W. Dollar, *A History of Fundamentalism in America* (Greenville, S.C.: Bob Jones University Press, 1973), pp. 160–61. This book is one of the few scholarly attempts from within Fundamentalism to describe and categorize the history of the movement.

7. Harry Emerson Fosdick, "Shall the Fundamentalists Win?" in William R. Hutchison, ed., *American Protestant Thought*, p. 172.

8. Ibid., pp. 179–80.

9. Ibid., pp. 173–74.

10. Ibid., p. 182.

11. Ibid., p. 179.

12. C. Allyn Russell, *Voices of American Fundamentalism* (Philadelphia: Westminster Press, 1976), p. 207. This is a book of fundamentalist biographies. Since Fundamentalism has been a movement of personalities, this book provides interesting insight into the people who led the movement. Russell includes in this book J. Frank Norris, John Roach Straton, William Bell Riley, J. C. Massee, J. Gresham Machen, William Jennings Bryan, and Clarence E. Macartney. This book is imperative to the student of the fundamentalist-modernist controversy.

13. Furniss, *The Fundamentalist Controversy, 1918–1931*, p. 137.

14. Kevin Tierney, *Darrow: A Biography* (New York: Thomas Y. Crowell, 1979), p. 3.

15. Ibid., p. 365.

16. Arthur Weinberg, ed., *Attorney for the Damned* (New York: Simon & Schuster, 1957), pp. 223–25.

17. Ibid., p. 365.

18. Quoted by DeWitte Holland, ed., *Preaching in American History*, p. 279.

19. Furniss, *The Fundamentalist Controversy, 1918–1931*, pp. 55–56.

20. Ibid., pp. 139–41.

21. Russell, *Voices of American Fundamentalism*, pp. 22–25.

22. Ibid., p. 25.

23. Dollar, *A History of Fundamentalism in America*, p. 133.

24. Russell, *Voices of American Fundamentalism*, p. 41.

25. Ibid., p. 32.

26. Ibid., p. 29.

27. Ibid., p. 30.

28. J. Frank Norris, *Inside History of First Baptist Church, Fort Worth and Temple Baptist Church, Detroit* (Toronto: Jarvis Street Church, 1938), p. 112. This book contains a number of sermons preached by J. Frank Norris. The *Gospel Witness* states concerning this book: "We question whether any book outside the Bible was ever published so full of inspiration and suggestion and explicit direction to Sunday School workers as this latest book by Dr. Norris."

29. Russell, *Voices of American Fundamentalism*, p. 194.

30. Ibid., pp. 139–40.

31. See pp. 127–41 of Furniss, *The Fundamentalist Controversy, 1918–1931*, for further discussion of the Princeton controversy.

32. J. Gresham Machen, *Christianity and Liberalism* (New York: Macmillan, 1923), p. 17. This book is the classic treatise on conservative Christianity and its antithesis, Liberalism. Machen provides a clear understanding of the real issues in the war with Liberalism.

33. Ibid., pp. 7–8.

34. Russell, *Voices of American Fundamentalism*, pp. 82–83.

35. Quoted by Dollar in *A History of Fundamentalism in America*, p. 114.

36. Russell, *Voices of American Fundamentalism*, pp. 102–3.

37. Ibid., p. 103.

38. Dollar, *A History of Fundamentalism in America*, pp. 106–12.

39. Ibid., p. 112.

40. Russell, *Voices of American Fundamentalism*, pp. 112–21.

41. Ibid., pp. 127–28.

42. Ibid., pp. 48–75.

43. Paul W. Glad, ed., *William Jennings Bryan: A Profile* (New York: Hill and Wang, 1968), pp. xix–xxi.

44. Ibid., p. 45.

45. Ibid., p. 39.

46. Lawrence W. Levine, *Defender of the Faith William Jennings Bryan: The Last Decade, 1915–1925* (New York: Oxford University Press, 1965), p. 365.

47. Harry Emerson Fosdick, *A Guide to Understanding the Bible* (New York: Harper & Brothers Publishing, 1938), p. xiv.

48. William R. Hutchison, *The Modern Impulse in American Protestantism* (Cambridge: Harvard University Press, 1976), p. 275. Hutchison traces the roots of Liberalism from the nineteenth century up to the "war" in the 1920s.

49. Ibid., p. 277.

50. Ibid., pp. 277–78.

51. Shailer Matthews, "The Affirmation of Faith," in William R. Hutchison, ed., *American Protestant Thought*, pp. 94–95.

52. Walter Rauschenbusch, "The New Evangelism," in William R. Hutchison, ed., *American Protestant Thought*, p. 109.

53. D. Bruce Lockerbie, *Billy Sunday* (Waco: Word Books, 1965), p. 63. Though Billy Sunday was not actively involved in the liberal-fundamentalist controversy, he was one of the leading conservative religious leaders of that era.

CHAPTER 5

1. Joel A. Carpenter, "Fundamentalist Institutions and the Rise of Evangelical Protestantism, 1929–1942," *Church History* 49 (Mar. 1980), p. 65. Carpenter shows a keen perception of the trends and organizations that emerged from the War with Liberalism. This is an excellent overview of the period.

2. "Bible Schools that are True to the Faith," *Sunday School Times* 72 (Feb. 1, 1930), p. 63.

3. Carpenter, "Fundamentalist Institutions," pp. 66–68.

4. Ibid., pp. 68–69. See also "Harvard of the Bible Belt," *Change* 6 (Mar. 1974), pp. 17–20.

5. R. K. Johnson, *Builder of Bridges: A Biography of Dr. Bob Jones* (Murfreesboro, Tenn.: Sword of the Lord, 1969), p. 173. This is an extensive biography of the ministry of Bob Jones.

6. Bob Jones, Jr., "A Tribute and a Pledge." Read by Dr. Edward Panosian at the funeral of Bob Jones on January 17, 1968.

7. George W. Dollar, *A History of Fundamentalism in America* (Greenville, S.C.: Bob Jones University Press, 1973), p. 221.

8. J. Murray Murdoch, *Portrait of Obedience: The Biography of Robert T. Ketcham* (Schaumburg, Ill.: Regular Baptist Press, 1979), p. 146.

9. Ibid., pp. 178–79. The role of Ketcham in Fundamentalism has been ignored by most writers when describing the movement. Norris was known for his harsh letters and attacks on other people. He would often attempt to intimidate other preachers into accepting his viewpoint.

10. Joseph M. Stowell is author of *A History of the General Association of Regular Baptist Churches* (Hayward, Calif.: Gospel Tracts, 1949). This is the most comprehensive story of the GARBC. The quotation is from J. Murray Murdoch, *Portrait of Obedience: The Biography of Robert T. Ketcham,* p. 314.

11. Dollar, *A History of Fundamentalism in America,* p. 223.

12. Norman H. Maring, *American Baptists Whence and Whither* (Valley Forge, Pa.: The Judson Press, 1968), pp. 46–47.

13. L. Russ Bush and Tom J. Nettles, *Baptists and the Bible* (Chicago: Moody Press, 1980), pp. 379–80.

14. Dollar, *A History of Fundamentalism in America,* p. 215.

15. Carpenter, "Fundamentalist Institutions," p. 71.

16. Daniel P. Fuller, *Give the Winds a Mighty Voice* (Waco: Word, 1972), pp. 140–41. On broadcaster M. R. De Haan, see J. R. Adair, *M. R. De Haan, the Man and His Ministry* (Grand Rapids: Zondervan, 1969).

17. Robert L. Sumner, *A Man Sent from God* (Grand Rapids: Eerdmans, 1959), p. 153.

18. Earle E. Cairns, *Christianity Through the Centuries* (Grand Rapids: Zondervan, 1954), p. 488.

19. Carl McIntire, *Servants of Apostasy* (Collingswood, N.J.: Christian Beacon Press, 1955), p. 1.

20. Bruce Shelley, *Evangelicalism in America* (Grand Rapids: Eerdmans, 1970), p. 70. For a thorough history of the formation of the NAE, see J. D. Murch, *Cooperation Without Compromise* (Grand Rapids: Eerdmans, 1956).

21. Ibid., pp. 81–82.

22. Harold J. Ockenga, "From Fundamentalism, Through New Evangelicalism, to Evangelicalism," Kenneth Kantzer, ed.. *Evangelical Books* (New York: Thomas Nelson, 1978), p. 38.

23. Ibid., p. 42.

24. Ibid., p. 43.

25. Ibid., p. 44.

26. Robert G. Torbet, *A History of the Baptists* (Valley Forge, Pa.: Judson Press, 1950), p. 477.

27. Dollar, *A History of Fundamentalism in America*, p. 226–33.

28. Ibid., pp. 247–48.

29. Murdoch, *Portrait of Obedience*, p. 179. A comprehensive history of the BBF is contained in its Twenty-fifth Anniversary booklet *The Beginnings* (Springfield, Mo.: Baptist Bible College, 1975).

30. Dollar, *A History of Fundamentalism in America*, p. 241.

31. Ian R. K. Paisley, *Billy Graham and the Church of Rome* (Greenville, S.C.: Bob Jones University Press, 1972), p. 47.

32. William E. Ashbrook, *Evangelicalism: The New Neutralism* (Columbus, Ohio: Calvary Baptist Church, 1963), p. 13.

33. Paisley, *Billy Graham and the Church of Rome*, pp. 57–58.

34. Ibid., p. 59.

35. Ashbrook, *Evangelicalism: The New Neutralism*, p. 13.

36. James Morris, *The Preachers* (New York: St. Martin's Press, 1973), p. 265.

37. William K. "Kenny" McComas, *Life Story of B. R. Lakin* (Orlando: Daniels Publishers, 1973), p. 120.

38. Kenneth S. Kantzer, "The Charismatics Among Us," *Christianity Today* (Feb. 22, 1980), p. 25.

39. John F. MacArthur, Jr., *The Charismatics: A Doctrinal Perspective* (Grand Rapids: Zondervan, 1978), p. 13.

40. Kantzer, "The Charismatics Among Us," p. 28.

41. Ibid., p. 27.

42. Ibid., p. 29.

43. MacArthur, Jr., *The Charismatics*, pp. 199–200.

44. Kantzer, "The Charismatics Among Us," p. 29.

45. Edward E. Plowman, "Conservative Network Puts Its Stamp on the Southern Baptist Convention," *Christianity Today* (July 18, 1980), pp. 50–51.

46. Much of the material related to the Southern Baptist Convention was secured in a personal interview with Judge Paul Pressler. A very kind and courteous man with a deep concern and love for the Southern Baptist Convention.

47. Ernest Pickering, *Biblical Separation: The Struggle for a Pure Church* (Schaumburg, Ill.: Regular Baptist Press, 1979), p. 217.

48. The material and statistics presented in this section were secured in interviews with official personnel from these churches.

CHAPTER 6

1. William J. Petersen and Stephen Board, "Where is Jerry Falwell Going?" *Eternity* 31:7 (July–Aug. 1980), pp. 18–19.

2. "Thunder on the Right: An Unholy War Breaks Out over Evangelical Politics," *People* (Oct. 13, 1980), p. 32.

3. Martin E. Marty, "Fundamentalism Reborn," *Saturday Review* (May 1980), p. 38.

4. Ernest Pickering, *Biblical Separation: The Struggle for a Pure Church* (Schaumburg, Ill.: Regular Baptist Press, 1979), p. 142. Pickering provides an excellent biblical exegesis of the issue of Christian separation. He struggles honestly with the issues within the context of scriptural principles. This is a scholarly attempt to dismiss prejudice and deal with concrete problems.

5. Ibid., pp. 143–44.

6. Merrill F. Unger, "Apostasy," *Unger's Bible Dictionary* (Chicago: Moody Press, 1966), p. 72.

7. D. Martyn Lloyd-Jones, *The Basis of Christian Unity* (Grand Rapids: Eerdmans, 1962), pp. 45–46. This book is a study of John 17 and Ephesians 4 in the light of Christian unity. He deals with the "nature and character" of unity, the plan of doctrine and belief as related to unity, and the struggle for unity (p. 6). He applies his principles to ecumenical evangelism. This is imperative reading.

8. Ibid., pp. 59–64.

9. Robert O. Ferm, *Cooperative Evangelism* (Grand Rapids: Zondervan, 1958), p. 87. Ferm's attempts to prove the validity of ecumenical evangelism from church history and Scripture are rather anemic. He succumbs to emotional arguments at the expense of rational, biblical defenses. Gary G. Cohen answers Ferm in *Biblical Separation Defended* (Philadelphia: Presbyterian and Reformed, 1966), and points to Ferm's errors in interpreting Scripture (p. 78).

10. Ibid., p. 45.

11. Ibid., p. 91.

12. Ibid., p. 94.

13. Cohen, *Biblical Separation Defended*. This is the most comprehensive answer to Ferm's defense of ecumenical evangelism. It articulates clearly the fundamentalist position. Cohen's exegesis of Scripture is credible. He clearly reveals the weaknesses of Ferm's arguments. See also Erroll Hulse, *Billy Graham—The Pastor's Dilemma* (Hounslow, England: Maurice Allan, 1966), pp. 34–78.

14. Cohen, *Biblical Separation Defended*, p. 83.

15. Ian R. K. Paisley, *Billy Graham and the Church of Rome* (Greenville, S.C.: Bob Jones University Press, 1972). Paisley is a strong anti-Romanist. His book traces Graham's relationship to the Roman Catholic Church. He calls for the complete rejection of Graham and asks Christians to forgive Graham "for sending converts back to the papal anti-Christ" (p. 32).

16. Hulse, *Billy Graham—The Pastor's Dilemma*. The author examines Graham's doctrine and seeks to establish that Graham does not preach the whole counsel of God. Hulse's major objection to Graham involves Graham's apparent rejection of traditional Calvinistic doctrine.

17. Harold J. Ockenga, "From Fundamentalism, through New Evangelicalism, to Evangelicalism," in Kenneth Kantzer, ed., *Evangelical Roots* (Nashville: Thomas Nelson, 1978), p. 44. Ockenga provides a concise understanding of Fundamentalism, New Evangelicalism, and neo-orthodoxy in this short article. A movement is best understood by those within it, and Ockenga's perception of his movement is imperative for Fundamentalist reading.

18. Ibid., p. 40.

19. Charles Woodbridge, *The New Evangelicalism* (Greenville, S.C.: Bob Jones University Press, 1969), p. 15. Woodbridge, one of the most academically credible Fundamentalists, represents his position well but has a tendency toward extreme separatism. Since the writing of *The New Evangelicalism* and his courtship of Bob Jones University, he has parted fellowship even with that Fundamentalist institution!

20. Ibid., p. 7.

21. William E. Ashbrook, *Evangelicalism: The New Neutralism* (Columbus: Calvary Bible Church, 1963), p. 5. This is an important booklet representing the fundamentalist cause. Ashbrook attempts to deal with all of the important issues and personalities of the early New Evangelical Movement.

22. Woodbridge, *The New Evangelicalism*, p. 23.

23. Ockenga, "From Fundamentalism," p. 44.

24. Woodbridge, *The New Evangelicalism*, p. 27.

25. Ockenga, "From Fundamentalism," p. 43.

26. Ibid., p. 40.

27. Woodbridge, *The New Evangelicalism*, p. 62.

28. Ockenga, "From Fundamentalism," p. 43.

29. Richard Quebedeaux, *The Young Evangelicals* (New York: Harper & Row, 1974), p. 22.

30. Jerry Falwell, "Let Us Hang Together," *Faith Aflame* magazine (May–June 1977), p. 2. This article caused a great flurry of reaction. Some Fundamentalists openly questioned where Falwell was really going. However, time has proved his fidelity to the historic fundamentalist position.

31. Quebedeaux, *The Young Evangelicals*, p. 22.

32. A Hyper-Fundamentalist is one characterized by negativism, pessimism, extreme separatism, and an exclusivism that rarely extends beyond his immediate circle (which is usually rather small). This definition is not intended to be a threat to any particular group or person, since most "hypers" rarely read books, let alone footnotes!

33. David Sproul, *An Open Letter to Jerry Falwell* (Tempe, Ariz.: Fundamental Baptist Press, 1979), pp. 5–6. Copies of this letter may be purchased directly from Sproul, 104 E. Riviera Drive, Tempe, Arizona 85282. At this time of writing, they cost $1.25 each for one to ten copies and $1.00 each for ten or more copies.

34. Ibid., p. 10.

35. Ibid., pp. 27–28.

36. Ibid., pp. 31–32.

37. Ibid., p. 32.

38. Robert E. Webber, *Common Roots* (Grand Rapids: Zondervan, 1978), pp. 32–33. His chart on p. 32 is helpful in understanding the broad spectrum of evangelical organizations. He identifies the major emphasis of each particular grouping and lists the major organizational representatives of that group.

39. Edward John Carnell, *The Case for Biblical Christianity* (Grand Rapids: Eerdmans, 1969), pp. 169–70. Harold J. Ockenga in "From Fundamentalism," correctly observes that Evangelicalism was a reaction to fundamentalist attitudes (pp. 41–42). Bruce Shelley described this same attitude, "The movement's 'wowser' worship, its cultural isolationism, its sectarian separatism, its monastic ethics, its theological hairsplitting . . ." in *Evangelicalism in America* (Grand Rapids: Eerdmans, 1967), p. 112.

40. Quebedeaux, *The Young Evangelicals*, pp. 37–41.

41. Carl F. Henry, "Winds of Promise," *Christianity Today* (June 5, 1970), pp. 829–30.

42. Richard Quebedeaux, *The Worldly Evangelicals* (New York: Harper & Row, 1978), p. 84. Quebedeaux clearly identifies and describes the new evangelical left, but he is not synchronized with the mainstream of orthodox Christianity. The resurgence of Fundamentalism has caused Quebedeaux and his middle-aged, anachronistic Jesus freaks to be *left* behind.

43. Ibid., pp. 126–27.

44. Ibid., p. 140.

45. Robert Webber and Donald Bloesch, eds., *The Orthodox Evangelicals* (Nashville: Thomas Nelson, 1978), p. 19. The book gives clear evidence of the major drift among many Evangelicals. In *The Battle for the Bible* (Grand Rapids: Zondervan, 1976), p. 33, Lindsell called the participants in the Chicago Call a "mixed bag."

46. See the review of *The Worldly Evangelicals* by Robert S. Ellwood in the *Anglican Theological Review* (July 1975), pp. 380–81.

47. Ernest D. Pickering, *The Fruit of Compromise* (Clarks Summit, Pa.: Baptist Bible College and School of Theology), pp. 44–45. This booklet is an evaluation of the status of New and Young Evangelicals. Pickering provides keen insight into the dangers of this movement from a fundamentalist perspective.

48. Quebedeaux, *The Worldly Evangelicals*, p. 166.

49. These statements came from a personal interview between Francis Schaeffer and Jerry Falwell in November, 1978, at Rochester, Minnesota, during Dr. Schaeffer's recovery from cancer treatment. It is interesting to note that they were both converted (at different times) while studying engineering in a college in Virginia.

50. See *Sojourners* and *Wittenburg Door* magazines and the political-mission discussion in C. Armerding, ed., *Evangelicals and Liberation* (Philadelphia: Presbyterian and Reformed, 1977); D. E. Hoke, ed., *Evangelicals Face the Future* (Pasadena: William Carey Library, 1978); and D. McGavran, ed., *The Conciliar-Evangelical Debate: The Crucial Documents 1964–1976* (Pasadena: William Carey, 1977).

51. B. Ramm, *The Evangelical Heritage* (Waco: Word, 1973), p. 14, goes so far as to include "evangelical neo-orthodoxy" under the evangelical banner. The term "evangelical" is becoming so broad and well accepted that it has become a catchall for almost every kind of theological mind.

52. Dean M. Kelley, *Why Conservative Churches are Growing* (New York: Harper & Row, 1972), p. 84. This book has been identified as one of the most important books ever written on church growth. It gives provocative and perceptive insight into the reasons for church growth among conservative groups and the decline in growth among the major denominations. (The following lists of characteristics of "strong" and "weak" groups—though not the discussion—are quoted from Kelley.)

53. Carl F. H. Henry, "Evangelicals: Out of the Closet but Going Nowhere?" *Christianity Today* (Jan. 4, 1980), p. 22.

54. Kelley, *Why Conservative Churches Are Growing*, p. 86.

55. During the 1970s an in-house war among Fundamentalists exploded over the value and significance of bus ministries and "bubble-gum" Evangelism.

56. The impact of Bill Gothard's "Institute of Basic Youth Conflicts" has helped significantly in this regard to focus attention on biblical principles of character development.

57. For example, the "King James Version only" defenders are violently vocal about their position because of a sincere desire to defend the Bible. However sincere they may be, their position is based upon almost complete ignorance. Some have gone so far as to claim that "the authorized King James Version of the Bible with the italicized words is the Word of God . . . all other versions preach another Jesus." One person claimed that even a modernization of "ye" to "you" would corrupt the Scripture by adding a letter to the Bible. I explained to him that the present form of the K.J.V. is a nineteenth-century modernization of the 1611 "original" and has changed the spelling of several words ("yee" to "ye" and "doe" to "do"). To this he merely said "Oh," and walked away!

58. When fundamentalist writers deteriorate to quoting bus drivers as authorities in leveling criticism at other ministries, their legitimate integrity must be questioned (Sproul, *An Open Letter to Jerry Falwell*, p. 16).

59. Ibid., p. 2. He lists Pillsbury, Maranatha, Bob Jones, Central, and San Francisco Baptist Seminary as the only true schools.

60. Truman E. Dollar and Grace H. Kelterman, *Teenage Rebellion* (Old Tappan, N.J.: Revell, 1979).

61. For another list of the weaknesses of Fundamentalism, see Leslie K. Tarr, "The Hermetically-Sealed World of Neo-Fundamentalism," *Eternity* (Aug. 1976), pp. 24–28. This is a perceptive article that merits the attention of every Fundamentalist.

FUTURE-WORD: AN AGENDA FOR THE EIGHTIES

1. H. O. J. Brown, *Protest of a Troubled Protestant* (New York: Arlington House, 1969), p. 72. See also the excellent study on the relationship of true revival to social action by R. F. Lovelace, *Dynamics of Spiritual Life: An Evangelical Theology of Renewal* (Downers Grove, Ill.: Inter-Varsity Press, 1979), and his more recent article, "Completing an Awakening," *The Christian Century* (Mar. 18, 1981), pp. 296–300.

2. Brown, *Protest of a Troubled Protestant*, p. 205.

3. R. Dingman, in *Moral Majority Report* (June 6, 1980), p. 4.

4. J. Gerstner, quoted in an article in the *Birmingham News* (Sept. 26, 1980).

5. T. La Haye, in *Moral Majority Report* (June 6, 1980). See also his incisive study on the influence of secular humanism in *The Battle for the Mind* (Old Tappan, N.J.: Revell, 1980). For a more technical study, see R. J. Rushdoony, *The Messianic Character of American Education* (Nutley, N.J.: Craig Press, 1979).

6. R. Burns, in *The Wanderer* (Oct. 2, 1980).

7. See this statement quoted in its fuller context in my book *Listen, America!* (Garden City, N.Y.: Doubleday, 1980).

8. Doug Badger, "Divinely Knit," *Sojourners* (Nov. 1980), p. 17. See this entire issue for a series of excellent articles on the abortion issue.

9. J. Loesch, "Fetus Is Latin for Unborn Child," *Sojourners* (Nov. 1980), p. 19.

10. F. A. Schaeffer and C. E. Koop, *Whatever Happened to the Human Race?* (Old Tappan, N.J.: Revell, 1979), p. 89. In this crucial work, theologian and apologist Schaeffer combines his expertise with the medical knowledge of Dr. Koop, formerly the surgeon in chief at the Children's Hospital in Philadelphia. The result is a brilliant evaluation of America's morality crisis.

11. M. F. Jefferson, as quoted in *Moral Majority Report* (Mar. 14, 1980) and *Listen, America!*, pp. 173–74.

12. La Haye, *The Battle for the Mind*, p. 26.

13. Mel Gabler, interview in *Moral Majority Report* (July 30, 1980), p. 5.

14. See the study of C. Chambers, *The SIECUS Circle* (Belmont, Massachusetts: Western Islands, 1977), *in toto*.

15. *Study Guide 9: Sex, Science and Values,* published by SIECUS.

16. B. DeMott, "The Pro-Incest Lobby," *Psychology Today* (Mar. 1980), pp. 11–18.

17. N. Gallagher, *How to Stop the Porno Plague* (Minneapolis: Bethany Fellowship, 1977), p. 13; quoted in *Listen, America!,* p. 202.

18. J. Dobson, quoted in *Moral Majority Report* (July 30, 1980), p. 11. An outstanding Christian writer, Dobson has produced such best sellers as *Dare to Discipline* (Wheaton, Ill.: Tyndale House, 1970).

19. See comments of H. Voth and W. Stanmeyer reported in *Moral Majority Report* (June 6, 1980), p. 5.

20. Quoted by G. Hall in *Moral Majority Report* (Mar. 14, 1980), p.5.

21. C. Keating, in *Moral Majority Report* (Oct. 15, 1980), p. 15.

22. R. Quebedeaux, *The Worldly Evangelicals* (New York: Harper & Row, 1978), p. 126. His honest assessment of the drift of Evangelicalism to the left is discussed in earlier chapters in this book.

23. Ibid., pp. 126 ff.

24. See this statement in full in *Listen, America!,* pp. 185–86.

25. For further information, see R. J. Billings, "Family Protection Act: Now is the Time for Passage," *Moral Majority Report* (Apr. 11, 1980), p. 16, and "Homosexual Rights Briefing: N.Y. Mayor Aide Attacks Falwell, Laxalt, Family Protection Act," *Moral Majority Report* (May 1, 1980), p. 6.

26. A. Billingsley, "Black Families in White America," *Black Family* (Nov.–Dec. 1981), pp. 16, 23.

27. Quoted by W. M. Kroll in "Test Tube Babies: A Giant Step Forward Improving the Quality of Life?" *Moral Majority Report* (May 1, 1980), p. 14.

28. Ibid.

29. Richard McCormick, as quoted by W. M. Kroll, "Selective Breeding Is Ethically Repugnant," *Moral Majority Report* (May 26, 1980), p. 14.

30. J. Rifkin and T. Howard, *Who Should Play God?* (New York: Dell, 1977), p. 115.

31. E. C. Koop, *The Right to Live; the Right to Die* (Wheaton, Ill.: Tyndale House), p. 115.

32. H. O. J. Brown, *Death Before Birth* (Nashville: Thomas Nelson, 1977).

33. L. W. Walt, *The Eleventh Hour* (New York: Caroline House, 1979), pp. xi, xii; see further quotations in *Listen, America!*, pp. 101–3.

34. Ibid., pp. xi, 3–4.

35. Leonid Brezhnev, as quoted in *Listen, America!*, p. 86.

36. Alexander Solzhenitsyn, as quoted in *Listen, America!*, pp. 87–88.

37. D. Boys, "The Separation Confusion," in *The Sword of the Lord* (Dec. 5, 1980), p. 12.

38. Billy Graham, "An Agenda for the 1980s," *Christianity Today* (Jan. 4, 1980), pp. 23–27.

39. J. R. Rice, *Earnestly Contending for the Faith* (Murfreesboro, Tenn.: Sword of the Lord, 1965), p. 13.

BIBLIOGRAPHY

Books

Ahlstrom, Sidney E. *A Religious History of the American People*. New Haven: Yale University Press, 1972.

Allen, James H. *Our Liberal Movement in Theology*. New York: Arno Press, 1972.

Altizer, Thomas J. J., and Hamilton, W. *Radical Theology and the Death of God*. Indianapolis: Bobbs-Merrill, 1966.

Anderson, R. M. *Vision of the Disinherited: The Making of American Pentecostalism*. New York: Oxford University Press, 1979.

Armerding, Carl E. *Evangelicals and Liberation*. Philadelphia: Presbyterian and Reformed, 1977.

Armstrong, Ben. *The Electric Church*. Nashville: Thomas Nelson, 1979.

Ashbrook, William E. *Evangelicalism: The New Neutralism*. Columbus, Ohio: Calvary Baptist Church, 1963.

Banks, William L. *The Black Church in the U.S.* Chicago: Moody Press, 1972.

Barr, James. *Fundamentalism*. Philadelphia: Westminster Press, 1977.

Bartlett, Billy Vick. *A History of Baptist Separatism*. Springfield, Mo.: Roark, 1972.

————. *The Beginnings*. Springfield, Mo.: Baptist Bible College, 1975.

Berger, Peter. *The Noise of Solemn Assemblies*. Garden City, N.Y.: Doubleday, 1961.

Blackwood, Andrew W. *The Protestant Pulpit*. Nashville, Abingdon Press, 1947.

Bloesch, Donald. *The Evangelical Renaissance*. Grand Rapids: Eerdmans, 1973.

Bridges, J. H. *The God of Fundamentalism*. Chicago: Pascal Covici, 1925.

Briggs, Charles A. *The Fundamental Christian Faith*. New York: Scribners, 1913.

Brink, G. H. *Baptist Fundamentals*. Philadelphia: American Baptist Press, 1920.

Brown, Dale. *Understanding Pietism*. Grand Rapids: Eerdmans, 1978.

Brown, Harold O. J. *The Protest of a Troubled Protestant*. New York: Arlington House, 1969.

Bush, L. Russ, and Nettles, Tom J. *Baptists and the Bible*. Chicago: Moody Press, 1980.

Cairns, Earle E. *Christianity Through the Centuries*. Grand Rapids: Zondervan, 1954.

——. *Saints and Society*. Chicago: Moody Press, 1960.

——. *The Christian in Society*. Chicago: Moody Press, 1973.

Carnell, Edward J. *The Case for Biblical Christianity*. Grand Rapids: Eerdmans, 1969.

Champion, John B. *Why Modernism Must Fail*. Philadelphia: Eastern Seminary Press, 1932.

Cherry, Conrad, ed. *God's New Israel: Religious Interpretations of American Destiny*. Englewood Cliffs, N.J.: Prentice-Hall, 1971.

Clabaugh, Gary K. *Thunder on the Right: The Protestant Fundamentalists*. Chicago: Nelson-Hall, 1974.

Cohen, Gary G. *Biblical Separation Defended*. Philadelphia: Presbyterian and Reformed, 1966.

Cole, Stewart G. *The History of Fundamentalism*. New York: Smith Publishers, 1931.

Cox, Harvey. *The Seduction of the Spirit: The Use and Misuse of the People's Religion*. New York: Simon & Schuster, 1973.

Cuddihy, John M. *No Offense: Civil Religion and Protestant Taste*. New York: Seabury Press, 1978.

Danker, Fredrick W. *No Room in the Brotherhood: The Preus-Otten Purge of Missouri*. St. Louis: Clayton, 1977.

Davie, Donald. *A Gathered Church: The Literature of the English Dissenting Interest*. New York: Oxford University Press, 1978.

Dawson, Joseph. *Baptists and the American Republic*. Nashville: Broadman Press, 1956.

Dayton, Donald. *Discovering an Evangelical Heritage*. New York: Harper & Row, 1976.

DeWolf, L. H. *The Case for Theology in Liberal Perspective*. Philadelphia: Westminster Press, n.d.

Dillenberger, John, and Welch, Claude. *Protestant Christianity*. New York: Scribners, 1954.

Dixon, A. C., et al. *The Fundamentals*. 12 vols. Los Angeles: Bible Institute of Los Angeles, 1909. 4-vol. ed. reprinted Grand Rapids: Baker Book House, 1970.

Dollar, George W. *A History of Fundamentalism in America*. Greenville, S.C.: Bob Jones University Press, 1973.

Durnbaugh, Donald F. *The Believers' Church: the History and Character of Radical Protestantism*. New York: Macmillan, 1968.

Erickson, Millard. *New Evangelical Theology*. Westwood, N.J.: Revell, 1968.

Estep, W. R. *Baptist and Christian Unity*. Nashville: Broadman Press, 1966.

Falwell, Jerry. *Church Aflame*. Nashville: Impact Books, 1972.

——. *Capturing a Town for Christ*. Old Tappan, N.J.: Revell, 1973.

——. *Listen, America!* Garden City, N.Y.: Doubleday, 1980.

Faulkner, J. A. *Modernism and the Christian Faith*. New York: Methodist Book Concern, 1921.

Feinberg, Charles. *The Fundamentals for Today*. Grand Rapids: Kregel, 1958.

Ferm, Robert O. *Cooperative Evangelism*. Grand Rapids: Zondervan, 1958.

Ferm, Vergilius, ed. *The American Church and the Protestant Heritage*. New York: Philosophic Library, 1953.

Forrest, W. M. *Do Fundamentalists Play Fair?* New York: Macmillan, 1926.

Fosdick, Harry Emerson. *New Knowledge*. New York: Harper, 1922.

——. *The Modern Use of the Bible*. New York: Macmillan, 1924.

Fuller, Daniel P. *Give the Winds a Mighty Voice*. Waco: Word Books, 1972.

Furniss, Norman F. *The Fundamentalist Controversy*. New Haven: Yale University Press, 1954.

Gabriel, R. W. *Christianity and Modern Thought*. New Haven: Yale University Press, 1924.

Gaebelein, Frank E. *The New Scofield Reference Bible.* New York: Oxford University Press, 1967.

Garrett, James L. *The Concept of the Believers' Church.* Scottdale, Pa.: Herald Press, 1969.

Gasper, Louis. *The Fundamentalist Movement.* The Hague: Moulton, 1963.

Gatewood, W. B., ed. *Controversy in the Twenties: Fundamentalism, Modernism and Evolution.* Nashville: Vanderbilt University Press, 1969.

Gaustad, Edwin S. *Dissent in American Religion.* Chicago: University of Chicago Press, 1973.

Goen, C. C. *Revivalism and Separatism in New England, 1740–1800.* New Haven: Yale University Press, 1962.

Green, Michael. *Evangelism in the Early Church.* Grand Rapids: Eerdmans, 1970.

Haldeman, I. M. *Why I Am Opposed to Modernism.* New York: Fitch, 1929.

Handy, Robert. *A Christian America: Protestant Hopes and Historical Realities.* New York: Oxford University Press, 1971.

Hebert, Gabriel. *Fundamentalism and the Church of God.* London: S.C.M. Press, 1957.

Henry, Carl F. H. *The Uneasy Conscience of Modern Fundamentalism.* Grand Rapids: Eerdmans, 1947.

———. *The Protestant Dilemma.* Grand Rapids: Eerdmans, 1949.

———. *Evangelical Responsibility in Contemporary Theology.* Grand Rapids: Eerdmans, 1957.

———. *Fifty Years of Protestant Theology.* Boston: W. A. Wilde, 1960.

———. *Aspects of Christian Social Ethics.* Grand Rapids: Eerdmans, 1964.

———. *A Plea for Evangelical Demonstration.* Grand Rapids: Baker Book House, 1971.

Hindson, Edward E. *Glory in the Church: The Coming Revival.* Nashville: Thomas Nelson, 1975.

———. *Introduction to Puritan Theology.* Grand Rapids: Baker Book House, 1976.

Hofstader, Richard. *Anti-Intellectualism in American Life.* New York: Random House, 1962.

Hoke, Donald E. *Evangelicals Face the Future.* Pasadena: William Carey Library, 1978.

Holland, DeWitte. *Preaching in American History.* New York: Abingdon Press, 1969.

Hopkins, C. H. *The Rise of the Social Gospel in America.* New Haven: Yale University Press, 1940.

Hudson, Winthrop. *Religion in America.* New York: Scribners, 1973.

Hutchison, William R. *American Protestant Thought: The Liberal Era.* New York: Harper & Row, 1968.

——. *The Modernist Impulse in American Protestantism.* Cambridge: Harvard University Press, 1976.

Inch, Morris A. *The Evangelical Challenge.* Philadelphia: Westminster Press, 1978.

Johnson, J. W. *Fundamentalism Versus Modernism.* New York: Century, 1925.

Johnson, R. K. *Builder of Bridges: A Biography of Dr. Bob Jones.* Murfreesboro, Tenn.: Sword of the Lord, 1969.

Jones, Bob Jr. *Scriptural Separation.* Greenville, S.C.: Bob Jones University Press, 1971.

Jorstad, Erling. *Politics of Doomsday: The Fundamentalists of the Far Right.* Nashville: Abingdon, 1970.

Kantzer, Kenneth S. *Evangelical Roots.* Nashville: Thomas Nelson, 1978.

Kelley, Dean M. *Why Conservative Churches are Growing.* New York: Harper & Row, 1972.

Kik, J. Marcellus. *Ecumenism and the Evangelical.* Philadelphia: Presbyterian and Reformed, 1958.

Krinsky, F. *The Politics of Religion in America.* New York: Macmillan, 1968.

Küng, Hans. *Signposts for the Future.* N.Y.: Doubleday, 1978.

La Haye, Tim. *The Battle for the Mind.* Old Tappan, N.J.: Revell, 1980.

Langford, Thomas A. *In Search of Foundations: English Theology 1900–1920.* Nashville: Abingdon Press, 1969.

Latourette, Kenneth Scott. *A History of the Expansion of Christianity.* New York: Harper & Brothers, 1954.

Lightner, Robert P. *Neoevangelicalism Today.* Schaumburg, Ill.: Regular Baptist Press, 1978.

Lindsell, Harold. *The Battle for the Bible.* Grand Rapids: Zondervan, 1976.

Livingston, James C. *Modern Christian Thought.* New York: Macmillan, 1971.

Lloyd-Jones, D. Martin. *The Basis of Christian Unity*. Grand Rapids: Eerdmans, 1973.

Lovelace, Richard. *Dynamics of Spiritual Life: An Evangelical Theology of Renewal*. Downers Grove, Ill.: Inter-Varsity Press, 1979.

MacArthur, John F. *The Charismatics: A Doctrinal Perspective*. Grand Rapids: Zondervan, 1978.

Machen, J. Gresham. *Christianity and Liberalism*. New York: Macmillan, 1923.

——. *The Christian Faith in the Modern World*. New York: Macmillan, 1936.

Manning, W. T. *Fundamentalism or Modernism*. Washington, D.C.: National Cathedral, 1923.

Marsden, G. *Fundamentalism and American Culture*. New York: Oxford University Press, 1981.

Marty, Martin E. *The New Shape of American Religion*. New York: Harper & Row, 1959.

——. *Righteous Empire: The Protestant Experience in America*. New York: Dial Press, 1970.

——. *A Nation of Behavers*. Chicago: University of Chicago, 1976.

Matthews, Shailer. *The Faith of Modernism*. New York: Macmillan, 1924.

McDonnell, K. *Charismatic Renewal and the Churches*. New York: Seabury Press, 1976.

McGavran, Donald. *The Conciliar Evangelical Debate*. Pasadena: William Carey Library, 1977.

McGiffert, A. C. *The Rise of Modern Religious Ideas*. New York: Macmillan, 1915.

McIntire, Carl. *Servants of Apostasy*. Collingswood, N.J.: Christian Beacon Press, 1955.

McLoughlin, William G. *Billy Sunday Was His Real Name*. Chicago: University Press, 1955.

——. *Modern Revivalism: Charles G. Finney to Billy Graham*. New York: Ronald Press, 1959.

——. *The American Evangelicals, 1800–1900: An Anthology*. New York: Harper & Row, 1968.

——. *Isaac Backus on Church, State and Calvinism*. Cambridge: Harvard University Press, 1968.

——. *New England Dissent, 1630–1833*. Cambridge: Harvard University Press, 1971.

Mead, Sidney E. *The Lively Experiment: the Protestant Experience in America*. New York: Dial Press, 1970.

——. *The Nation with the Soul of a Church*. New York: Harper & Row, 1975.

Mecklin, J. M. *The Story of American Dissent*. New York: Kennikat Press, 1972.

Menendez, A. J. *Religion at the Polls*. Philadelphia: Westminster Press, 1977.

Mitchell, C. *Those Who Came Forward*. Philadelphia: Chiton Books, 1966.

Moberg, David. *The Great Reversal: Evangelicals Versus Social Concern*. Philadelphia: Lippincott, 1972.

Montgomery, John W. *The "Is God Dead?" Controversy*. Grand Rapids: Zondervan, 1966.

——. *Ecumenicity, Evangelicals and Rome*. Grand Rapids: Zondervan, 1969.

Morris, James. *The Preachers*. New York: St. Martin's Press, 1973.

Mouw, Richard. *Politics and the Biblical Drama*. Grand Rapids: Eerdmans, 1976.

Murch, J. D. *Cooperation without Compromise: A History of the National Association of Evangelicals*. Grand Rapids: Eerdmans, 1956.

——. *The Protestant Revolt*. Arlington, Va.: Crestwood Books, 1967.

Nash, Ronald H. *The New Evangelicalism*. Grand Rapids: Zondervan, 1963.

Niebuhr, H. Richard. *The Kingdom of God in America*. New York: Harper & Brothers, 1937.

Norris, J. Frank. *The Inside Story of the First Baptist Church, Fort Worth, and Temple Baptist Church*. Detroit: Temple Baptist Church, 1938.

Orr, James. *The Faith of a Modern Christian*. London: Hodder & Stoughton, 1910.

Orr, J. Edwin. *The Second Evangelical Awakening in America*. London: Marshall, Morgan & Scott, 1952.

——. *The Eager Feet: Evangelical Awakenings 1792 and 1830*. Chicago: Moody Press, 1973.

——. *The Fervent Prayer: Evangelical Awakenings 1858–1899*. Chicago: Moody Press, 1974.

——. *The Flaming Tongue: Evangelical Awakenings 1900–*. Chicago: Moody Press, 1975.

Packer, J. I. *Fundamentalism and the Word of God*. Grand Rapids: Eerdmans, 1964.

Paisley, Ian R. K. *Billy Graham and the Church of Rome*. Greenville, S. C.: Bob Jones University, 1970.

Parks, Leighton. *What is Modernism?* New York: Scribners, 1924.

Patton, F. L. *Fundamental Christianity*. New York: Macmillan, 1926.

Pickering, Ernest. *Biblical Separation: The Struggle for a Pure Church*. Schaumburg, Ill.: Regular Baptist Press, 1979.

——. *The Fruit of Compromise: The New and Young Evangelicals*. Clarks Summit, Pa.: Baptist Bible College and School of Theology, n.d.

Pierard, Richard. *The Unequal Yoke: Evangelical Christianity and Political Conservatism*. Philadelphia: Lippincott, 1970.

Pollock, John. *Billy Graham: The Authorized Biography*. New York: McGraw-Hill, 1966.

——. *Billy Graham: Evangelist to the World*. New York: Harper & Row, 1979.

Quebedeaux, Richard. *The Young Evangelicals*. New York: Harper & Row, 1974.

——. *The New Charismatics*. Garden City, N.Y.: Doubleday, 1976.

——. *The Worldly Evangelicals*. New York: Harper & Row, 1978.

Ramm, Bernard. *A Handbook of Contemporary Theology*. Grand Rapids: Eerdmans, 1966.

——. *The Evangelical Heritage*. Waco: Word Books, 1973.

Rice, John R. *Earnestly Contending for the Faith*. Murfreesboro, Tenn.: Sword of the Lord, 1965.

——. *I Am a Fundamentalist*. Murfreesboro, Tenn.: Sword of the Lord, 1975.

——. *Come Out—or Stay In?* Nashville: Thomas Nelson, 1974.

Rifkin, J., and Howard, T. *The Emerging Order: God in the Age of Scarcity*. New York: G. P. Putnam's Sons, 1979.

Riley, W. B. *The Menace of Modernism*. New York: Alliance, 1917.

Rogers, Jack, ed. *Biblical Authority*. Waco: Word Books, 1977.

Rudnick, Milton L. *Fundamentalism and the Missouri Synod*. St. Louis: Concordia, 1966.

Ryrie, Charles C. *Neoorthodoxy*. Chicago: Moody Press, 1956.

——. *Dispensationalism Today*. Chicago: Moody Press, 1965.

Sandeen, Ernest R. *The Roots of Fundamentalism: British and American Millenarianism 1800–1930.* Chicago: University of Chicago Press, 1970.

Shelley, Bruce. *Evangelicalism in America.* Grand Rapids, 1967.

Shields, T. T. *The Plot that Failed.* Toronto: Gospel Witness, 1937.

Shipley, Maynard. *The War on Modern Science: A Short History of the Fundamentalist Attacks on Evolution and Modernism.* New York: Alfred Knopf, 1927.

Shriver, G. H., ed. *American Religious Heretics.* Nashville: Abingdon Press, 1966.

Smith, Timothy L. *Revivalism and Social Reform.* New York: Harper & Row, 1965.

Sodergen, C. J. *Fundamentalism and Modernism.* Rock Island, Ill.: Augustana, 1925.

Stedman, Murray S. *Religion and Politics in America.* New York: Harcourt, Brace & World, 1964.

Sterrett, J. M. *Modernism in Religion.* New York: Macmillan, 1922.

Stevick, Daniel. *Beyond Fundamentalism.* Richmond: John Knox Press, 1964.

Stoeffler, F. E. *Rise of Evangelical Pietism.* Leiden: E. J. Brill, 1971.

——. *Continental Pietism and Early American Christianity.* Grand Rapids: Eerdmans, 1976.

Stonehouse, Ned. *J. Gresham Machen.* Grand Rapids: Eerdmans, 1954.

Stott, John R. W. *Fundamentalism and Evangelism.* Grand Rapids: Eerdmans, 1959.

Straton, John R. *The Battle over the Bible.* New York: Doran, 1924.

Streiker, L. D., and Strober, Gerald. *Religion and the New Majority.* New York: Association Press, 1972.

Strober, Gerald, and Tomczak, Ruth. *Jerry Falwell: Aflame for God.* Nashville: Thomas Nelson, 1979.

Sumner, Robert L. *A Man Sent from God: A Biography of Dr. John R. Rice.* Grand Rapids: Eerdmans, 1959.

Sweet, William W. *Revivalism in America.* Nashville: Abingdon Press, 1944.

Tarr, Leslie K. *Shields of Canada.* Toronto: Gospel Witness, 1967.

Tautum, Ray. *Conquest or Failure: A Biography of J. Frank Norris.* Dallas: Baptist Historical Foundation, 1966.

Torbet, Robert G. *A History of the Baptists.* Valley Forge: Judson Press, 1963.

Torrey, R. A., et. al. *The Fundamentals: A Testimony to the Truth.* 4 vols. repr. Grand Rapids: Baker Book House, 1970.

——. *Higher Criticism and the New Theology.* New York: Gospel Publishing House, 1920.

Towns, Elmer L. *The Ten Largest Sunday Schools.* Grand Rapids: Baker Book House, 1969.

——. *America's Fastest Growing Churches.* Nashville: Impact Books, 1972.

——. *Is the Day of the Denomination Dead?* Nashville: Thomas Nelson, 1973.

Tulga, Chester A. *The Case Against Modernism.* Chicago: Conservative Baptist Fellowship, 1949.

Tuveson, E. L. *Redeemer Nation: The Idea of America's Millennial Role.* Chicago: University of Chicago Press, 1968.

Van Allen, Roger. *American Religious Values and the Future of America.* Philadelphia: Fortress Press, 1978.

Vanderlaan, E. C., ed. *Fundamentalism Versus Modernism.* New York: Wilson, 1925.

VanDusen, Henry P. *The Vindication of Liberal Theology.* New York: Scribners, 1963.

Van Til, Cornelius. *In Defense of the Faith.* Philadelphia: Presbyterian and Reformed, 1960.

——. *The New Modernism.* Philadelphia: Presbyterian and Reformed, 1972.

Watts, Michael R. *The Dissenters from the Reformation to the French Revolution.* Oxford: Clarendon Press, 1978.

Webber, Robert E. *Common Roots: A Call to Evangelical Maturity.* Grand Rapids: Zondervan, 1978.

Webber, Robert E., and Bloesch, Donald. *The Orthodox Evangelicals.* Nashville: Thomas Nelson, 1978.

Weber, Timothy P. *Living in the Shadow of the Second Coming: American Premillenialism 1875–1925.* New York: Oxford University Press, 1979.

Weisberger, Bernard A. *They Gathered at the River.* Chicago: Quadrangle Books, 1958.

Wells, David F., and Woodbridge, John D., eds. *The Evangelicals.* rev. ed. Grand Rapids: Baker Book House, 1977.

Westin, Gunnar. *The Free Church Through the Ages.* V. A. Olson, trans. Nashville: Broadman Press, 1958.

Williams, George H. *The Radical Reformation.* Philadelphia: Westminster Press, 1962.

Wilson, John F. *Church and State in American History.* Boston: Heath, 1965.

Wirt, Sherwood E. *The Social Conscience of the Evangelical.* New York: Harper & Row, 1968.

Woodbridge, Charles. *The New Evangelicalism.* Greenville, S.C.: Bob Jones University Press, 1969.

Woodbridge, John D., et al. *The Gospel in America: Themes in the Story of America's Evangelicals.* Grand Rapids: Zondervan, 1979.

Wright, J. E. *The Old-Fashioned Revival Hour.* Boston: Fellowship Press, 1940.

Wright, Melton. *Fortress of Faith.* Grand Rapids: Eerdmans, 1960.

Periodicals

Alexander, C. D. "The Failure of Evangelicalism," *Eternity,* May 1953.

Amerding, H. T. "What's right about evangelicalism," United Evangelical *Action,* fall 1968.

Armstrong, B. "Opinion polls and predictions," *Religious Broadcasters,* Feb. 1980.

Ashbrook, W. "The New Evangelism—the New Neutralism," *Central C.B. Quarterly,* summer 1959.

Bayly, J. "Yes, there are semi-evangelicals," *Christianity Today,* July 1977.

Bender, T. W. "What's New in Theology?" *Bulletin of the Evangelical Theological Society,* summer 1959.

Bisset, J. Thomas. "Religious Broadcasting: Assessing the State of the Art," *Christianity Today,* Dec. 12, 1980.

Blaiklock, E. M. "Conservatism, liberalism, and neo-orthodoxy," *Eternity,* Aug. 1960.

Board, S. "The great evangelical power shift," *Eternity,* June 1979.

Brackney, W. H. "American evangelicalism: an analysis and its evolution," *Christian Librarian,* Jan. 1977.

Bromiley, G. W. "Fundamentalism-modernism: a first step in the controversy," *Christianity Today,* Nov. 1957.

Brown, H. O. J. "Church of the 1970's: a decade of flux?" *Christianity Today,* Dec. 1979.

Carnell, E. J. "Post-fundamentalist Faith," *The Christian Century,* Aug. 1959.

Carpenter, J. A. "Fundamentalist Institutions and the Rise of Evangelical Protestants, 1929–1942," *Church History*, Mar. 1980.

Cerillo, A., Jr. "Survey of recent evangelical social thought," *Christian Scholar's Review*, 1976.

Chandler, R. "Conservative Fallout," *Christianity Today*, Sept. 1971.

"Christianity Today–Gallup Poll: An Overview, The," *Christianity Today*, Dec. 21, 1979.

Clearwaters, R. V. "The Double Divisiveness of the New Evangelicalism," *Central C.B. Quarterly*, summer 1958.

Collins, C. "We did it His way (or did we?)," *United Evangelical Action*, fall 1979.

Dahlin, J. "Another Look at this New Evangelicalism," *Evangelical Beacon*, May 1960.

Davis, D. C. "Evangelicals and the Presbyterian Tradition: an alternative perspective," *Westminster Theological Journal*, fall 1979.

Dollar, G. W. "Early days of American Fundamentalism," *Bibliotheca Sacra*, April 1966.

———. "Facts for Fundamentalists to Face," *Bibliotheca Sacra*, April 1967.

Edwards, R. R. "Some thoughts on fundamentalist infallibility," *Eternity*, Sept. 1957.

"Evangelicalism in the United States," *Evangelical Quarterly*, July 1967.

"Evangelicals and Fundamentals," *Christianity Today*, Sept. 1957.

"Evangelicals in a Corner," *Christianity Today*, May 1966.

Feinberg, C. L. "An Answer to 'Is Christianity Changing?'" *The King's Business*, Jan. 1957.

"Fundamentalism and Neo-Evangelicalism—Whither?" *The Sunday School Times*, Feb. 1961.

Graham, Billy. "An Agenda for the 1980's," *Christianity Today*, Jan. 4, 1980.

Grounds, V. "Nature of evangelicalism," *Eternity*, Feb. 1956.

"Growing emergence of the evangelical," *Moody Monthly*, Mar. 1971.

Harman, G. "Evangelical principles and practices," *Christianity Today*, Jan. 1967.

Henry, C. F. "Agenda for evangelical advance," *Christianity Today*, Nov. 1976.

———. "Contemporary Evangelical Thought," Great Neck, N.Y.: Channel Press, 1957.

———. "Dare we renew the modernist-fundamentalist controversy?" *Christianity Today*, June–July 1957.

——. "Decade of gains and losses," *Christianity Today*, Mar. 1976.

——. "Demythologizing the evangelicals," *Christianity Today*, Sept. 1968.

——. "Evangelical Renewal," *Christianity Today*, Jan. 1973.

——. "Evangelicals: out of the closet but going nowhere?" *Christianity Today*, Jan. 1980.

——. "Evangelical Summertime?" *Christianity Today*, Apr. 1977.

——. "Evangelical Underground," *Christianity Today*, Apr. 1970.

——. "Future of evangelical Christianity," *World Vision*, Jan. 1978.

——. "House divided: an interview with Carl Henry," *Eternity*, Oct. 1976.

——. "The Kingdom and the Empire," *Eternity*, Mar. 1980.

——. "Perspective for Social Action," *Christianity Today*, Jan. 1959.

——. "Resurgence of evangelical Christianity," *Christianity Today*, Mar. 1959.

——. "Revolt on evangelical frontiers," *Christianity Today*, Apr. 1974.

——. "Signs of evangelical disunity: Part 4," *Christianity Today*, Apr. 1976.

——. "Somehow, let's get together," *Christianity Today*, June 1967.

——. "Tensions between evangelism and the Christian demand for social justice," *Fides Et Historia*, spring, 1972.

——. "Toward a brighter day," *Christianity Today*, Aug. 1976.

——. "We need each other," *Christian Life*, June 1970.

——. "Who are the evangelicals?" *Christianity Today*, Feb. 1972.

Hill, B. "Evangelical boom," *Christian Life*, Jan. 1971.

Hine, L. D. "Is evangelicalism dying of old age?" *Eternity*, Mar. 1972.

"Is Evangelical Theology Changing?" *Christian Life*, Mar. 1956.

Jaberg, R. L. "Is there room for fundamentalists?" *Christianity Today*, July 1960.

Kahoe, R. D. "Religious conservatism in a quasilongitudinal perspective," *Journal of Psychology and Theology*, winter 1977.

Kik, J. M. "Are evangelicals literalists?" *Christianity Today*, Nov. 1956.

Kromminga, J. H. "Evangelical Influence on the Ecumenical Movement," *Calvin Theological Journal*, Nov. 1976.

Kucharsky, D. "Year of the Evangelical," *Christianity Today*, Oct. 1976.

Lazear, R. W. "Fundamentalism's facades," *Eternity*, Dec. 1956.

Love, R. L. "Evangelical students: alive and well," *Christianity Today*, May 1970.

Lovelace, R. F. "Contemplating an Awakening," *The Christian Century*, Mar. 18, 1981.

Mackay, J. A. "Toward an evangelical renaissance," *Christianity Today*, Feb. 1972.

Marsden, G. "Defining Fundamentalism," *Christian Scholar's Review*, winter 1971; a reply: E. Sandeen, *Christian Scholar's Review*, spring 1971.

———. "Demythologizing evangelicalism: a review of Donald W. Dayton's *Discovering an Evangelical Heritage*," *Christian Scholar's Review*, 1977.

———. "Fundamentalism as an American Phenomenon." *Church History*, June 1977.

Martin, W. R. "Love, Doctrine and Fellowship," *Eternity*, Nov. 1960.

Marty, Martin E. "Born Again—Faith or Fanaticism," *U.S. Catholic*. June 1979.

Marty, Martin E. "Fundamentalism and the Church," *The Christian Century*, Nov. 1959.

———. "Fundamentalism Reborn," *Saturday Review*, May 1980.

———. "Old Time Religion on the Offensive," *U.S. News and World Report*, April 7, 1980.

Masters, D. C. "Rise of Evangelicalism," *Evangelical Christian*, Dec. 1960.

Moore, L. "Another look at fundamentalism: a response to Ernest R. Sandeen," *Church History*, June 1968.

Moral Majority Report (An ongoing documentary on the political-moral issues to today.) Published by Moral Majority, Inc., Washington, D.C. 20003.

Morris, L. "Conservative Evangelicals," *Christianity Today*, Nov. 1971.

Murch, J. D. "*Christian Century* renews the controversy," *United Evangelical Action*, Apr. 1958.

Nash, R. L. "Unbowed to Baal: the fundamentalist remnant in America: A review essay of George W. Dollar's *A History of Fundamentalism in America*," *Fides Et Historia*, fall 1974.

"The New Evangelicalism," *Christian Beacon*, Jan. 1958.

"New Right Comes of Age, The," *The Christian Century*, Oct. 22, 1980.

Noll, M. A. "Catching up with the evangelicals," *Christianity Today*, Dec. 1975.

Ockenga, H. J. "The New Evangelicalism," *The Park Street Spire*, Feb. 1958.

Ockenga, J. J. "Resurgent evangelical leadership," *Christianity Today*, Oct. 1960.

Olson, A. T. "Evangelicals in today's world," *United Evangelical Action*, spring 1969.

"On not leaving it to the liberals," *Eternity*, Feb. 1977.

Packer, J. I. "Fundamentalism Controversy: retrospect and prospect," *HIS*, Jan. 1959.

Payne, B. P. "Hermeneutics as a Cloak for the Denial of Scripture," *Bulletin of the Evangelical Theological Society*, fall 1960.

"Perils of Ecumenicity, The," *Christianity Today*, Nov. 1956.

"Perils of Independency, The," *Christianity Today*, Nov. 1956.

Petticord, P. P. "True Ecumenicity," *United Evangelical Action*, May 1958.

Pickering, E. "New Evangelicalism: Its Present Status," *Voice*, Jan. 1959.

Pierard, Richard V. "Billy Graham and the U.S. Presidency," *Journal of Church and State*, winter 1980.

———. "Quest for the historical evangelicalism: a bibliographical excursus," *Fides Et Historia*, spring 1979.

Pinnock, C. H. "Evangelical theology: Conservative and contemporary," *Christianity Today*, Jan. 1979.

"Preachers in Politics," *U.S. News and World Report*, Sept. 24, 1979.

Rausch, D. "The Fundamentals and the Jews," *Fides Et Historia*, fall 1977.

"Resurgent Evangelical Leadership," *Christianity Today*, Oct. 1960.

Rice, John R., ed. *The Sword of the Lord* (leading fundamentalist publication).

Rogers, M. L. "Fundamentalist church as an autonomous community and its relationship to the larger community," *Journal of Psychology and Theology*, summer 1975.

Runia, K. "Evangelical responsibility in a secularized world," *Christianity Today*, June 1970.

———. "When is separation a Christian duty?" *Christianity Today*, June–July 1967.

Sanasac, R. "The Basics of New Evangelicalism," *Central C.B. Quarterly*, summer 1960.

Sandeen, E. R. "Toward a historical interpretation of the origins of fundamentalism," *Church History,* March 1967.

Sanderson, J. W., Jr. "Fundamentalism and Its Critics," *The Sunday School Times,* Jan. 1961.

Schaeffer, F. A. "Watershed of the evangelical world," *United Evangelical Action,* fall 1976.

Shelley, B. "Evangelical Christianity Today," *United Evangelical Action,* Apr. 1967.

————. "Sources of pietistic fundamentalism," *Fides Et Historia,* spring 1973.

Tarr, L. K. "Evangelical passwords," *Evangelical Christian,* July 1967.

————. "Hermetically-sealed world of neo-fundamentalism," *Eternity,* Aug. 1967.

"Theology, Evangelism, Ecumenism," *Christianity Today,* Jan. 1958.

"Tide of Born-Again Politics, A," *Newsweek,* Sept. 15, 1980.

Tinder, D. "Why the evangelical upswing?" *Christianity Today,* Oct. 1977.

Towns, E. L. "Trends among fundamentalists," *Christianity Today,* July 1973.

Vinz, W. L. "Politics of protestant fundamentalism in the 1950's and 1960's," *Journal of Church and State,* spring 1972.

Wagner, C. Peter. "Aiming at Church Growth in the Eighties," *Christianity Today,* Nov. 21, 1980.

Walvoord, J. F. "What's right about Fundamentalism?" *Eternity,* June 1957.

"What's wrong with born-again politics? A Symposium," *The Christian Century,* Oct. 22, 1980.

"Who and where are the evangelicals?" *Christianity Today,* Dec. 1979.

Willoughby, W. F. "New Evangelical surge," *Christianity Today,* May 1971.

Woodbridge, C. J. "Gray Shades," *The King's Business,* May 1958.

Woods, C. S. "The Neutral Protestants," *Evangelical Action,* Jan. 1961.

Young, C. D. "What is this New Evangelicalism?" *The Evangelical Beacon,* Apr. 1960.

Young, W. C. "Whither Evangelicalism?" *Bulletin of the Evangelical Theological Society,* winter 1959.

JERRY FALWELL is a leading American fundamentalist preacher. He is pastor of the 18,000-member Thomas Road Baptist Church in Lynchburg, Virginia, and the Chancellor of Liberty Baptist College and Seminary. He was named Clergyman of the Year in 1979 by the Religious Heritage Society and Humanitarian of the Year in 1980 by Food for the Hungry, International. His television and radio broadcasts of "The Old-Time Gospel Hour" reach millions of people every week. He is undoubtedly one of the most influential religious leaders in America today.

ED DOBSON is the Dean of Student Affairs and Director of Pastoral Training at Liberty Baptist College, Lynchburg, Virginia. He holds B.A. and M.A. degrees from Bob Jones University and is presently engaged in doctoral studies at the University of Virginia. In addition he serves as an associate pastor of Thomas Road Baptist Church.

ED HINDSON is Professor and Chairman of the Division of Religion at Liberty Baptist College and also serves as an associate pastor of Thomas Road Baptist Church. His degrees include: M.A., Trinity Evangelical Divinity School; Th.M., Grace Theological Seminary; Th.D., Trinity Graduate School of Theology; D.Min., Westminster Theological Seminary. He has previously authored seven books and edited the *Liberty Bible Commentary*.